THE ECONOMIC CONSEQUENCES
OF LIABILITY RULES

The Economic Consequences of Liability Rules

IN DEFENSE OF COMMON LAW LIABILITY

EDITED BY
Roger E. Meiners
&
Bruce Yandle

Q

Quorum Books

NEW YORK · WESTPORT, CONNECTICUT · LONDON

Library of Congress Cataloging-in-Publication Data

The Economic consequences of liability rules : in defense of common
  law liability / edited by Roger E. Meiners and Bruce Yandle.
      p.   cm.
  Includes bibliographical references and index.
  ISBN 0–89930–649–7 (alk. paper)
    1. Liability (Law)—Economic aspects—United States.   I. Meiners,
  Roger E.   II. Yandle, Bruce.
  KF1250.E26   1991
  346.73′02—dc20
  [347.3062]   91–185

British Library Cataloguing in Publication Data is available.

Library of Congress Catalog Card Number: 91–185
ISBN: 0–89930–649–7

First published in 1991

Quorum Books, 88 Post Road West, Westport, CT 06881
An imprint of Greenwood Publishing Group, Inc.

Printed in the United States of America

The paper used in this book complies with the
Permanent Paper Standard issued by the National
Information Standards Organization (Z39.48–1984).

10 9 8 7 6 5 4 3 2 1

Contents

Acknowledgments

Preparation of these chapters was supported by the Center for Policy Studies at Clemson University through a grant provided by the John M. Olin Foundation. The Olin grant made it possible for the authors to focus sharply on liability issues that had surfaced in their research but had not been examined in depth. Additional appreciation is expressed to Ryan C. Amacher, Dean of Clemson University's College of Commerce and Industry, who fosters a fertile research environment, but is not liable for any of the faults contained in the chapters.

1

Addressing the "Liability Crisis"

Roger E. Meiners and Bruce Yandle

This book focuses on the economic consequences of rules of liability. Despite the clamor about what some call the liability crisis, which has resulted in a decade-long effort to obtain passage of federal legislation that would limit common law liability rules, the authors of this collection do not examine that "crisis." Nor do they claim to have the wisdom necessary to prescribe major tort law reforms or call for a return to past rules, although advocates of such changes might find ammunition for their views in some of the chapters. Rather, the purpose of this book is to study the role of liability rules to help us understand the possible consequences of statutory tampering with common law liability rules. In constructing this volume, we intended to help explain how public (statutory) and private (common law) liability rules evolve, how they work, and how changes in rules can alter economic outcomes in significant and unintended ways.

The body of economic logic called price theory is the main analytical engine employed in the chapters. The focus is on individual decision making: how incentives faced by individuals are affected by liability rules, and how the collective actions of purposeful individuals working in private markets and through the political process affect social outcomes. In addition to price theory, there is also a richness of institutional detail that helps us understand the structure and operation of the forces at work.

In the sense that the logic of price theory can be applied to legal institutions, this collection is an exercise in law and economics.[1] In another sense, the book can be termed political economy, since most of the chapters focus on the institutions of government. Discussions of the workings of government demand that politics and collective choice be considered. Price theory applied in a political setting implies public choice analysis.[2]

In sum, the focus on liability found in this volume carries with it the belief that economic logic can provide insights in the investigation of legal institutions that are formed in a free society where politics matters. We believe this book provides evidence that attempts to remedy alleged defects in the common law by legislative edicts are not well grounded. To introduce the volume in more detail, it is necessary to speak to some issues and principles that form bedrock for the work undertaken herein. After that, we provide a sketch of the chapters in the book.

LIABILITY RULES AND MARKET FUNCTION

Legal rules are fundamental to the working of a market economy. Rules that define rights and liabilities are inherent in all transactions. Sometimes rules are explicitly specified in detail in contracts or in statutory requirements. At the same time, common law and statutory rules are applied to solve unanticipated controversies that arise among parties that did not account for the solution of a problem that could arise under a contract, or are needed to solve the problem that arises when a party violates its legal responsibility. The combination of explicit and default legal rules forms a framework in which economic activity occurs.

Decisions made in advance of transactions about which party will be liable also allocate costs across future contracting parties. If the liability rule makes producers responsible for the costs incurred by consumers of faulty products, producers can buy insurance, self-insure, and take action to reduce defects. In competitive markets, the costs of producer-initiated actions will be passed along to consumers. Without recognizing it, consumers indirectly bear the costs of producer liability and insurance. If the liability rule calls for consumers to bear the costs imposed by faulty products, they can insure to cover the costs of the harm they may suffer and take actions to avoid likely harm. In either case, consumer or producer liability, the costs are borne by consumers.

Economies in managing liability on either side of the transaction are revealed through the market process and generally dictate which party assumes liability. Court or legislative decisions that alter economizing arrangements that have been worked out previously by producers and consumers can result in higher liability costs and a breakdown of linkages that tie individual actors to the cost of their actions.

Parties not directly involved in transactions can have a role in determining liability, and parties to transactions can attempt to reassign liability, when politicians become active in defining and redefining legal rules.[3] Certain voters and interest groups are likely to benefit by shifting the liability costs they bear to others. One way this can be done is when government, through taxpayers, assumes liability for losses previously handled by producers and consumers of particular products and services.

For example, political pressures may lead politicians to offer subsidized flood damage insurance to those who build homes on flood plans. Where developers and homeowners previously bore the liability costs of their risky actions, those costs can be shifted to unknowing taxpayers. Spreading costs across taxpayers in small doses shifts the liability burden. Moral hazard,[4] a problem to be minimized in private contracts, enters the picture. The value of flood-risk real estate rises, subsidizing those who paid lower prices for accepting the flood risk, and the volume of construction in flood-prone areas rises, increasing the damage likely to be suffered by floods. Liability rules that disguise the true cost of hazardous behavior cause socially undesirable behavior to increase.

Political action directed toward redefining property rights[5] can also affect liability rules. Efforts to increase air and water quality or to reduce the hazardous disposal of waste products often result in new liability rules that force waste dischargers to bear more costs, even when waste receivers might be the low-cost avoiders of the problem. Again, a particular definition of liability can lead to higher costs and, in some cases, more rather than less harm.

Regulation of production and consumption by government can be viewed as a substitute for rules of liability. To illustrate, hazardous products can simply be banned from the market, eliminating the need for the contract and tort liability rules for the products in question. Alternately, regulations can specify uniform standards for product design that induce relatively uniform behavior by consumers. By eliminating choices, which results in lost benefits to consumers, uniform rules reduce uncertainty when writing contracts and reduce the risk-measurement problems faced by insurers who seek to underwrite potential liabilities. At the same time, a move to uniformity usually benefits those who previously preferred the rule that is chosen, while imposing costs on those who did not. Since federal regulation leaves no choice but to follow the rule, some groups gain at the expense of others.

THE LIABILITY CRISIS

A crisis is usually declared to exist when there is a sharp rise in relative prices that surprises those who pay for the goods or services affected by the price increase (or when one suffers from an unexpected price drop). The insurance industry suffered financial difficulties in the mid–1970s and mid-1980s that have, in part, been attributed to the rise in tort judgments paid by insurers. Similarly, companies that self-insure have suffered a price shock from tort judgments.

Ignoring how problems may be compounded by state regulation of insurance that in some cases has forced companies to incur noncompetitive rates of return, there is no question that insurance companies (and self-insurers) were surprised by the change in tort liability over the past two decades. Premiums or product prices were not set high enough to cover the payouts that were later incurred. Matters that used to be covered by contracts have been declared to be subject to tort liability, and tort liability has significantly expanded. Common law liability rules changed, causing economic disruptions.

Insurance studies indicate that a far greater problem was caused for the industry by the inflation bouts of the early 1970s and 1980s that were followed by deflation. During inflation the industry earned what appeared to be high rates of return on their portfolios, allowing premium rates to be held down or cut, which caused problems when deflation hit, rates of return fell, and payouts increased. By 1991 the aftershocks of inflation-deflation have been largely washed out.

Since there is little the insurance industry can do to influence future inflation rates, the industry naturally looks to influence policy where damage can be controlled: hence the focus on the change in liability standards and the resulting increase in damage awards. The industry has worked with private industry, which either self-insures or pays insurance premiums, to achieve passage of state legislation limiting the size of judgments that may be awarded in common law cases. Success in this area has been limited as several of the statutes have been declared to be in violation of the state constitution.

PROPOSED FEDERAL PRODUCTS LIABILITY LEGISLATION

Of greater significance has been the decade-long attempt to obtain passage of federal legislation, backed by the Reagan and Bush administrations, to set some statutory standards for tort liability, especially as they apply to consumer products.[6] The proposed statute would impose time limits on actions, affirm some traditional defenses, and reestablish the negligence standard in certain cases. In our opinion, the proposed legislation would establish sensible standards. However, the purpose of this volume is to show that statutory tampering with common law standards usually produces bad results.

In the case of the proposed product liability legislation, those who have legitimate concerns about liability rules are seeking a solution that could have long-run negative effects not intended by the supporters. There is no doubt that significant economic losses have been incurred as a result of the unexpected changes in tort liability rules. However, to blame this change on ignorant or ideologically motivated judges, lawyers, and juries in hundreds of independent court cases seems a weak explanation for what has happened in three decades of common law litigation.[7]

What has not yet been explained is why the motives of lawyers, judges, or juries would be different in the last three decades than in the decades before that. We are not original when we suggest that the world is very complicated. To the best of our knowledge, there is no general understanding of why common law rules have changed with respect to products liability or any other part of the law. What we do have a better understanding of is, first, the merits of the common law relative to statutory law and, second, the ability of private interests and political entrepreneurs to exploit the statutory law process for special interest purposes.

That is what this collection addresses. We intend to shed light on the merits of statutory tinkering with common law rules. We do not claim that specific common law rules are "optimal" in an economic sense or that mistakes, some of which are costly, are not made. However, we believe that the discussion here indicates that there are sound theoretical reasons to believe that the common law works well relative to the statutory alternative, and we present some case studies that illustrate, in situations small and large, that statutory meddling with liability rules is often not done for the public welfare and can have disastrous economic results.

HOW THIS COLLECTION ADDRESSES THESE ISSUES

This volume addresses these issues and more. Some chapters focus more sharply on general principles and theoretical discussions of liability rules. Some chapters make little reference to particular laws, actions, or industries. Instead, they analyze major features of liability rules. The chapters in the latter part of the book concern particular situations and pay careful attention to tracing the evolution and consequences of changes in public or private liability rules. These case studies use economic theory to explain the effects of changes and, in some cases, why the changes emerged in particular ways. Taken together, the chapters provide the reader with lessons in political economy, law and economics, and public choice, with all of the lessons focused on liability rules.

Chapter 2, by Robert J. Staaf and Bruce Yandle, is an economic examination of the two sources of liability rules in the American legal system. Common law rules that specify liability arrangements, which individuals can contract around by mutually beneficial agreements, shape one branch of the legal tree. Statutory laws that specify liability rules that cannot be avoided legally, even if parties to a contract say otherwise, form the other branch of the liability tree. The two systems or processes compete in their evolution and offer private and public choices to members of society who wish to specify liability rules.

Staaf and Yandle see common law as private, which is to say individuals specify their own rules. Those who do not like the choices voluntarily adopted by others cannot change them unless they are willing to contract for a change agreeable to all parties. Statute law provides an opportunity for everyone to write rules. What was private law can be made public law. The legislative process offers opportunities for special interest groups and politicians to address special cases and write rules that can redistribute wealth. The dynamics of the process discussed in the paper lead to the conclusion that the common law will gradually lose its market when forced to compete with statute law.

David D. Haddock and Fred S. McChesney, authors of chapter 3, develop a theme that is related to the Staaf-Yandle chapter by examining more closely the relationship between property and liability rules. Exploring the fact that property rules require agreement in advance of an asset transfer, while liability rules allow for payment after a taking, the authors develop and apply a theoretical discussion of the boundaries of the two institutional approaches. Their analysis is applied in private and public settings, where they examine institutional deterrents that limit the unintended transfer of property. In particular, they provide an economic rationale for the application of punitive damages in certain cases. To some extent, this analysis contradicts the notion touted by tort law "reformers" that a statutory limitation on common law remedies is economically justified. The chapter ends with an analysis that contrasts the incentives of political agents and private economic agents in the context of liability and property rules. It should be noted that in note 2 of their chapter they discuss the definitions of property rights and property rules to help clarify how economists and lawyers use those terms.

James L. Huffman addresses government liability in chapter 4. Here we find a more detailed discussion of the statute-making case discussed by Staaf and Yandle. Huffman describes how the federal government historically assumed liability in some cases and not in others. He goes on to examine how government liability has expanded and how this federalization has affected the behavior of economic agents who previously had to work out their own liability and property arrangements. The chapter illustrates the riskiness of government efforts to reduce and manage risk and shows how moral hazard expands with growth of government liability.

It is difficult to enforce tort liability rules in situations involving generic products and unidentifiable producers. While statutory and common law rules may dictate ways to allocate damages, they usually assume that cause and effect between producers and consumers can be linked. In chapter 5, Robert J. Staaf and Bruce Yandle address one method used by courts when generic liability surfaces, the allocation of liability by market share. Logical on its face and relatively simple to apply, market-share liability requires each producer of a generic good found harmful to assume a pro rata part of the total liability imposed. Like other apparently logical approaches to problems, market-share liability has hazards of its own. The authors point out plausible situations in which the production of hazardous products will rise as a result of this rule. The rule itself introduces moral hazard in markets for risky products. The market-share liability rule illustrates a weakness with the common law—judges can issue new rulings that break from precedent, that are economically destructive. The genius of the common law is that bad rules are recognized as such in other jurisdictions and are not adopted. The market-share liability rule has not spread nationwide as had been feared when first announced in California. Unlike "bad" liability rules that issue from Congress, "bad" liability rules from a court are not binding.

Chapter 6 describes the interaction of liability rules with rules of taxation. Here, Robert J. Staaf explains how income tax laws provide producers with incentives to adjust their behavior away from one form of liability in favor of another. In other words, what might be the least-cost method for society, and is, therefore, preferred, can become more costly for private parties. Staaf's chapter illustrates the general importance of considering all institutional arrangements affecting the behavior of firms when developing or altering liability rules.

Hugh H. Macaulay's chapter on environmental quality asks the question: Who should be liable for environmental quality? Macaulay forms his answer to the question by way of the Coase Theorem.[8] He asks the reader to consider opportunity cost when evaluating environmental quality. The standard answer to the question is that industrial users should be liable for environmental harm; that is, polluters are liable, consumers and lovers of environmental quality have the property rights. After reviewing the theoretical arguments put forth by economists who share the popular view, Macaulay develops a consistent model that questions the answer. In his view, all parties who use environmental resources should be liable for the costs they impose on others. His model of a market for environmental quality sees a system of property rights and associated liability rules.

Continuing the environmental theme, the next chapter focuses on Superfund, the federal program devised to fund the cleanup of abandoned hazardous waste sites. Bruce Yandle examines an issue similar to market-share liability where identification of the causal parties is very costly or irrelevant. Superfund's requirement of joint and several liability is related to the demise of commercial insurance, an escalation of litigation, and little progress in cleaning up waste. The Superfund story illustrates how changes in liability rules can redistribute income, introduce institutional hazards, and have perverse effects on the goal of improved environmental quality.

Social regulation of the 1970s that brought federal approaches to environmental management also delivered a new wave of regulation to consumer markets. Out of the newly formed Consumer Product Safety Commission (CPSC) came efforts to regulate the manufacture of sleepwear in an attempt to reduce the incidence of burns. Gordon Shuford and Bruce Yandle trace the evolution of the CPSC flammability rule, how it affected international markets, and then what happened when the chemicals used for treating fabrics were found to be carcinogenic. Questions of private and government liability surface in the episode where wealth redistribution is a major theme.

Insurance is one method for handling the losses that come with liability assignment. An important element in several of the volume's chapters, insurance is the major focus in the chapter by Roger E. Meiners and Bruce Yandle. They address one of the major financial issues of recent years, the collapse of a large part of the savings and loan industry, and identify the federal deposit insurance mechanism as a major cause of the insolvency. Their study traces the history of the industry, the insurance mechanism, and shows how taxpayer insurers of the last resort subsidized risk taking in the industry. Their review of current legislation to solve the S&L problem shows that the insurance flaw, which imposes liability on taxpayers who have no control over the risks, is still with us.

The last chapter, by Robert Kneuper, looks at the history of automobile air-bag regulations. Because of the expense involved, air bags generated substantial industry intervention in the political and legal process—by automakers and by insurance companies. The role of the automakers is obvious, but Kneuper asks why the insurance industry played such a major role in the push for air bags. His conclusion is that the industry had an incentive to force adoption of air bags so as to reduce uncertainty about driver habits. An insured driver might not use a seat belt but cannot avoid an air bag. By pushing for a regulation that produces a more certain result, the insurers could reduce their liability, largely at the expense of the automakers and the consumers.

These case studies illustrate a major purpose of this book. By exploiting the political system—or by having politicians exploit private parties who must respond to their threats—the rules of liability and the operation of the market can be moved away from where they would be under consistent rules of common law liability restraining free market behavior.

NOTES

1. The study of law and economics has gone beyond its original, rather narrow focus on the relationship of economic efficiency and the law. For a good discussion, see Randy Barnett and Jules Coleman, eds., "Symposium on Post-Chicago Law and Economics," 65 *Chicago-Kent Law Review* 1 (1989).

2. The foundation of public choice as a discipline is generally credited to Nobel Laureate James Buchanan and his colleague, Gordon Tullock, for their original work *The Calculus of Consent* (Ann Arbor: University of Michigan Press, 1962).

3. For an insightful discussion of politicians as managers of opportunities to change rules, see Fred McChesney, "Rent Extraction and Rent Creation in the Economic Theory of Regulation," 16 *Journal of Legal Studies* 101–18 (1987).

4. Moral hazard is the incentive created by insurance for people to engage in more risky behavior than they would in the absence of insurance (or a technological improvement that improves safety).

5. How economists view property rights is discussed by David D. Haddock and Fred S. McChesney in chapter 3.

6. For a summary of the basic arguments and an overview of the legislation, see

Dan Quayle, "Now Is the Time for Product Liability Reform," *Product Safety & Liability Reporter*, March 23, 1990, pp. 306–9.

7. One of the most cited works critical of the change in liability standards is Peter W. Huber, *Liability: The Legal Revolution and Its Consequences* (New York: Basic Books, 1988). Huber's indictment of tort liability is largely based on recounting tort cases in which liability was assigned in seemingly dubious circumstances and criticizing the judges and lawyers as being motivated by profit and ideology. Other than that, he presents no consistent explanation for why the common law has changed.

8. The Coase Theorem, which arises from Ronald Coase, "The Problem of Social Cost," 3 *Journal of Law & Economics* 1–44 (1960), is perhaps the most important article written for helping economists understand the consequences of alternative liability rules.

2

Common Law, Statute Law, and Liability Rules

Robert J. Staaf and Bruce Yandle

I. INTRODUCTION

Rules of liability emerge in the United States from two routes. Common law rules are applied by judges in disputes among parties to contracts and in tort cases. These common rules, which have evolved over the centuries, can be altered by firms when they explicitly choose to do so, though consumers may not have the same latitude. For example, the common law standard of liability for all firms (e.g., negligence or strict liability) can be contracted around. Statute law, which always supersedes common law in the event of a clash between the two, specifies rules of liability in many specific areas of commerce. For example, regarding the damages caused by flammable sleepwear there are rules of strict liability that cannot be escaped by producers and vendors. There are also statutory rules of joint and several liability that apply to chemical producers whose past disposal of solid waste contributed to a hazardous waste site identified by the U.S. Environmental Protection Agency. These statute-based rules of liability cannot be altered by contracting parties. A chemical producer may not contract away its liability to a waste-site operator, even if the operator agreed to those terms in a contract.

To understand the dynamic legal processes through which common law and statutory rules evolve, it is helpful to employ theoretical models that explain the behavior of parties who agree to mutually beneficial contracts (common law) and of collective bodies that write statutes. Two bodies of developed theory can be employed for that purpose. The central theory in *The Calculus of Consent* (the *Calculus*)[1] and the Coase Theorem[2] are generally interpreted as addressing collective decision making, in the first instance, and private (common law) contracting, in the second.

The *Calculus* applies economic logic to explain political decision making and portrays voting decisions in the context of various marginal benefit and marginal cost relationships. Voting rules, whether simple majority or supramajority, determine the cost of gaining agreement among voting parties and the cost of exclusion when the voting rule is less than unanimity. Coase examine rules of liability in the context of disputes over damages involving two parties. Coase shows that under certain conditions the rules of liability do not matter, which is to say that either party may be held liable but compensation across parties will lead to the same decision while yielding different distributional outcomes.

Many notable writers, such as John R. Commons, Bruno Leoni, and F. A. Hayek have emphasized the harmonious relationship of the common law with markets and the incongruence of statute law with markets. Commons, using a historical perspective, focuses on common law as a basis for market capitalism and draws an analogy between common law and common (open) markets.[3] He ascribes the rise of capitalism to the rise of the use of common law. Commons also emphasizes the point that the common law was not used for the purpose of redistributing wealth from one group to another, but that statutory law surely was.[4]

Hayek sees common law as a foundation that supports markets and observes legislation (policy) as expediency that typically interferes with markets. He sees the anticipated effects of specialized statutes as making them more attractive to politicians than the common law and the markets that generate unidentifiable benefits or opportunities for unpredictable recipients.

This chapter uses a comparison of the *Calculus* and Coase to address the issues raised by Commons and Hayek. In doing so, we focus on the competition between common and statute law and the distributional effects of that competition when outcomes affect rights and liabilities. Section II of the chapter describes similarities and differences between the Coasian and *Calculus* frameworks by comparing common and statute law.

Section III presents a synthesis of Coase and the *Calculus* in a single framework, allowing comparisons to be drawn between disputes resolved under unanimity voting rules (the *Calculus* and statute law) and then under rules of property (Coase and common law).We show that it is possible for the same outcome to occur under either process in a static world; that is, legislators seeking to pass a liability rule could write a law having the same effective content as one agreed to by contracting parties. However, the symmetry breaks down in a dynamic world. Transfers in the form of outcomes (statutes) specialized and modified to various constituents can occur with voting, whereas under the common law specialized interests contract around rules rather than make investments to change the rules.[5] In other words, special interest groups can gain more by seeking a specialized statute than by contracting in the market.

The final part of the chapter concludes that systems of law in competition with the common law generally prevail while never completely appropriating the common law; that is, the common-access domain of common law is gradually eroded to accommodate special interest statutory law.[6]

II. THE THEORETICAL FRAMEWORK

Some Distinctions

Legislative choice or statute making, which is the focus of the *Calculus*, concerns public dispute resolution where public actions occur in a large-number setting.[7] The Coase Theorem applies to common law and private dispute resolution—private actions in small-number settings.[8] While there are differences that reach beyond this private versus public distinction, both the *Calculus* and Coase deal with a common issue of internalizing externalities in the presence of transaction or decision-making costs.

Ironically, statute law, the product of collective decision making produced by large legislative bodies, is often tailored to meet special interest demands of small groups. By contrast the common law, produced in a small-numbers setting, creates standards that are generalized to a large-number setting. Common law, thought to be private law, is often applied more generally than statutory law.

This does not mean that specialized rules of liability, such as those that relate to flammable sleepwear, do not emerge in common law settings. The common law defines the broad parameters of liability, permitting the market to operate by creating more specialized rights and liabilities (standards) through mutually beneficial private agreements that contract within or even around the common law. Theoretically, each and every contract can contain a unique standard. On the other hand, contracting around statutory law is generally prohibited. Statutory law is not a two-stage process whereby private individuals can create their own law in abrogation of existing statutes.

Legislative action can also be distinguished from market transactions on the basis of an emphasis on process versus substantive rules. The *Calculus*, which seeks to describe political decision making, has little to say about the substantive law that emerges under various decision-making rules. It is almost exclusively process oriented. It shows that for any given voting rule external costs will vary for different substantive issues. Institutional arrangements that define specific rights and liabilities are not discussed. On the other hand, Coase is also a process framework that focuses on reciprocal costs, but is less abstract than the *Calculus* in that the institutional structure of existing rights and liabilities is used to define reciprocal costs. Coase analyzes the "judicial process," not the "legislative process" or "constitutional process," although many economists blur this distinction.

The *Calculus* framework implies that all rights and liabilities emanate from the Constitution or collective, a view shared by most lawyers.[9] From the perspective of the *Calculus*, all property is, in a sense, undefined collective property subject to reallocation by legislatures that are constrained by constitutions. U.S. constitutional constraints, such as the "equal protection" and "due process" clauses, can be interpreted as requiring a sort of common access approach in the exercise of legislative authority. The treating of unequals as equal under the law, defined as the common access approach, provides protection against using the process for specialized interests. These clauses operate in ways similar to the use of supramajority rules in the *Calculus*.

Parallels of the Common Law and Constitutional/ Statutory Law

The common law sets some broad (exogenous) parameters by which individuals are permitted the freedom generally to contract around when it is in their interest to do so; that is, agreements that are mutually beneficial are made that represent specialized interests. In this sense, common law outcomes are the result of a two-stage process. The first stage is set by the evolution of rules constrained by precedents, the second by contracting around the rule.[10] Similarly, the Constitution is analogous to the common law in that it sets broad (exogenous) parameters in which legislators, but not private individuals, are permitted to contract among themselves (the statute-making process) and at least implicitly contract with constituents and interest groups. The enactment of statutes generally prohibits subsequent contracting around. Therefore, all affected interests must logroll (contract) at the time. Hence, all contracts are telescoped into one stage under the legislative process.

While both processes allow for gains from trade in the formation of law, these two frameworks treat transactions costs differently. Transactions costs in Coase concern defined and exclusive rights and are primarily the costs associated with engaging in voluntary exchanges. There is a status quo defining rights and liabilities prior to exchange. Costs are incurred in transacting away from the status quo.[11] The rights to undefined future rents associated with specific assets are defined before all transactions occur. No arbitrary reallocation or division of rents occurs exogenously.[12]

By contrast, when legislatures vote to take action (the *Calculus*), decision-making costs (transactions costs) can be interpreted as the costs of converting undefined collective or common property rights into private rights. Rents can be created and reallocated in the process. These costs are appropriately defined as decision-making rather than transactions costs. The status quo, existing statutes, the common law and precedents are not binding constraints on the legislature other than through the influence these rights have in defining one's position in the collective. Thus, property rights defined under the common law are not exclusive if collective decision making can evade or can change those rights.

This raises the question, what are the external costs generated by the statute-making process? Can there be external costs in the absence of defined rights and liabilities or an institutional setting? Are external costs the cost of not being in the winning or prevailing coalition? Such a definition seems consistent with the notion that all external costs are internalized (are zero) under a rule of unanimity. To consider this question, it is necessary to distinguish between the pre- and postconstitutional stage. In the postconstitutional stage, with a rule of unanimity and zero transactions costs, substantive rights and liabilities are likely to emerge. The initial distribution of property (wealth) is the default position. Movement away from that position implies gains from trade as legislators exchange votes. The logrolling process involves the formation and exchange of specialized benefits. Thus, as the decision-making rule expands toward unanimity, the laws that emerge are likely to become more specialized and less of a commons.[13] This is why some sort of "veil of ignorance" or a long-run view of not knowing one's place or position in the future is imposed at the constitutional stage.

Judicial Legislation

It might be argued that common law is similar to statute law in that judges act as legislators. These arguments put little emphasis on the doctrine of *stare decisis*. If each judge made up the law for each dispute before him on the basis of personal preferences, then the special interest, small-numbers argument would be valid. The doctrine of *stare decisis*, the common law doctrines of standing and justiciability, constrain judicial legislating.[14] Finally, Articles 1 through 3 (Separation of Powers) of the U.S. Constitution also constrain judicial legislating.[15] These constraints on the common law process maintain a commons. For example, the common law property interest called "fee simple" has not only affected the decisions of millions of individuals in this country, but also millions of people in other common law countries, in this and numerous past generations. Statute laws of common law countries are not comparable in duration and scope. While tariff and other statutes endure in a general sense, there is continual tinkering with specific content.

Supraplurality rules such as unanimity are the parallel to common law precedents that could constrain legislatures. Unanimity supports the status quo, a reference to existing statutes, the existing constitution, and the common law. If a simple majority vote could amend the Constitution, its essence would be lost. Thus the Constitution can be thought of as the vehicle for creating precedents by supraplurality voting rules.

External Costs versus Reciprocal Costs

In the *Calculus*, analysis focuses on the expected external costs of collective decision making. Coase focuses on reciprocal costs associated with the assignment of rights and liabilities. Are external costs equivalent to reciprocal costs? To examine this issue, assume zero transactions costs and zero decision-making costs. Coase emphasized that the assignment of a right or liability in the common law will always impose a (reciprocal or external) cost on others. This cost would seem to be similar, if not identical, to the (reciprocal or external) cost imposed by some portion of the collective on the other portion (minority) of the collective under various decision rules (except unanimity) under the *Calculus*.

However, use of the term "external cost" in the context of constitutional choice creates a vagueness not associated with Coase's term of reciprocal cost. The difficulty with the term external cost is related to, but goes beyond, Steven Cheung's criticism of the term.[16] Consider the externalities (discomforts) that might be created by cigarette smoke. Thought immediately turns to the notion that the smoker imposes costs on nonsmokers. The term externality connotes a causation or unidirectional meaning for which Coase criticized A.C. Pigou.[17] Reciprocal costs, however, convey no such meaning.

Clarifying this confusion is Coase's major contribution.[18] As he points out, all costs are reciprocal.[19] Reciprocal costs are simply another term for opportunity costs. If rights are not assigned, reciprocal (opportunity) costs are the costs of the party or parties not designated to receive the right. If rights are assigned or established, reciprocal (opportunity) costs are the costs (payments) that the party with the right forgoes by not exchanging his right. In the smoking example, smokers held the right to smoke that has been gradually shifted by statutes and ordinances to become rights of nonsmokers. The reciprocal (opportunity) cost in this case is, of course, the value smokers place on the right to smoke in prohibited areas.

The reciprocal nature of costs is also recognized in discussions of voting rules, especially made apparent by a rule of unanimity. It is commonly believed that a rule of unanimity allows one individual to impose significant costs on the collective by the exercise of a veto. Under unanimity, each individual can be thought of as the potential owner of the benefits (rights) under the collective agreement. Each individual has the independent right to contract with the collective, and the collective is required to contract with each individual in reaching agreement. The reasoning here is a collapsed version of Coase in which any contracting around the collective rule must occur at the time of the collective agreement or not at all. Rules short of unanimity result in fewer (less) contracts (logrolling) among members of the collective, a point to be discussed later.[20]

III. LIABILITY RULES: COASE VERSUS THE CALCULUS

Assigning a rule of liability and then contracting around the rule under common law can be viewed as having the same effect as requiring unanimity for the passage of a liability statute in the *Calculus*. But this does not mean that the outcomes with respect to transactions and transfers will be the same under Coase and the *Calculus*, even if there were no transactions costs or decision-making costs. The difference can be understood by comparing externalities that are internalized to those that are economically irrelevant.

Suppose that, under the common law of nuisance, A has the right to create smoke using his barbecue. A's neighbor, B, may highly value a smoke-free environment and contract with A to change the location of the grill. Another of A's neighbors, C, may also value a smoke-free environment, but not enough to induce A to change the location or reduce the smoke or for C to take avoidance measures. The A–B transaction is called the internalization of a (Pareto) relevant externality where gains from trade are realized. The externality (cost) imposed on C by A is called (Pareto) irrelevant because there are no gains from trade. This is the equilibrium position regardless of A's right to create smoke.

However, if the rule of liability held that A had no right to use his barbecue if anyone objected, the internalization of the Pareto relevant externality is the C–A transaction, and the B–A externality is now irrelevant. By changing the definition of rights, the transfers have changed in direction, and presumably in magnitude.

Now consider a collective decision among A, B, and C with a rule of unanimity. If A values the right to use his barbecue more than B and C value a smoke-free environment, and they have such a right initially, then A must compensate both B and C to reallocate the right. If B and C value a smoke-free environment more than A values the use of his barbecue, and A has such a right initially, then A can extract transfers from both B and C. A rule of unanimity means that all externalities are relevant in the sense that all voters have a right in the collective outcome and, therefore, may require compensation even if the imposed cost is slight. If compensation is produced by the logrolling process, then it is easy to see why statutes with a unanimity rule would be very specialized. Any gains from trade, and binding agreements about subsequent trades, must occur with the vote, and that is the equilibrium. There are no postvoting opportunities for gains from trade unless the collective agrees.[21] To permit contracting around the collective agreement would be tantamount to not requiring unanimity, or for that matter not abiding by a collective decision rule.

If a legislative rule of less than unanimity is required, there are fewer transactions (contracts) required across individual voters and thus fewer transfers. It is tempting to refer to such transfers under collective decision making as rent-seeking or income transfers. The distinction between (Pareto) relevant and irrelevant actions requires a reference point, a starting point like the status quo. If A values using his barbecue at $100 and B suffers a cost of $10 from such use, B's cost can be considered a Pareto irrelevant externality or simply an irrelevant cost that will not be internalized by A, provided A has the right. On the other hand, if B has the right to prevent

A's use of his barbecue, then B can impose a $100 (external) cost on A that is relevant or will be internalized to B if there are zero transaction costs.

All right (liability) assignments have opportunity costs. So it is with collective decision making. Congress has certain powers to define and redefine rights and liabilities subject to the Constitution. But a representative (or constituent) does not have exclusive rights to the process. The rights are more like "common property." For example, suppose there is a rule of unanimity, and a measure is being voted on that provides $5 billion net benefits to 10,000 people and imposes a cost of $10 on one person. The $10 cost is not irrelevant to the group or the single individual, since that person has the right not to be injured by collective action. Moreover, the single individual may extract a significant portion of the total gains of $5 billion.[22] It is questionable to call the individual's behavior extortion unless receiving rent or surplus in voluntary trades is defined as extortion.[23] Under such a definition, all market gains could be considered as extortions. Moreover, while the individual may have the right to extract significant gains, he is not likely to monopolize the power since each participant holds the marginal vote that can veto whatever deals are struck.

Rights Evolution under Less-than-Unanimity Rules

Now consider a less-than-unanimity voting rule to determine rights and liabilities. The individual who held out would be unlikely to receive a transfer since he does not have a right to prevent collective action. The cost imposed on the individual is also irrelevant (i.e. is, will not be internalized by the collective). Thus, as the decision rule moves from unanimity to less than unanimity, the initial rights before logrolling move from common rights toward exclusive rights, in that minorities can be and are excluded from claims to the benefits of collective decision making. The exclusion results in fewer deals or logrolling to give up one's right (vote) to block collective action; that is, there are fewer special interest groups required to form a winning coalition.[24]

The currency of logrolling is the exchange of private special interest laws. Common law enactments that treat unequals as equals are not currency that can be used to logroll common rights associated with voting into private specialized interests.[25] As the plurality required to make collective decisions increases, the common rights associated with collective decision making increase. This common right eventually becomes privatized by special interest legislation. Thus, the reason there are more transfers involved in statutory law relative to common law is that there are "common property" rights, whereas common law is confined to individual private rights. The argument that transfers will be larger and will involve irrelevant effects under the *Calculus* versus Coase approach is important to the central point of this chapter.

The argument regarding the relative size of transfers is based on the notion of special interest demand for government (rent seeking). But all legislative actions do not conform to that notion. There are some rules or rights that are so broadly supported that logrolling is not needed for their passage. True public good actions (in the technical sense of the term) that generate benefits to all·parties and perhaps reduce costs to all would draw unanimous support, if that were required. For example, rules requiring all vehicles to drive on a particular side of the road are superior to no rule at all.[26] A proposal for such an action would hardly require negotiation across legislators. However, when there are distributional effects, legislators who broker statutes hold a superior position over judges who create common law, with the consequence that we should still expect to observe meaningful erosion of common law over time.

Voting for Rights with a Perpetual Commons

The above voting solution is based on comparative statics, a once-and-for-all voting solution (the *Calculus*), compared to the common law/contracting solution (Coase). Reconsider the legislative process or agenda as common property subject to constitutional constraints. As before, assume that the legislative commons is jointly owned community property, not undefined or public property. The problem of the legislative process is the same problem associated with all common property. The traditional problem has been recognized as overgrazing, overharvesting, and overfishing. In our case it is overlegislating, where the average product of legislating exceeds the marginal product of legislating.[27]

This commons problem may be the essence of what is meant by the need for limited government. While we can conceptualize this common property becoming privatized into special interest legislation in a comparative static sense, in a dynamic sense it is never permanently privatized or made exclusive.[28] There is less invested in privatization or exclusivity because it is understood that the next round of legislation begins with the potential of converting the prior, special private interests into a commons once again.[29] There are few institutional constraints, other than the Constitution, that permit private interests to become truly private in the exclusionary sense for a prolonged time period to permit a transfer or capture of the capitalized value of special interest legislation. Special interest legislation is more like the creation of rental interests. In addition, the horizon problem tends to cause decisions to be made that do not maximize the long-run value of assets compared to a private property right arrangement. Legislative bodies can invade what they previously created as exclusive rights for special interests.[30]

Beyond the Constitution, there is a limiting counterforce, which may be embodied in party leadership, that disciplines an otherwise chaotic legislative process. The legislature must have some degree of contract credibility in order to expand and contract marginal contracts. For government actions to be broadly consistent across time, durable commitments must be made to major groups and the general public, even though short-term opportunities for political gain tempt politicians to open debate on previously settled issues.[31] The time consistency constraint forces politicians to search for new social issues that can lead to the amending of settled contracts or to the expansion of the contracting domain.

Under current institutional arrangements, the legislature can change property rights on the basis of public policy. This leads to overlegislating, the churning of property rights. If common rights could be permanently privatized, there would be fewer investments in legislating in the long run. Eventually, all special interests would be covered by legislation. The legislative body would then focus its energies on other matters.

This dynamic view presents a different conclusion from the static view presented earlier and is at odds with the position taken by Gary Becker on the efficiency of the legislative process.[32] Our previous argument assumes the commons could be permanently privatized. However, under this dynamic view, if there are no constraints on privatization (e.g., legislation can rearrange rights or the administration can vary public enforcement based on public policy), then there is an atrophy in the value of previously determined special interest rights.

The situation can be visualized in terms of fishing from a body of water with common rights such that the average product exceeds the marginal product. From our previous discussion it would follow that commercial fishermen would lobby for private property or exclusive rights to fish. They have the highest value use and therefore would be the successful lobbyists, even though other groups may value the commons for such things as sport fishing or pristine views of placid waters. These other groups may require compensation (logrolling) depending on the decision-making rule. But legislators cannot grant exclusive or private rights into the future with perfect certainty. Still recognizing that some political contracts are out of bounds for time consistency reasons, legislators are assumed to be legislators in an active sense, not simply acting to defend or refine prior legislation. The latter is the task of the judiciary.

This atrophy of legislative rights that cannot guarantee exclusive rights means that the magnitude of transfers through lobbying (logrolling) is considerably smaller in any single period than has been previously discussed in this chapter.[33] The transfers are short-term rents rather than transfer of exclusive property rights in fee simple. Moreover, transfers can also occur by shifting from private rights to common rights to private rights and so on, whereas the traditional view is that private rights are simply reallocated by the special interest lobbying process. Put differently, the legislature has only limited constraints that emerge from opportunity costs derived from a stable and durable set of property rights, and those relate to one category of actions that ensure durability to the process. Under this analysis it is understandable why, despite all the rhetoric, privatization or contracting out has generally not been favored by legislators. A commitment to privatization could reduce the scope of the legislative commons and thus limit temporarily the power and control of legislators and bureaucrats. Even with privatization, politicians have the opportunity to extract rents in the contracting-out process.[34]

Common Law and Markets

This dynamic framework also explains why the common law is fundamental to markets as emphasized by Commons, Leoni, Hayek, and others. Precedents or the doctrine of *stare decisis*, in conjunction with the right to contract around the common law, prevent the common law from becoming a vehicle for making special interest transfers. One might argue that statute law evolves in a manner similar to the common law since there are similar traditions (jurisprudence) among the courts regardless of the type of law adjudicated. However, the requirement of standing, *inter alia*, distinguishes the process of common law from statute law. Except for a claim of unconstitutionality, an individual normally does not have standing to challenge statutes. Moreover, most statutes are enforced by a state or federal agency, that is; usually only these agencies have standing.[35]

However, agencies are subject to political pressures and bureaucratic incentives that result in varying enforcement patterns. Whatever the evolution of agency law, it is not going to resemble the private dispute-resolution process that evolves under the common law. For example, there were significantly different types and numbers of both antitrust and consumer protection actions brought by the Federal Trade Commission (FTC) in the 1980s compared to the 1970s. Just as the current legislature cannot bind future legislatures, it is also not possible to guarantee that current FTC patterns will extend into the future.

This analysis highlights the importance of the taking of property and freedom of contract clauses in the U.S. Constitution as limiting the legislative commons. The definition and scope that the courts give these clauses and their interpretation have varied dramatically as in the Lochner and post-Lochner eras.[36] This variability means the residual of rights can be considered common rights subject to privatization and redefinition with time by legislatures and judges.

Becker and others suggest that the choice of forum for satisfying specialized individual interests depends on the costs of transacting in the private market versus the collective (public) market. Thus, collective choice is efficient if there are lower transactions costs compared to market choice. This conclusion is misleading. A decision to use the market by, say, purchasing an easement, does not affect the common law or statute law. It is an endogenous choice within an exogenous legal framework. On the other hand, a decision adopted by the collective, say imposition of eminent domain, is not only a change in statute law but also may result in the elimination of common law and generate a restriction on the scope of private market activities.

The legal framework, except for a Constitution based on common law principles, is endogenous. The choice of a new statute (social contract) means forgoing the common law, whereas the choice of a contract within the common law does not mean society forgoes statute law. Thus collective choice transactions have an opportunity cost of fewer market transactions. This opportunity cost may be what Hayek had in mind when discussing interference with the market order: "the more indirect and remote effects will mostly be unknown and will therefore be disregarded."

IV. CONCLUSION

This chapter has compared the *Calculus* and Coase frameworks as alternative rights evolution processes. Disputes within a Coasian framework are resolved primarily by contracting around exogenous common law property and liability rules. Disputes in the *Calculus* are also resolved by contracting (logrolling), but the laws and rules are determined endogenously subject to a constitution, which places limits on legislators.

The Coasian framework and common law deal with small-number controversies that evolve into slowly changing precedents that are applied to a large number of undefined economic agents. The *Calculus* and statutory law relate to controversies resolved in a large-numbers setting that often evolve into specialized statutes that apply to a small number of well-defined agents. The common law process has requirements such as case in controversy, standing, and the doctrine of *stare decisis* that diminish profitable opportunities for making specialized transfers. The absence of precedents, the absence of supraplurality voting rules, and the inability to contract around statutes may result in significant transfers occurring in the legislative process relative to the common law process.

Our comparisons of outcomes under the Coasian and the *Calculus* frameworks lead to the conclusion that transfers are larger in the *Calculus* setting. Transfers under the Coasian framework are exclusively economically relevant. What may be economically irrelevant under the common law and markets becomes relevant with voting rights. The analysis supports the notion that legislative brokering can be expanded by substituting statutory law for common law.

Our static comparison of Coase and the *Calculus* with a rule of unanimity shows that allocative outcomes are invariant with respect to those two frameworks, although the magnitude of transfers is larger under the *Cal-*

culus. A rule of unanimity is in essence a contractarian approach to government and the counterpart to the Coasian framework. However, a comparative analysis of the two processes in a dynamic setting predicts a gradual decay in the value of special interest rights and transfers in the legislative framework. Legislatures are only able to grant, and special interests to receive, rental rights. The uncertain status of property rights inherent to the legislative process coupled with cyclical efforts to privatize the legislative commons ultimately atrophies the common law and, as some have argued, the commonwealth as well. We conclude that competitive struggles between common law and statute law processes for settling disputes and determining liability rules will systematically favor the latter. Statute law stands above common law in the legal hierarchy, and the relatively unconstrained legislative commons offers numerous opportunities for rearranging rules to facilitate wealth transfers. Common law is anchored by precedents, yet made flexible by the ability to contract around. Except for the Constitution, legislation has no such anchor and all contracting that occurs must occur in the legislative process.

Much has been written about legislative transfers in a normative sense under the heading of rent seeking. Our analysis presents a positive analysis of transfers by examining property rights. We conclude that legislative transfers (rents) have probably been overstated because of the inability of legislatures to bind future legislatures and thereby permanently privatize rights afforded special interests. The rent-seeking literature appears to have ignored what is perhaps the highest opportunity cost of legislation. Our analysis explicitly identifies the opportunity costs by showing that legislation tends to erode the common law, which is the foundation for markets.

NOTES

The authors express appreciation for criticisms and comments provided by Bill Dougan, Thomas Hazlett, Roger E. Meiners, Anthony Ogus, and Gordon Tullock.

1. James M. Buchanan and Gordon Tullock, *The Calculus of Consent* (Ann Arbor: University of Michigan Press, 1962).
2. Ronald Coase, "The Problem of Social Cost," 3 *Journal of Law & Economics* 1 (1960).
3. John R. Commons, *Legal Foundations of Capitalism* (Madison: University of Wisconsin Press, 1968).
4. Along these lines, Bruno Leoni notes: "[T]here is much more than an analogy between the market economy and a judiciary or lawyer's law, just as there is much more than an analogy between a planned economy and legislation." (See Bruno Leoni, *Freedom and the Law* [Los Angeles: Nash Publishing Co., 1972], p. 22.)
5. Hurst compares the use of common law to legislation for special interest purposes: "Doctrines of standing, justiciability, and precedent hedge in lawmaking

by judges.... Anyone who can persuade a legislature to introduce a bill can cause subject matter of interest to him to be put into the legislative machinery.... That a proposed measure will use law for a purpose or in a way that lawmakers never pursued before, or that it will change prior common law or statute law, raises no legal barrier to adopting it. Not even Constitutional limitations bar bringing any given matter in the legislative arena." (See James Willard Hurst, *Law and Markets in United States History* [Madison: University of Wisconsin Press, 1982], p. 124.)

6. One might argue that the common law prevails over statute law when a statute is repealed. This is not entirely true. The courts are likely to look to legislative intent in why the statute was repealed rather than simply revert back to the previous common law rule. (See Leonard Liggio and Tom Palmer, "Freedom and the Law: A Comment on Professor Aranson's Article," 11 *Harvard Journal of Law & Public Policy* 713 [1988], p. 715, for examples of statutes preempting the common law in the broad areas of electromagnetic broadcasting, water rights, and intellectual property rights. Another example is seen in the Federal Trade Commission Act [1914] that preempted much of the common law on unfair trade.)

If there is a conflict between the Constitution and a statute or common law, then the Constitution prevails. Thus, the common law prevails only when there has been no preemption by the Constitution or statutes. These three types of laws can be interpreted as alternative institutional arrangements in that one could choose (1) to operate within the common law and either accept the rule or contract around the rule, (2) to litigate the rule in an attempt to change the rule, (3) to lobby legislators to adopt a new rule, and (4) to lobby to change the Constitution. Each of these actions is likely to be mutually exclusive and the chosen action will depend on relative expected costs and benefits.

7. The term *public good* is not used in a public goods context. Rather, the term *public* is used to mean actions taken by a collective subject to constitutional constraints. The public goods argument for collective action is raised later in the paper.

8. The class action suit is an exception but limited in use because of restrictions requiring members of the class to be similar in terms of the manner of injury and the extent of the injuries.

9. For example, constitutional law casebooks criticize the legal reasoning of the Lochner era, named after *Lochner v. New York*, 198 U.S. 45 (1905). During this period, the U.S. Supreme Court struck down numerous regulations on the basis of infringing on freedom of contract under the Fourteenth Amendment. Since that period, which ended in the 1930s, the predominant legal view is that rights can be defined only by a sovereign government and not on the basis of some natural rights theory.

10. There are, of course, areas of the common law that do not permit contracting around (e.g., some areas of tort and criminal common law), just as there are statutes that permit contracting around (e.g., general incorporation statutes). However, most market transactions rest fundamentally on the common law of contract and property that in general permits contracting within and around the rule. (But see Richard Epstein, "Beyond Foreseeability: Consequential Damages in the Law of Contract," 18 *Journal of Legal Studies* 105 [1989] for a discussion of the court's use of generalized principles of damages based on tort in place of explicit damages stated in contracts as an example of limitations on the right to contract around the rule.)

11. The common law, even under the doctrine of *stare decisis*, evolves (changes)

and is not static for all time. Our emphasis is on the relative evolution of common law compared to statute law. There is no counterpart to *stare decisis* in the process of making statute law that could constrain the evolution. Moreover, even though products liability can be interpreted as changing a rule of *caveat emptor*, at the beginning of the century, to *caveat venditor* today, common law products liability is still based on broad principles rather than special interest demands. The right to contract around the common law, unlike statute law, permits adaptation to changing technology and values. Criticism of the common law as preserving the status quo fails to recognize the importance of the right to contract around the common law. In this sense, statute law is based on a preservation of the status quo because of the absence of the right to contract around. See Lawrence E. Blume and Daniel L. Rubinfeld, "The Dynamics of the Legal Process," 2 *Journal of Legal Studies* 405 (1982) for a criticism of the common law efficiency literature on the basis that it is static and explicitly or implicitly gives little weight to precedents. They in turn argue that an optimal weight be given to precedents. Also see George L. Priest, "Measuring Legal Change," Civil Liability Program, Working Paper 58, Yale Law School (April 1987), which uses settlements as a measure of change.

12. In another sense, transactions costs are used in avoiding exchange, rather than reflecting the costs associated with exchange. Coase urged judges to allocate property rights in a way to reduce transactions even when market transactions were feasible. This type of transaction cost is not associated with the status quo or an established set of rights.

13. This is likely to be true only if there are zero transactions costs. Transactions costs increase the price of transfers, and transactions costs increase as the rule approaches unanimity. (See William R. Dougan and James M. Snyder, "The Logic of Inefficient Regulation," Unpublished manuscript, Clemson University [1989].)

14. See *supra* note 6.

15. Obviously, this constraint is more binding as applied to statutory law relative to common law, where the conflict of making versus finding the law is not as apparent.

16. See Steven Cheung, "The Structure of a Contract and the Theory of a Non-Exclusive Resource," 13 *Journal of Law & Economics* 49 (1970), who argues there are no externalities but only problems of contracting or very high transaction costs.

17. A. C. Pigou, *The Economics of Welfare*, 4th ed. (London: Macmillan, 1946). Pigou's analysis is a good example of ignoring the reciprocal nature of costs. It is natural to think of cause and effect, a unilateral externality, in discussing costs. Coase, *supra* note 2, of course, questions the usefulness of causation in allocating rights and duties. This criticism seems valid when rights or duties are not established. However, when rights are established, it is natural to think of cause and effect. If A punches B, it is correct to say that A caused injury to B. When rights are defined there is causation in that A has a duty of liability to avoid injuring B's property including his body. On the other hand, there are opportunity costs of maintaining this right that would preclude one from the boxing profession. Thus, one can ask what the opportunity (reciprocal) costs of established rights are while maintaining causation.

18. But see Richard Epstein, "Causation and Corrective Justice: A Reply to Two Critics," 8 *Journal of Legal Studies* 477 (1979).

19. James M. Buchanan and William C. Stubblebine, "Externality," 29 *Economica* 371 (1962), further clarify the point.

20. Serious discussions of unanimity voting rules, of the sort presented here, are often viewed as being out-of-bounds with reality. We note one brief, but meaningful experience when under the Articles of Confederation (1786–1788) unanimity was required of all actions taken by the confederation of American states. We also note that John C. Calhoun, while a U.S. Senator (1820s), argued strongly for a system of concurring majorities, which effectively gave each state a veto right. His proposal had the same effect as a unanimity rule. (We are grateful to Peter Aranson for having called these two items to our attention.)

21. For a discussion of postequilibrium bargaining, see Ralph Turvey, "On the Divergences between Social Cost and Private Cost," 30 *Economica* 309 (1963).

22. See Fred McChesney, "Rent Extraction and Rent Creation in the Economic Theory of Regulation," 16 *Journal of Legal Studies* 101 (1987), for a discussion of legislators acting as "market makers" in the rent-seeking process.

23. See Gordon Tullock, "The Cost of Rent Seeking: A Metaphysical Problem," 57 *Public Choice* 15 (1988), on the difficulties of defining rent seeking in some normative sense as waste when property rights such as voting are considered.

24. Obviously, there are as many potential interest groups under majority rule as a rule of unanimity. We do not suggest any stability or unique property in the winning coalition as per the Arrow Impossibility Theorem. Such a property is not necessary for showing that there will be fewer transfers under less-than-unanimity rules compared to unanimity rules. Zero transactions costs are also assumed.

25. This analysis ignores public goods in the general sense of light or a signal from a lighthouse or television station. Specialized interest legislation generally benefits some group, and in that sense it is a public good. Even if public goods such as national defense were considered, logrolling is still likely given different preference intensities and the difficulties with a Wicksellian tax scheme. An omnibus bill with special interest legislation is a substitute for discriminatory taxes in providing public goods.

26. This example is taken from and discussed in Geoffrey Brennan and James M. Buchanan, *The Reason for Rules* (Cambridge: Cambridge University Press, 1985).

27. See Bruce Yandle, "Conflicting Commons," 38 *Public Choice* 317 (1982), for a more detailed discussion of legislative overgrazing as a commons problem.

28. The standard property rights terminology does not exactly correspond to the type of right discussed, since right referred to here is something of a hybrid. The standard characteristics of common property are usually thought to consist of non-exclusive and nontransferable rights. Private rights are thought to consist of exclusive and transferable rights. We are considering a bundle of rights consisting of limited transferability and limited exclusiveness; that is, there is a common right that can be transformed to an exclusive right, but only for limited time periods with the possibility of a reversion to common rights after some nonspecified period. Limited time shares in a condominium are somewhat similar but have more certainty or exclusiveness than the hybrid property right discussed above.

29. This argument reinforces Anthony Downs' "rational ignorance" argument. (Anthony Downs, *An Economic Theory of Democracy* [New York: Harper & Row, 1957], chs. 11–13.) It is not only the small probability of effecting the outcome of

an election that leads voters to be rationally ignorant, it is also the limited time horizon and ability to capitalize on more complete information that leads to rational ignorance in a commons.

30. This is subject to constitutional constraints such as the taking clause or freedom of contract. Note that this is not the standard efficiency argument of why common rights exist such as enforcement and transactions costs associated with exclusive rights exceeding the benefits of these rights (e.g., Demsetz's public parking lot or the provision of public "common" goods).

31. On the time consistency problem, see Finn E. Kydland and Edward C. Prescott, "Rules Rather than Discretion: The Inconsistency of Optimal Plans," 473 *Journal of Political Economy* 84 (1977): 473–91.

32. See Gary Becker, "A Theory of Competition among Pressure Groups for Political Influence," 98 *Quarterly Journal of Economics* 371 (1983). His argument seems to assume that all rights are exclusive and private, as we previously discussed in the static model. Becker's model does not permit a change in rights from the commons to private and back to commons. The legislators, as brokers, can in essence be considered to "churn the process" in a way similar to stockbrokers, where their wealth depends on the number of transactions (transfers) and not on maximizing wealth in some social sense. (Also see McChesney, *supra* note 22.)

33. See William R. Dougan and James M. Snyder, "Are Rents Fully Dissipated?" Unpublished manuscript, Clemson University (March 1989), for a different interpretation of why rents are not fully appropriated or dissipated. But see Richard Higgins, William Shughart, and Robert Tollison, "Free Entry and Efficient Rent Seeking," 46 *Public Choice* 247 (1985).

34. For empirical evidence in support of this statement, see Randall G. Holcombe, "The Tax Cost of Privatization," 56 *Southern Economics Journal* 732 (1990).

35. There are exceptions primarily in the antitrust, consumer protection, and environmental areas. Plus, in many cases, private causes of actions can piggyback the public cause of action.

36. See Bruce Yandle, "Property in Price," 9 *Journal of Economic Issues* 501 (1975), for an interpretation of prices as property or a commons. The concept provides insight into judicial interpretations of market regulation from the *Slaughter House* cases (1872) to *Nebbia v. New York* 291, U.S. 502 (1934), a period that includes the Lochner area.

3

Do Liability Rules Deter Takings?

David D. Haddock and
Fred S. McChesney

Protecting property rights by rules that require *ex ante* compensation is fundamentally different from protecting them by rules that tolerate *ex post* compensation. Some exchanges are legally permissible only through negotiated *ex ante* agreements. At this time and in this culture, marriage is an example: a man can only acquire a wife through proposal and acceptance in advance, not by carrying off a woman and compensating her for her losses later. Carrying off a prospective mate against her will is a serious crime (kidnapping), as is treating her as if she were one's wife (the crime of rape, among others). But in other situations, taking now with compensation to be paid later (if at all) is perfectly legal. As a commonplace example, automobile drivers are characteristically permitted to take (damage or destroy) another's property—even another's life—and to compensate the victim (or his estate) *ex post*. Indeed, depending on the jurisdiction in which the accident occurred, the driver may not be required to pay any compensation at all, providing his behavior, though clearly such as to increase the risks faced by others, is adjudged to have been within acceptable bounds, that is, was not "negligent."

Economists have paid little attention to the difference between rules requiring negotiation *ex ante* and those that require compensation *ex post*. But the distinction is a fundamental one in the law.[1] Whether physical or intangible, assets—or "entitlements" as they are often called in the law—that can be lost only by *ex ante* negotiation are said to be protected by "property rules"; those which can simply be taken, subject possibly to a requirement of *ex post* compensation, are protected by "liability rules."[2] This chapter first provides an economic rationale for the legal distinction and then discusses several issues that are related to the distinction.

In Section I we use an Edgeworth box to illustrate the difference between property and liability rules. Both sorts of rules are used in our legal system.

An important problem looms whenever a liability rule is in effect, however. In a sizable number of situations, the law's ordinary remedies for takings are intentionally and, we will show, understandably less than negotiated payments would be. In consequence, there is often an opportunistic incentive to take and pay compensation rather than to enter negotiation. As Section I discusses, the incentive to take opportunistically imposes social costs. Consequently, to dissuade opportunistic takings, additional remedies, which we have called "extraordinary sanctions," have evolved in the law as complements to ordinary compensatory damages.[3]

Section II expands the basic model of property versus liability rules. There are important reasons why an efficient legal system (or any other efficient system of precepts) would use property rules to protect some entitlements against some potential takers, while according other takings only liability protection. The choice between those protective rules has conventionally been analyzed as being determined solely by the magnitude of the transactions costs that must be borne during negotiation. But that analysis is incomplete, because it fails explicitly to take into account legal process costs. Acquisition of assets through the use of a liability rule imposes litigation costs directly on individuals, and it increases the costs that must be borne by society as a whole to maintain the judicial system itself. Failure to consider such costs is a considerable oversight, because legal process costs are positively correlated with transactions costs. Even more seriously, conventional models also ignore opportunism costs.

With the determinants of the choice of rules thus established, Section III focuses on one situation in which private actors themselves, as opposed to the judicial system, demonstrably alter their choices in response to those determinants. Within corporations, shareholders voluntarily opt for liability rules in some contexts, but select more complete property-rule protection in other contexts. The choice of the protective rule is implicit in the basic relationships among shareholders, in relations between shareholders and management, and in the ways that shareholders themselves define various rights in the face of potential corporate takeovers. By and large, it is seen, shareholders are effectively able to select their own combinations of property and liability protection for their entitlements and seem to make the selections in predictable ways. Opportunistic takings are not a problem, because shareholders themselves can change the "law" that protects their entitlements if opportunism threatens.

Protecting entitlements by individual choices apparently works well in purely private contexts like the corporation. But as discussed in Section IV, rule choices fail conspicuously in the typical public context, where the potential taker is the sovereign, upon whom private parties typically depend for definition and enforcement of the protective rules. The same possibilities for opportunism (i.e., to take rather than negotiate) by which private takers are tempted also tempts governmental takers. But governmental takers have several advantages over private opportunists. Government defines the terms and conditions of its own legal liabilities; it defines as well the sorts of compensation for which it agrees to be liable. But perhaps most important of all, it is extremely rare for the individuals within the government who are actually the takers to be personally liable for their opportunism, whether or not the government itself has accepted liability. In that regard, governmental agents are treated in a fashion that is totally at odds with the way private agents are treated. Governmental agents almost always can pass on to their principals—the taxpayers—the sanctions imposed as a result of the agents' behavior; private agents almost never can. Even if egregiously wrongful, governmental takings almost never result in personal liability for the responsible individuals.

I. PUNISHING PRIVATE TAKINGS

Property Rules versus Liability Rules

At common law, a "taking" is treated as a tort—the tort of conversion. In the standard economic model of torts,[4] legal sanctions internalize the external costs of socially beneficial activities such as driving an automobile, where the external costs are taken to be unambiguously ascertainable. Efficiency, and hence "optimal deterrence," requires that one take into account all the costs that one's actions impose on oneself and on others in the course of such beneficial activities. A potential defendant will choose the efficient level of an activity as long as expectationally he must always compensate the plaintiff by an amount that "makes the plaintiff whole."[5] Such awards are compensatory and will be referred to as "ordinary damages."

Note, however, that the standard tort model shows how to optimize externality, producing activities that are socially valuable on net, but not at the margin. That model says nothing about activities—theft is one example—that are socially injurious at any level, and for which, consequently, the optimal rate of occurrence is zero. To eradicate such activities, efficient law would instead try to "make the defendant whole," meaning that it would *reduce* the defendant's utility back to the level he could have enjoyed had he never undertaken the socially injurious activity.[6] The defendant must have anticipated attaining a level of utility greater than that, at least as a statistical expectation, or he would not have undertaken the forbidden activity.

The dichotomy between making plaintiffs whole and making defendants whole points to the fundamental difference between liability and property rules. Edgeworth boxes can be used to summarize a model, which we developed with Menahem Spiegel, that analyzes the distinction between the two rules and that investigates the sanctions that an efficient law would use to enforce those rules.[7] In Figure 3.1, the utility function of some person

Figure 3.1
Private Bargaining versus Strict Liability at Law

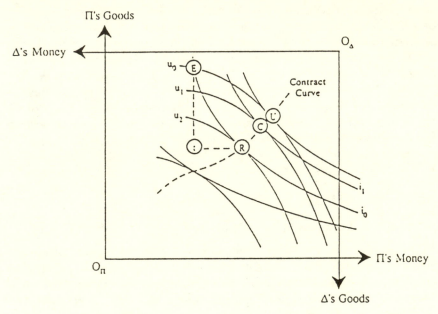

Patty Plaintiff is mapped over Patty's alienable entitlements: a composite good (on the vertical axis) and money (horizontally), with the origin in the lower left corner. The corresponding mapping of another person, Duke Defendant, has an origin at the upper right. Assume for now that each map is observable by Patty, Duke, and a court. Given that assumption, there need be no error in ascertaining an award that will make a plaintiff whole. Assume, however, that nobody can gauge relative bargaining skills. Initial entitlements are at E.

Property protection is illustrated for a "thin" or "illiquid" market—one with no "standard price quotation."[8] Assume for the moment that there are no transactions costs. With complete property protection an exchange results, if at all, from bargaining. Any reallocation will leave Patty and Duke on the contract curve between R and U, but at neither of those end points. Let the contract point be C. Neither Patty nor Duke is "made whole" by that transaction, because each is on a higher indifference curve at C than at E; that is, Patty and Duke share the available "gains from exchange."

Ex ante, however, bargaining outcomes in thin markets are not determinable; one cannot say in what proportions the gains from exchange will be shared. The parties have a common interest in reaching the contract curve, but as regards the exact point on the curve that is attained, their interests are totally opposed. Hence, although both Patty and Duke have been assumed for the moment to know each other's utility maps (and thus the contract curve), the location of point C will depend on the relative ability and willingness of the parties to negotiate. That process includes threatening to withdraw from the negotiation, running the risk of a failed negotiation, cajoling the bargaining partner while criticizing his apparent greed and lack of understanding of the realities of the market, and otherwise bargaining for an outcome more to the party's liking. Each party's degree of success in the bargaining process will depend on intelligence and negotiating experience, the opportunity cost of time, and beliefs (which may be erroneous) about the other's intelligence, negotiating experience, opportunity cost of time, and indifference map.

If a taking by Duke from Patty were substituted for negotiation, a strict liability remedy following litigation would be for ordinary damages. That award would make Patty "whole" by returning her to the indifference curve that passes through the original entitlement—here, the curve i_0 that passes through E. For illustration, assume that there are no legal process costs—there are no costs to the parties for litigating, or to the court for enforcing its judgment. Also assume that the court neither mistakenly imposes liability when no right has been violated nor fails to impose liability when a violation has occurred. Then a taking by Duke of Et units of Patty's goods will lead to a monetary remedy of tR. Et is Duke's preferred taking if he expects to have to compensate Patty, because at R Duke reaches the highest indifference curve (u_2) attainable, subject to the legal constraint that Patty must be returned to i_0.

Strategic Abuse of Liability Rules

Under present assumptions—thin markets, universal knowledge of Patty's and Duke's indifference maps, zero transactions, and legal process costs—one inference that typically is drawn from the Edgeworth box model is that there is no welfare preference between the Kaldor-Hicks equivalents R and C. R and C reflect only different asset distributions that each exploit all gains from exchange. Thus, there seems to be no welfare rationale for strict liability rather than property protection, or vice versa.

That inference is incorrect, because it ignores opportunism. Despite the apparent "social welfare" equivalence of R and C, Patty and Duke have personal preferences—Patty for C, Duke for R. If Duke expects to pay only a liability award, an incentive exists to expend resources to be a taker, who gets all gains from exchange. But Patty has an incentive to expend resources to prevent a taking and preserve some of those gains.[9] Because a taker in an illiquid market extracts all gains from exchange, *ex post* strict liability remedies that compensate Patty in a legal sense (tR) are undercompensatory in a larger sense. They leave unrestored some preexisting potential opportunities for exchange value—opportunities to share any gains from exchange that may be discovered. The now-impossible trade would have made Patty more than whole. Full compensation for the Et taken would be to a point on i_1, or even back to E, whence Patty still could negotiate to i_1 at point C.[10]

The distinction between full property and mere liability protections explained in the model above, and the problem of opportunism created by the distinction, can be illustrated for a simple, two-person setting by a recent court case. Rather than negotiate *ex ante* with Bette Midler for use of her voice, the advertising agency Young and Rubicam simply used a "soundalike" vocalist to record a song that had earlier appeared on one of Midler's albums, with the song being altered slightly to imply that the singer endorsed the products of a Young and Rubicam client, Ford Motor Company.[11] Young and Rubicam clearly wanted the public to believe that Midler endorsed the product: They had approached her first, but had been unsatisfied with the way negotiations progressed. Only then did they approach the Midler soundalike. They did not use the Midler soundalike to sing a Fleetwood Mac song, nor did they use a Stevie Nicks soundalike to sing a Midler song. Instead, they created a series of hints to listeners, all of which were consistent with a listener hypothesis that "this is Bette Midler, and she is endorsing Ford automobiles."

When Midler sued, suppose that Young and Rubicam had been required to "make her whole," that is, simply restore her to the level of utility she enjoyed prior to the unauthorized use of her voice. Ordinary damages would seemingly have been purely nominal—Ford Motor Company is a respectable enterprise, and Midler's reputation, album sales, and concert attendance were probably little changed (maybe even enhanced somewhat) as a result of having what seemed to be Midler singing her song over the national airwaves time and again. Moreover, Midler told the court that "I don't do commercials," so the court could reasonably conclude that Young and Rubicam had not spoiled the advertising market for her. Hence, ordinary damages, imposed on the advertising agency *ex post*, would actually have been a bargain for them. Had Young and Rubicam pursued negotiations until Midler agreed to have her distinctive voice heard in the fashion they proposed, the cost to them would surely have been substantially greater.

If an opportunistic Duke like Young and Rubicam can take and pay ordinary compensation (liability rules) rather than negotiate and share the gains from exchange (property rules), potential traders are in a prisoner's dilemma in illiquid markets. Even if compensation will be required, everyone's dominant strategy is to try to convert property protection that covers others' entitlements to liability protection in order to garner more potential gains from exchange. But the collectivity of traders will be disadvantaged if individuals can strategically substitute liability rules for negotiation.

Liability rules make thin-market entitlements a sort of commons, so gains otherwise available from exchange will be dissipated by searches for and

Figure 3.2
Effect of Imposing Punitive Damages

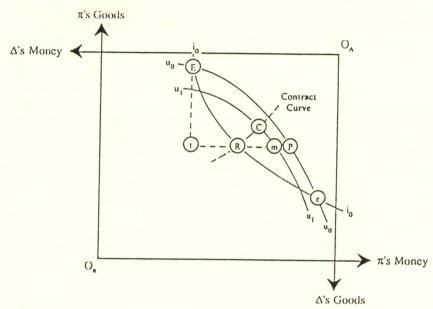

defense of takeable assets,[12] and resources available for investment will be diverted toward less takeable forms.[13] As explained more fully in Section II below, societies willingly bear such costs only when circumstances make property rules untenable. Property protection for entitlements is properly the norm; liability protection, and hence the standard tort model—or what we should properly call the standard *liability* model—are exceptional responses to exceptional circumstances.

Controlling Private Takings: Punitive Damages

A defendant is better off with a liability remedy of ordinary damages than with a contractual outcome, given the present assumptions. Thus, if legal remedies always imposed ordinary damages, as in the standard liability model, incentives would exist to forgo consensual exchange in favor of socially costly takings. To discourage a taking, the remedy must be expected to leave the defendant with no advantage vis-à-vis a bargain. When properly employed, punitive damages provide one way to strip defendants of their gains from abusing liability rules.

If return of the taken entitlement will be impossible, a taking of Et requires a remedy that moves allocations from t to m or beyond in Figure 3.2, thus leaving Duke with no more utility than the market would have provided.

But even if a court is assumed to know indifference maps, the court ordinarily would not know what voluntary bargain could have been struck between the parties—that is, the court would not know to which one of the infinity of points along the contract curve the parties would have negotiated. Thus, the court cannot know u_1, the critical level of Duke's utility to which he must be returned in order to discourage similarly placed potential defendants from bypassing negotiations with potential plaintiffs.

A court could only be sure that Duke would have been better off with a negotiated outcome (i.e., through respecting Patty's property protection) if the remedy for the taking puts Duke at or to the right of P. But moving Duke to P makes whole (or "compensates" in the economist's sense) the defendant by restoring Duke's pretaking utility. Compensation in that instance requires stripping away all the gains Duke expected from the action *ex ante*.[14] Therefore, the appropriate remedy for a violation of a property protection ("property violation" henceforth) is "punitive": It leaves Duke worse off than a negotiation would have. Merely compensatory damages would be insufficient to discourage takings and encourage negotiation.

In a thin market, a remedy that makes the defendant whole (strips all gain but nothing more) rarely makes the plaintiff whole (restores all loss but nothing more); in Figure 3.2 only point e, where i_0 and u_0 intersect, is equivalent for both Patty and Duke to point E, where i_0 and u_0 again intersect. Because a remedy that compensates the plaintiff (tR) often fails to compensate the defendant (tP), the form of the award that is appropriate for each dispute must be selected. When a property violation has occurred, restoring the defendant's initial utility has desirable properties—it removes incentives for a rational party to ignore the protection.

The standard liability model sees efficient law as being designed to mimic a missing market transaction—as is sometimes appropriate, but only when circumstances make it unreasonable or unnecessary to nurture a market. In contrast, the extraordinary sanctions model shows that efficient law would try to eradicate property violations, not help optimize them.[15] An efficient law would not help mimic a missing exchange in a property violation case, but instead would encourage individuals who are facing other potential exchanges to bargain. The marginal conditions applying to Duke's activity level would be irrelevant. Only totals would matter—Duke's expected costs, including punitive damages, would have to exceed Duke's expected benefits.

II. THE CHOICE BETWEEN PROPERTY RULES AND LIABILITY RULES

Transactions, Legal Process, and Opportunism Costs

Transactions Costs. It was noted above that liability protection is an exceptional response to exceptional circumstances. Those exceptional circumstances are typically taken to arise from high transactions costs. Automobile accidents are the commonplace example; it just seems too costly to negotiate in advance with all parties a driver would place at increased risk by some proposed change in his driving procedures, such as an increase in speed. When transactions costs for a particular potential exchange are high, people are less likely to enter negotiations in the first place. As a consequence, exchanges that otherwise might have afforded substantial gains will be thwarted. Under such circumstances, it is argued, the law ought to condone nonnegotiated takings.[16] The party that has lost an asset under those conditions will be permitted only to appeal to a court of law for the compensation that would make her whole.[17]

But the view that high transactions costs alone explain the choice between property and liability rules of protection for entitlements is too narrow. The benefit of moving from property to liability rules is indeed the saving of market transactions expenses. But that benefit must be compared to the cost incurred. To understand fully the cost/benefit calculus of property rules versus liability rules, it is necessary to relax two unrealistic assumptions made heretofore: that transactions costs are zero, and that legal process costs are zero.

The cost of a liability rule is twofold. First, acquisition of assets through the use of a liability rule entails legal process costs. Some external institution must set the terms of compensation *ex post*. Second, the use of liability rules leads to the costs associated with opportunistic potential defendant takers seeking takeable assets and the cost that potential plaintiffs incur to defend their assets, that is, the "opportunism costs" discussed above. In an efficient legal system one would not necessarily expect to observe liability rules merely because transactions costs are high, but rather because they are *higher* than the sum of legal process and opportunism costs. The chapter now focuses on those costs in turn.

Legal Process Costs. First, it is important to note that transactions and legal process costs are positively correlated with each other. Transactions costs will be high, *ceteris paribus*, when information costs are high. In situations in which it is difficult for one to know the reservation price of one's potential trading partner, one is apt to expend considerable resources trying to discover that magnitude. The discovery, however, will be made especially difficult because the trading partner will simultaneously be attempting to impede it; the party with superior information will be able to reach a superior position on the contract curve, and one's relative informational position will be improved both by augmenting one's own information and by retarding the acquisition of information by one's trading partner. Nevertheless, a mutually beneficial deal may ultimately be frustrated altogether if one is too intransigent, and that imposes constraints on a trader's behavior. Consequently, adequate information often will eventually dribble into negotiations, and an exchange will be concluded, though admittedly at considerable transactions costs.

But a nearly parallel argument can be made for legal process costs. A court cannot know whether a particular compelled exchange (taking) was desirable unless it can ascertain whether the reservation price of the defendant was higher than the reservation price of the plaintiff. In the same way, the court cannot ascertain an appropriate remedy without knowing what will make the plaintiff whole. And, again in parallel with the discussion of transactions costs, while maneuvering to obtain the best possible outcome for oneself in litigation, a party has an incentive to misrepresent relevant information and so increase the cost of discovering it. But, in distinction to the transactions costs discussion, a taking is often an accomplished fact prior to litigation. Hence, there is no constraint imposed on the defendant to give up relevant information eventually in order to continue the "negotiations." The "deal" has been concluded whether or not the parties can ever achieve a meeting of the minds.

Therefore, an efficient legal system would at times expect traders to incur high transactions costs imposed by property protection for a particular entitlement—or to forgo negotiations, and thus an exchange, altogether—because the legal process costs required if the system governed the exchange through a liability rule would impose even higher costs. Conversely, a liability rule may at times be acceptable to the law even though transactions costs would be low, because legal process costs are lower still.

Opportunism Costs. Now consider opportunism costs. When liability rules govern, there is the danger that potential takers will expend resources searching for takeable assets and that the assets' owners will expend resources defending the assets. But one would expect the elasticity of those expenditures with respect to the strength of property protection to vary across entitlements. For example, there are apt to be variations across assets in the economies of scale for both taking and defending; there are fewer car thieves per capita in the Dakotas than in the Bronx in part because car-thieving skills are worth less where the market for used automobile parts is smaller. Similarly, potential takers devote no resources to searching for victims when plaintiffs' losses are an unintended by-product of the takers' activities; the mere increased likelihood of killing automobile passengers does not induce railroads to reschedule trains to times of heavy traffic at railroad crossings.[18] Hence, when deciding whether to impose punitive damages, courts consider the state of mind of the defendant, in particular whether the act that led to the plaintiff's loss was "willful," and whether the potential injury could have been foreseen by the defendant.[19]

In summary, liability rules are more likely to be appropriate when the elasticity of opportunism costs with respect to the strength of property protection is low. Even with a low elasticity, however, liability rules will be inappropriate when legal process costs are high relative to transactions costs, whether or not the latter are high in some absolute sense. Indeed, as the next section illustrates, courts readily apply liability rules to takings that occur in one important group of markets in which transactions costs are extremely low.

Market Liquidity and the Choice between Punitive and Ordinary Damages

If plaintiffs received as remedies the allocations that would have resulted from negotiation—a "full liability" remedy, so to speak—no opportunistic use of the courts would occur. But such an award is infeasible in thin markets, particularly once the implausible assumption that courts know the litigants' indifference curves has been relaxed. The task of making Patty whole, difficult though it is, pales in comparison with ascertaining a counterfactual bargaining outcome. Determining a bargaining outcome requires ascertaining all conceivable bargains that might have been reached, then *guessing* which particular bargain would have been struck.[20] In effect, from the court's vantage the precise cost Patty has suffered from the taking is already ambiguous and unascertainable with precision. The court's task would be several orders of magnitude more difficult if it then went on to estimate market outcomes rather than simply making plaintiffs whole.

But if the assumption of a thin market is relaxed, and it is assumed instead that a reasonable quantity of the good is available at a well-defined price, full liability protection becomes feasible. As Figure 3.3 indicates, there is no role for extraordinary damages in thick markets. In a thick market each party faces a budget constraint passing through the initial endowments and having a slope determined by the goods' price, as shown in Figure 3.3. If Duke takes Et of Patty's goods, the proper remedy will restore Patty's original budget constraint at R′ rather than Patty's original utility at R. Patty regains the exchange value available at E; Patty can again trade to C, or back to E if no exchange had originally been attractive.[21] Strict liability and a property rule merge, but only because the meaning of compensation is altered still again when it is cheap to estimate a counterfactual market transaction. In effect, in a thick market strict liability *is* full liability.

Hence, the proper way to "make the plaintiff whole" depends on the degree of market liquidity. In a thick market, a remedy at C (or even R′) is preferable to E, because transactions costs are lower. Efficiency-minded courts would rarely grant equitable relief for thick-market takings, but will award damages instead. But an efficient remedy for a taking of Et in a thick market (tR′) will exceed ordinary damages for a similar taking in a thin market (tR), reflecting the court's lower information costs of recognizing the full value of a taken entitlement. For the same reason, the thick-market remedy will fall short of the punitive remedy a court will try to impose on an opportunistic taker in a thin market (tP).

Figure 3.3
Congruence of Bargaining and Strict Liability in Thick Markets

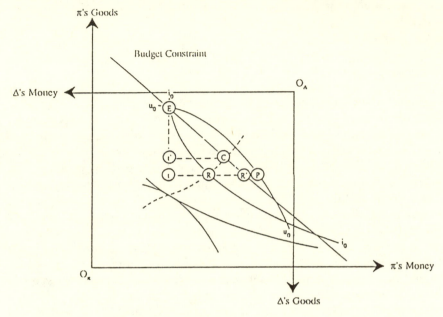

In summary, the definitions of property and liability rules of protection, plus the role of extraordinary sanctions, all depend on market liquidity. A strict liability rule and a property rule converge as markets become more liquid, so incentives for Duke's opportunism diminish, and the motivation for extraordinary damages is reduced apace.[22] An allocation at R′ makes both Patty and Duke whole relative to the contractual outcome at C (neglecting transactions costs), because each of them can exchange to C from R′. The thick-market setting requires little sacrifice of the benefits of property protection when a court acquiesces to takings, because movement to the budget constraint restores both Patty's full potential for exchange value and full use value.

Hence, even though transactions costs are ordinarily low in thick markets, courts willingly adjudicate liability takings that occur there and rarely (if ever) impose punitive damages where strict liability rules apply. That is because legal process costs also are low in thick markets, and opportunism costs are absent, since the defendant will have expected the court to arrive at a full liability remedy.

III. PRIVATE RULES AGAINST PRIVATE TAKINGS: THE CORPORATION

Use of liability rules creates an incentive for those who want to acquire an entitlement to behave opportunistically. Rather than negotiate *ex ante* for voluntary transfer, an acquirer (e.g., the Young and Rubicam advertising agency) actually benefits by simply taking an entitlement (e.g., the characteristics of Bette Midler's voice) and paying compensation *ex post*. As noted above, such opportunistic takings require that the law impose on a taker some extraordinary sanction such as punitive damages, in addition to compensatory awards to the victim, in order to mitigate the temptation to take rather than negotiate.

However, the simple two-person illustration of taking risks is misleading in two ways. First, the incentive to take rather than negotiate arises in considerably more complex institutional settings. As will be discussed below, taking rather than negotiating describes many of the strategic settings observed today in the world of corporate takeovers.

Second, as also illustrated by corporate takeovers, individuals often are able to set rules privately that minimize the potential for unwanted takings; that is, legal remedies such as punitive damages may be sufficient to control undesirable takings, but they are not always necessary. Corporations themselves adopt rules, which courts ordinarily will enforce, that define whether, and under what circumstances, their shareholders are prepared to acquiesce to a taking. Moreover, the corporate rules define lower bounds to the compensation that must be paid in the event of a taking. Any individual corporation's choice of rules reflects the various costs and benefits described above.

Internal Organization of Firms

The ability of private actors to set their own rules for protecting entitlements in a complex, multiparty situation is well illustrated by the internal organization of large corporations. With thousands of shareholders, a public corporation[23] faces relatively high transactions costs in obtaining shareholder approval for various policies that would be of benefit to owners. It is ordinarily too costly for outside contracting parties (creditors, suppliers, potential purchasers of the firm's assets, etc.) to negotiate individually with all of a firm's shareholders as a prelude to undertaking particular contractual or quasi-contractual acts. Moreover, requiring shareholder approval of every potentially beneficial action would create an opportunity for holdout strategies that might be used by some shareholders against others.[24]

As a consequence, shareholders appoint agents—corporate management—to represent them in contractual negotiations. Shareholders recognize that as a group they are better off when they are not consulted *ex ante* about every management initiative. Rational ignorance would guarantee that shareholders would rarely understand managements' proposals; the holdout problem would mean that important decisions would often be made more poorly if each shareholder's position had to be taken into account. Thus, corporate charters (articles of incorporation) and bylaws typically provide that management need not consult with shareholders prior to undertaking many sorts of new policy initiatives, nor need they submit the matter to a shareholder vote.

Should management behave negligently,[25] shareholders are limited to recovery of ordinary damages *ex post*, that is, to the sum that makes them whole after the fact. In effect, shareholders have voluntarily chosen to employ agents to run their corporation, and they have voluntarily chosen to protect their entitlements against agent negligence through a liability rule.[26] But note that the choice of rules that protects shareholder entitlements *is* largely voluntary. Shareholders are always free to specify in their charters those matters for which management will be required to obtain shareholder approval in advance; they are free to negotiate stipulated damages clauses in the contracts of their managers, and those damages need not be those that make shareholders whole. In such situations, property protection has been chosen instead of liability rules, but transactions costs necessarily will be higher as well.[27]

Corporate Takeovers

Hence, against their manager-agents, shareholders typically opt for liability protection against negligent behavior. But against outside acquirers, shareholders usually decide to protect their entitlements more strongly. They retain a certain self-specified level of property protection, albeit not full property protection, by the use of their corporate charters and bylaws.

Shareholders could insist that any would-be acquirer obtain their individual consent to any merger or acquisition; in effect, they could insist on full property protection. That arrangement would require that those hoping to acquire a firm negotiate with every shareholder, with a unanimity rule protecting each entitlement. But the high transactions costs of negotiating with a large number of dispersed shareholders, plus the notorious holdout costs associated with unanimity voting rules, mean that owners ordinarily agree to forgo complete property protection for their shares and adopt a weakened alternative instead.[28] Alternatively, when approached by a potential acquirer, shareholders could adopt the pure passivity posture propounded by some scholars.[29] As discussed in more detail below, that policy would essentially amount to the selection of a liability rule to protect shareholder entitlements.

Where potential takeovers are concerned, shareholders ordinarily opt for neither the strongest property protection they can design—a requirement of unanimity—nor for the near-liability protection that pure managerial passivity would entail. Instead, they appoint agents (usually the firm's managers) to negotiate for them, while retaining ratification powers, again short of unanimity, over the exchange that the agents negotiate. The shareholders expect the agents to obtain for them a part of the gains from the exchange, and hence expect to be made more than whole. The shareholders attempt to select the strength of entitlement protection that maximizes their expected benefits from potential takeovers, net of the costs they incur, which include any residual holdout costs.

In fact, there are rather fine gradations in the choice between property and liability protection for corporate entitlements, and rarely (if ever) will one observe two different firms opting for the same strength of protection for shareholder entitlements. There are different ways that would-be acquirers ("raiders") can obtain control of a firm. A merger requires approval of management and shareholders alike. But shareholders are free to set the number of votes needed for approval of mergers and typically require a proportion well short of unanimity (majority, two-thirds).

And there is ordinarily more than one way for a potential acquirer to obtain the requisite number of votes. The acquirer may persuade existing shareholders to vote to restructure the firm, the acquirer may purchase enough shares so that he owns the votes needed to restructure the firm, or the acquirer may pursue a strategy that mixes the other two. If the corporation's rules make it too easy for the acquirer to proceed by direct purchase of shares, which would make it unnecessary to obtain the approval of any of the preexisting entitlement owners, the dispersed target-firm shareholders run a risk of being placed in a prisoner's dilemma through an unwanted tender offer, with a dominant strategy to tender their shares.[30]

Without some prearranged defensive mechanisms, a successful tender offer/prisoner's dilemma could mean that shareholders would surrender their shares and the raider would acquire control for an offer only minimally in excess of current market price.[31] A tender offer allows the bidder to avoid negotiation with the shareholders' agents, management, and instead obtain the shares for a price that just barely makes shareholders whole. Like the opportunistic advertising agency that took rather than negotiated for the use of Bette Midler's voice, the tender offeror gains by substituting liability-rule compensation for more complete property protection of shareholder entitlements.

But that can occur only if shareholders and managers fail to institutionalize the degree of property protection that they have chosen. Firms are free to install defensive devices like poison pills, "fair price" amendments, and super-majority voting provisions, and to empower their agent-managers to undertake ad hoc maneuvers to resist acquirers' advances. All of those tactics make it more difficult for a bidder to avoid negotiating with the shareholders' agents, and hence make it more difficult to acquire control for a price that just makes shareholders whole.

The other side of the coin, of course, is that stronger property protection decreases the likelihood that any acquirer will materialize in the first place.[32] Stronger property protection reduces bidders' shares of the gains from exchange, holding the aggregate value of the target population constant, and that reduces the bidders' incentives to locate and bid for a target in the first place. But under present law the precise degree to which shareholders wish to protect their entitlements—ranging continuously from mere liability protection to complete property protection—is up to them.[33] Shareholders' choice in effect resolves the trade-off between the probability of and the gains from being acquired.[34]

There are many other situations in which owners of assets are able to decide for themselves what kinds of protection they want for their entitlements. The choice made will depend on the relative costs and benefits of the alternative systems for protecting entitlements. In such situations, the role of law is simply to enforce the contract that shareholders and managers have agreed to (explicitly or implicitly) among themselves. The fact that negotiated outcomes are not always achieved is not worrisome, because the corporate actors themselves choose the sorts of entitlement protection they want. They choose in light of the realization that their choices will frustrate some potential beneficial exchanges, but will also retard efforts at opportunistic exploitation, either by dissident shareholders or by unwanted bidders.[35] As circumstances change, the parties are free to (and often do) alter the types of protection that they utilize.

IV. REWARDING GOVERNMENTAL TAKINGS

Government's Incentives to Take

In the corporate context, it was seen, relatively high transactions costs and potential holdout problems often motivate shareholders to opt for something less than maximal property protection of their entitlements. As conventionally analyzed, similar problems can arise in the production of so-called public goods, that is, goods that can be used simultaneously (at least up to some point) by many persons. National defense and highways are commonly cited as examples.[36] When the Pentagon puts up a missile system covering the East Coast, all citizens from Maine to Florida are protected. Likewise, a highway from Maine to Florida allows millions of citizens to benefit from the road simultaneously.

Under the conventional analysis, the problems of creating public goods like national defense are similar to those arrangements discussed for corporations. Any effort management exerts to locate and bargain with an acquirer, for example, benefits all the shareholders and so is a public good in the economic sense of that term. At the same time, all shareholders bear a portion of the costs imposed on the corporation by those management efforts, but those who own more shares bear a larger portion. Similarly, since all citizens will share in the protection afforded by the defense system, all should pay; since some citizens have more to protect than others, some should pay more for protection.[37] But the transactions costs of collecting voluntary payments (which individually would be relatively modest) from all the citizens (who may number in the millions) are prohibitive. Moreover, there is something very closely akin to the holdout problem that a corporation operating under a shareholder-unanimity rule would face. Citizens will not voluntarily reveal their true valuation for national defense if revelation of that information means that they then will have to pay accordingly.

Similarly, if a transportation artery is to be built, the transactions costs of reaching agreement with hundreds or thousands of landowners in order to acquire the parcels needed for the right-of-way seem prohibitive. More important, if property owners are aware of the construction plans before the right-of-way is assembled, smart owners will let other owners sell their land first, then hold out for higher sums (up to the full gains from exchange) for themselves. If everyone has an incentive to be the last to sell, the assembly of land parcels for the right-of-way may never begin.

Collectively, we attach considerable value to public goods. But financing and producing them through voluntary negotiation (or so it is argued) may be infeasible, given the transactions costs and holdout problems that predictably will arise in a regime of private bargaining. In such cases, one might voluntarily agree in advance to replace negotiation with takings for the transfer of some entitlements.[38] That is the conventional explanation for the Fifth Amendment of the U.S. Constitution, which permits the taking of private property "for public use," subject to payment of "just compensation." Thus, road building typically involves eminent domain taking of land, with compensation at a level that makes landowners whole rather than at a price negotiated by the parties.

The extraordinary sanctions model implies, however, that any system that constitutionally legitimizes some government takings must anticipate opportunism costs. Once citizens have agreed to mere liability protection in limited situations, politicians predictably will be tempted to try to take when negotiation would have been the preferable path. A taking avoids irritating numerous voters with a direct appeal for the added tax revenues necessary to negotiate for the asset that is sought, rather than simply taking it. There is little fundamental distinction between many governmental takings and the situations discussed earlier in which private actors have an incentive to take rather than to negotiate. Taking means that all of the gains from trade go to the taker. In effect, a politician can take all the gains from exchange in a particular transaction in order to cultivate support from those voters whose entitlements have not been taken. But finding entitlements that are politically appropriate to take consumes resources, and the threat that they may be taken encourages private parties to misconfigure assets in ways that are less vulnerable to opportunistic takings by governmental actors.

A current example is found in Burlington, Vermont. Burlington's waterfront on Lake Champlain has become choked with garbage and weeds. Much of that land, which is adjacent to Burlington's downtown, is a railyard of the Central Vermont Railway, located on landfill authorized in the mid-1800s by state legislation. The railyard is too large for the company's present operations, and in 1989 the company unveiled plans to use thirty-two acres of it for new development—marinas, a hotel, condominiums, town houses, offices, and retail space. But the city quickly announced its own plans to use the same space for a very similar project. Central Vermont subsequently said it would consider selling the property to the city for fair market value, thus permitting the city's design for the land, rather than the company's, to proceed.[39]

But rather than purchasing the land it wanted—for a project that would go forward in one form or another in any event—Burlington went to court, contending that land beneath navigable waters is protected from private use. Although by legislative authorization navigable water has not lain above the land at issue for a century and a half, during which time the city and the state have treated the land as the rail company's for tax purposes, the Supreme Court of Vermont held for the city, ruling that the legislation was binding only as long as the company uses the land for railroad operations. The company is planning an appeal to the U.S. Supreme Court. If the appeal fails, however, Central Vermont plans to continue using the land as a rail-yard: Although the value of the land is not being maximized that way, at least it has positive value to the company. In this example, then, one readily observes both a governmental attempt to appropriate an asset rather than negotiate for it and the evolution of a private plan to misconfigure usage of that asset in a way that will better shield it from such appropriation.

Or consider what happened to the Oakland Raiders football team.[40] In 1966, the Raiders negotiated with the city of Oakland an agreement for the use of the municipal stadium. The agreement had five three-year renewal options, which the Raiders exercised three times. The team declined to exercise its option the fourth time and instead entered into negotiations with Oakland over a new agreement. When negotiations proved unavailing, the owners of the Raiders indicated that they would move the team to Los Angeles. Rather than continue negotiating, Oakland began an eminent domain proceeding to "condemn" the Raiders and the team's assets (the most valuable of which was its franchise from the National Football League).[41]

The city's attempt to "take" the Raiders was ultimately (and rightly, according to the analysis here) struck down as unconstitutional.[42] But many similar governmental attempts to take rather than negotiate have succeeded. Sometimes, taking is of direct benefit to the government itself. In the instance of the Raiders, for example, "condemning" the Raiders would have preserved the tax revenues, employment, publicity, and other benefits that the local government itself enjoyed as a result of having an NFL team in Oakland. There were also the political benefits the city fathers would have realized from having made a live football game available to local voters/fans.

In other situations, the beneficiaries of government's ability to take rather than negotiate are more concentrated. That is hardly surprising; it is now well understood that government frequently acts to benefit certain well-organized interest groups at the expense of the general population. But if that is so, governmental power would predictably be used to take on behalf of politically powerful private interests and at the expense of more diffuse, less powerful victims.

The phenomenon of governmental taking for the benefit of private interests sometimes passes euphemistically for "urban renewal" or "industrial development." The case of *Berman v. Parker*[43] is typical. Berman owned land that was to be condemned by the District of Columbia government, which intended to convey his land to a private developer, who in turn wanted the land for commercial development. A similar dispute arose in *Poletown Neighborhood Council v. City of Detroit*,[44] in which the Poletown residents contested Detroit's condemnation of their neighborhood. The condemnation was apparently motivated by Detroit's desire to maintain General Motors' level of local employment. GM had decided to close two outmoded assembly plants in the city, but offered to build a new assembly operation in Detroit if a suitable parcel of land could be found and acquired. The Poletown neighborhood was a suitable spot, but neither Detroit nor GM entered into negotiations with Poletown's property owners for acquisition of the land. Instead, the city invoked its power of eminent domain to condemn the entire neighborhood and make it available to GM. Both the *Berman* and the *Poletown* takings, benefiting private developers at the expense of private landowners, were upheld when challenged in court.[45]

Consider also governmental taking of labor for the military via the draft. One cannot be compelled to work for a private individual's enterprise merely because that enterprise was prepared to pay the salary that one was already receiving from some alternative enterprise, that is, to make one whole. Instead, the potential employer must negotiate to persuade the recruit to leave the present employment, meaning the new employer will find it necessary to offer a wage premium or some other inducement that leaves the recruit with part of the gains from the exchange. In the terminology of the present chapter, private employment relationships are controlled by property rules.

The same is not always true of governmental employment relationships. A government can often benefit in its role as a demander of both goods and services by using its power to take rather than negotiate for what it wants. For example, raising and maintaining an army can be done through contracts: one sets a wage and other terms of employment so that this particular labor market clears at the desired level of employment. Current American experience with the volunteer army illustrates the ease of contracting for military forces. At any selected level of benefits that the military offers, some recruits will be at the margin in an economic sense, meaning that they will be indifferent between being in the military and holding an alternative private position. But since many labor markets are thin ones, a large number of recruits will be inframarginal, and so they will receive a surplus in the wage arrangement that they receive from the military.

Volunteer armies are the historical exception, however, both in this country and elsewhere; military manpower is mustered more frequently by taking—a draft—than by purchase. Indeed, few nations maintain volunteer armies at present, and the ultimate fate of the volunteer army in the United States is in doubt. Many American politicians continue to espouse a conscripted army, in part because it would be cheaper (to the government treasury, not to society as a whole) than maintaining armed forces by individual labor contracts.

The government, of course, does not even have to pay conscripted military personnel a wage that would make them whole, that is, the wage that the personnel could have received as a private employee. Based on military pay scales and civilian wage rates in the early 1960s, Walter Oi calculated the average implicit tax rate imposed on draftees as 45 percent.[46] That is to say, military pay, including in-kind benefits, amounted to only 55 percent of an inductee's alternative civilian pay. Thus, though taking by conscription clearly results in a much lower wage bill for government than would an army raised by contract, the reduction in the government's accounting costs is not reflected by any reduction in the cost to the nation. Instead, the entire procedure effectuates a transfer from conscripted military personnel to the remainder of the populace, who pay conscripts 55 cents for labor that would cost at least $1 in the market. At the same time, the draft imposes an economic distortion, meaning that the gains to the beneficiaries fall short of the costs being imposed on draftees.

But even if the government paid military personnel a wage that would make them whole, conscription would still work as an implicit tax on draftees. The size of that tax would be the difference between what the draftee was earning elsewhere and the wage necessary to induce that individual to contract into the army. In addition, draftees must bear the additional tax implied by the difference between the amount that would have made them whole—the real income that they would have earned elsewhere—and what they are actually paid by the military, both pecuniarily and in the in-kind form of food, clothing, housing, and so forth.

Failure of the Law

Takings in both the private (corporate) and governmental context illustrate a fundamental tension in the use of liability rules. On the one hand, individuals may voluntarily surrender full property protection for their entitlements and instead install liability protection. That entails a foreseeable cost, but one voluntarily incurred in order to facilitate other activities that produce net economic benefits. Mere liability protection for shares thus enables the large firm to act more quickly and more surely than would be the case if all shareholders were required to assent contractually to every corporate activity.

Similarly, the taking of land, subject to the payment of "just compensation," may be the only way to build at least some roads. Prohibitive transactions costs and impossible holdout problems might mean that some beneficial new road construction would not even be attempted if individualized negotiation with existing owners were required. But even if one grants all that, the existence of only liability protection creates an incentive for would-be acquirers opportunistically to overreach, taking in situations where negotiation with current owners would be preferable.

Thus, successful use of liability rules will require some discouragement of opportunistic takings, that is, of takings in situations where negotiation is preferable. In some contexts, owners may be able to devise their own ways to avoid opportunistic takings. In corporate takeovers, shareholders can install various defensive devices to require negotiation when unwanted attempts to take are foreseen. In a similar fashion, an efficient legal system will install legal devices to discourage opportunistic takings in other settings where prearranged agreements will not suffice. At common law, as discussed above, such takings are often deterred by the imposition of punitive damages, among other extraordinary sanctions.

However, legal sanctions to guard against illegitimate takings work poorly against one taker: the government. That is so for several reasons. First, government itself defines what is a legitimate or an illegitimate taking. Second, government itself defines the sanction that it will accept to have imposed against itself, in the event that it is liable. And finally, the system of property rights within government means that the truly liable parties are not the ones who bear the brunt of any penalties imposed.

Liability. The first barrier to avoiding opportunistic governmental taking is government's ability to exclude itself from the legal system altogether for acts that are deemed not to implicate constitutional values. Under the doctrine of sovereign immunity, for example, government has simply claimed exemption from suit by private victims of defamation, trespass, and other torts, except insofar as the government has consented to be sued. Government has in some instances allowed suits for its misdeeds, but on terms it defines. Thus, in the Federal Tort Claims Act of 1946 the government waived sovereign immunity for many of its torts, but refused to subject itself to strict or absolute liability, the legal standards that are frequently imposed on private tort defendants. Instead, injured plaintiffs must prove actual negligence by the government.

Even in the constitutional context, government has increasingly been allowed to define the distinction between acceptable and unacceptable taking. Thus, in *Berman* and *Poletown*, courts approved blatantly opportunistic takings that had been undertaken solely to avoid the surplus sharing that would have been necessary in the event of negotiation with then-current entitlement owners. Since no private party is permitted to take in a similar setting, one suspects that transactions costs in such settings are not higher than legal process costs plus the costs of opportunism.

The Fifth Amendment was intended to limit takings to narrowly circumscribed purposes. But over time, courts' willingness to use the Fifth Amendment to distinguish legitimate from opportunistic takings has eroded substantially. Thus, it is becoming increasingly unlikely that government will be held liable under any circumstances for opportunistic takings.[47]

Sanctions. It is equally noteworthy that government does not face all of those sanctions that may be meted out against private defendants, even when the government is found liable for a taking. At common law, one of the most important sanctions for frustrating opportunistic takings is punitive damages, as discussed above. But just as government defines the terms of its own potential liability under the Federal Tort Claims Act, so too does it specify the damages for which it will be liable. The statute states that the government "shall not be liable for interest prior to judgment or for punitive damages."[48] Thus, an award of punitive damages, a fundamental common law device used to frustrate the opportunistic conversion of property into liability protection, explicitly is rendered impossible against the government as defendant.

Not only are punitive damages unavailable against the governmental defendant, but private plaintiff-victims of government takings are often denied even consequential damages. As Epstein notes, "just compensation" as interpreted under the Fifth Amendment has been measured by "the values that have been transferred to the government and not those that are lost to the owner when the government is unable to use them in its own business."[49] Therefore, if a condemnation entails loss of goodwill or destruction of perishable goods that the government did not intend to use anyway, a taking victim may not recover for those items, which were of no value to the governmental taker.[50]

In short, government defines many of the terms on which it will be liable for takings, and many of the sanctions that will flow from any liability. It is hardly surprising that such a system leads to reduced probabilities of any liability being imposed and reduced penalties when liability is imposed, when the taker is government itself.

Property Rights and Sanctions for Taking. It might seem, in view of the discussion above, that most problems of inappropriate governmental takings could be rectified by enabling plaintiffs to recover punitive damages from the government in the face of unjustifiable governmental takings. As it happens, however, that solution would be unlikely to work well. Moreover, it would not mirror the rules of punitive damages that common law courts apply to private takings. Assume, *arguendo*, that government and private defendants were judged by the same legal standards when plaintiffs challenged a taking as illegitimate and that the government itself could be found liable for both ordinary and punitive damages on the same facts as could a private defendant. It would still be true that the governmental defendant would be less deterred from illegitimate takings than a potential private defendant would be. That is because governmental actors would not bear the full consequences of their improper takings. It is not "the government" that chooses to take rather than negotiate, but some particular agent—a politician or bureaucrat.

In fact, principal/agent distinctions in the common law implicitly recognize the problem and are well worked out with respect to punitive damages. If a private agent is guilty of an illegitimate taking, the resulting punitive sanction is imposed on that individual, not on the principal. The usual rule bars vicarious liability for punitive damages: "In the federal courts and in the majority of state courts, a principal cannot be held for exemplary [that is, punitive] damages for acts done by an agent unless it be proven that the principal has participated in or ratified the agent's wrongdoing."[51]

When government does the taking, however, damages (such as are permitted) are usually paid out of the treasury, that is, by taxpayers—the principals.[52] *Ex ante*, each citizen is potentially a plaintiff and potentially a defendant for illegitimate governmental takings. Before it is apparent which citizens will be among the injured, the main interest of taxpayer-principals is to avoid the cost of the additional litigation that would be entailed if punitive damages could be imposed against the government. Why expend resources merely to transfer resources from one's taxpaying-defendant pocket into one's plaintiff pocket? Perhaps that seems to the naive as a perfectly adequate rationale for shielding illegitimate governmental takings from punitive liability.

But that is *not* an adequate rationale; it is a rationale for placing the punitive sanction on the agent rather than on the principal, just as is done when private punitive damages are at issue. To control opportunistic takings by government, punitive sanctions would have to be imposed directly on culpable politicians and bureaucrats who are responsible for takings in the name of the government when negotiation is preferable. In other words, the law that applies to privately employed agents would have to apply to governmentally employed agents as well. And merely trying to get the goods for less should serve no better as a defense for governmentally employed defendants than it would for any other thief.

V. CONCLUSIONS

Modern public choice literature offers scant reason to expect politicians and bureaucrats to seek the general "public interest" when formulating their actions. Instead, those governmental agents who are "honest," that is, who recognize their fiduciary duty not to seek their private interest simply and directly regardless of the preferences of the rest of society, will strive to advance the interests of the politically powerful, but often at the expense of the politically weak. It is the politically powerful, by definition, who maintain politicians in office and who indirectly maintain the agency budgets of the bureaucrats.

The founding fathers were well aware of the danger that the powerful will tread on the interests of the powerless, and so they intentionally placed certain actions beyond the boundaries of acceptable governmental behavior by institutionalizing constitutional barriers. That is hardly news; constitutional lawyers of every political stripe constantly underline the importance of our Constitution for protecting the neglected or unpopular interests of the politically powerless.

But constitutional barriers against politically opportunistic behavior work against politicians and bureaucrats only if the courts will enforce those barriers. At least where takings are concerned, however, courts have proved ever more hesitant to rely on the Constitution, paying increasing respect to the now-discredited theory that a popularly elected legislative branch can be expected to seek the welfare of all the members of the body politic.

As a result of the growing judicial neglect, individuals acting as legislators can obtain judicial approval for actions that they could never undertake in their role of private citizen. Private real estate can be taken in a low-transactions-cost/high-legal-process-cost setting, often to be made available for purely private uses. Private employment agreements among law-abiding citizens can be forcibly terminated, with the worker then being pressed into involuntary service in the military. All such actions impose opportunism costs—governmental actors search too avidly for assets of the politically powerless that can be made available for use by the politically powerful, while the politically powerless themselves misconfigure their assets in an effort to render them less attractive to governmental takers.

Similar behavior in the private sphere is controlled through the imposition of extraordinary sanctions, such as punitive damages, on individuals who have the temerity to circumvent a readily available market in favor of a litigational alternative. Yet, not only are governmental actors immune to the imposition of extraordinary sanctions for improper takings, but also plaintiffs often cannot even retrieve awards that make them whole for their losses. If the general public interest is truly to be served, our judicial system must disabuse itself of the notion that a legislature is publicly interested *because* it is popularly elected. In truth, it is because a legislature is popularly elected that it is interested in the *private* welfare of the politically powerful. Politicians and bureaucrats can be made to advance the general public interest, but only if they are restrained by a properly devised constitution, and only if the courts insist that those agents operate scrupulously within the boundaries provided for them by that constitution.

NOTES

Grateful acknowledgment is made to the Morris R. Shapiro Fund for support received.

1. Guido Calabresi and A. Douglas Melamed, "Property Rules, Liability Rules, and Inalienability: One View of the Cathedral," 85 *Harvard Law Review* 1089 (1972).

2. A continuing source of confusion to observers is that economists and legal scholars often use the same or very similar words and phrases for ideas that may be related but nevertheless are distinct. For instance, that which is a "property right" to an economist is an "entitlement" coupled with a specified "rule of protection" to a legal scholar. As the text notes, the protective rule that a legal scholar perceives may be a property *rule*, but that is not a property *right*, only a component of one. The economist may term an entitlement protected by a property rule a "strong property right," while an entitlement protected by a liability rule may be called a "weak property right."

But the economist's weak property right may mean something else altogether, for example, an entitlement ostensibly protected by a property rule, but with neither the state nor the individual being capable of enforcing the protection. An individual who took such an entitlement would be seen by the legal scholar as violating the protective rule, but with no practical recourse available to the entitlement's owner.

Moreover, virtually every entitlement actually has a number of rules of protection that apply to it, depending on the party that wishes to acquire it and the circumstances prevailing at the time. In effect, there are no *perfectly strong* property rights. Instead, the strength of protection varies continuously from the relatively strong (for some entitlements, in some circumstances, and against some potential takers) through an infinite number of degrees of weakening protections, and finally down to no protection at all. As an example, one can never have a property rule protecting any entitlement against the sovereign, if the sovereignty is real instead of nominal. The protection would depend on the will and might of the sovereign; if the sovereign decided to ignore it, or if the sovereign were overthrown, the claimed protection could melt away. Indeed, that is one of the matters discussed below.

Although few property rights economists will have found anything in this note to be objectionable or really surprising, precision and clarity have value. Because legal scholars seem to have developed the more fine-grained, and hence precise, vocabulary for discussing property rights, it is largely the legal vocabulary that will be utilized in this chapter.

3. See David D. Haddock, Fred S. McChesney, and Menahem Spiegel, "An Ordinary Economic Rationale for Extraordinary Legal Sanctions," 78 *California Law Review* 1 (1990).

4. Ronald H. Coase, "The Problem of Social Cost," 3 *Journal of Law & Economics* 1 (1960); Guido Calabresi, *The Costs of Accidents: A Legal and Economic Analysis* (New Haven: Yale University Press, 1970); John Prather Brown, "Toward an Economic Theory of Liability," 2 *Journal of Legal Studies* 323 (1973). See Charles J. Goetz, *Law and Economics: Cases and Materials* (St. Paul: West Publishing Co.,

1984), pp. 516–23 for an extensive, though now somewhat outdated, bibliography; and Robert D. Cooter and Thomas Ulen, *Law and Economics* (Glenview, Ill.: Scott, Foresman and Co., 1988), pp. 475–76 for a brief but updated one.

5. Judges have defined ordinary damages as those that make the plaintiff whole— or alternative phrasing to that effect—in a vast number of opinions. A particularly clear statement can be found in *Beaulieu v. Elliott*, 434 P.2d 665 (Alaska 1967): "[A]n injured person is entitled to be replaced as nearly as possible in the position he would have occupied had it not been for the defendant's tort."

Economists employ a similar definition of compensation when we discuss "compensated" demand curves, which, for example, add enough income to a budget to restore a consumer to the indifference curve he would have enjoyed in the absence of a specified disadvantageous event, such as a price increase.

6. Again, this terminology parallels the meaning of compensation in the ordinary parlance of economists, who conceptually subtract income from a budget in order to restore a consumer's utility to its original level following a specified advantageous event, such as a price decrease.

7. Haddock, McChesney, and Spiegel, *supra* note 3.

8. Markets such as those for common agricultural commodities, minerals, unskilled labor, or modest blocks of securities are characterized by a definite price for each grade, time, and location, and are said to be "thick" or "liquid." Other markets, such as those for houses, art, skilled labor, or controlling blocks of a corporation's shares, exhibit no "market price" on a continuous basis. Instead, transaction prices are negotiated sporadically by those few buyers and sellers who are interested in making a transaction at any moment. Such markets are called "thin" or "illiquid."

9. The portion of the model developed here derives from the original work (in a very different context) of Gordon Tullock, "The Welfare Implications of Tariffs, Monopoly, and Theft," 5 *Western Economics Journal* 224 (1967). Substituting liability for property protection opens new avenues for Tullock-type rent seeking.

10. Efficient caretaking by potential defendants is achieved in the standard tort model if tortfeasors can expect to bear the full costs that their actions have imposed on potential plaintiffs. The Haddock-McChesney-Spiegel model presented here makes plain, however, that the cost imposed on plaintiffs when their assets are taken is ambiguous in a thin market; the utility from owning and using an asset (i_0) is not generally the same as the utility obtainable from exchanging it (i_1).

11. *Midler v. Ford Motor Co.*, 849 F.2d 460 (9th Cir. 1988). For a discussion of the subsequent trial court judgment and award, see "Soundalike Suit: Bette Midler Doesn't Wanna Dance, Wins $400,000," *ABA Journal*, January 1990, p. 24. There was no violation of copyright, because Young and Rubicam had obtained a license from the song's owner.

12. Terry L. Anderson and Peter J. Hill, "The Race for Property Rights," 33 *Journal of Law and Economics* 177 (1990); Yoram Barzel, "Optimal Timing of Innovations," 50 *Review of Economics & Statistics* 348 (1968); H. Scott Gordon, "The Economic Theory of a Common-Property Resource: The Fishery," 62 *Journal of Political Economy* 124 (1954); David D. Haddock, "First Possession versus Optimal Timing: Limiting the Dissipation of Economic Value," 64 *Washington University Law Quarterly* 775 (1986); Garrett Hardin, "The Tragedy of the Commons," 162 *Science* 1243 (1968).

13. David D. Haddock and Fred S. McChesney, "Bargaining Costs, Bargaining

Benefits, and Compulsory Non-Bargaining Rules," 7 *Journal of Law, Economics and Organization*, Fall 1991; David D. Haddock, Jonathan R. Macey, and Fred S. McChesney, "Property Rights in Assets and Resistance to Tender Offers," 73 *Virginia Law Review* 701 (1987): 712–17.

14. Note that the proper focus is on *ex ante* expected utility of defendants. It may happen, for example, that a potential defendant unilaterally decides to impose an increased risk on a potential plaintiff, even though an expectation that the parties would negotiate to allocate the risk would not have been unreasonable. Perhaps the defendant realizes that under certain states of the world both parties will be injured in conjunction with the defendant's actions. Yet the defendant is willing to bear the risk of injury to self and is simply endeavoring to reduce the expected payment that must be made to the plaintiff by substituting (1) *ex post* litigation within a subset of possible outcomes, those wherein the potential plaintiff actually is injured, for (2) *ex ante* negotiation with all potential plaintiffs in all states of the world, whether or not an injury occurs. The defendant's motivation is that the expected cost of a liability award (ordinary damages if an injury occurs times the probability of the plaintiff's injury) is less than the cost of obtaining the potential plaintiff's agreement to bear the increased risk, given that the plaintiff will expect to negotiate into the trading lens of the Edgeworth box, not along its edge.

Whether or not the defendant ultimately is also injured as matters transpire is largely immaterial to our discussion. What has been taken by the defendant is the *ex ante* risk premium that would otherwise have gone to the plaintiff; the reason it has been taken is that expected ordinary damages were less than the premium the plaintiff would have demanded; making the defendant whole consists of extracting the difference, appropriately adjusting for the probability that the potential defendant will ultimately be compelled to pay a damage award. If, *ex post*, the defendant has also been injured, that is unfortunate, but it is a separate matter.

15. This assumes there are no court costs. In practice, it is costly to discourage property violations, so efficient law would not seek total eradication. But the restraint would be intended to optimize court behavior, not that of potential defendants. See David D. Friedman, "An Economic Explanation of Punitive Damages," 40 *Alabama Law Review* 1125 (1989).

16. For example, William M. Landes and Richard A. Posner, *The Economic Structure of Tort Law* 31 (1987); James M. Buchanan and Roger Faith, "Entrepreneurship and the Internalization of Externalities," 24 *Journal of Law & Economics* 95 (1981); Calabresi and Melamed, *supra* note 1 at 1106–10.

17. Landes and Posner, *supra* note 16 at 30. Some authors have argued that plaintiffs ought not be compensated at all for certain sorts of takings. See Lawrence Blume, Daniel Rubinfeld, and Perry Shapiro, "The Taking of Land: When Should Compensation Be Paid?" 99 *Quarterly Journal of Economics* 71 (1984); Louis Kaplow, "An Economic Analysis of Legal Transitions," 99 *Harvard Law Review* 509 (1986). In effect, those articles urge that a negligence remedy be substituted for a strict liability remedy under the circumstances they examine.

18. Admittedly, the present theory does not account for the bumper sticker that reads "So Many Pedestrians, So Little Time."

19. "Courts have found punitive damages especially appropriate when the plaintiff's harm has resulted from the defendant's strategic gambit. For instance, in *Melchior v. Madesco Investment Corp.*, 622 S.W.2d 362 (Mo. Ct. App. 1981), "the

defendant deliberately punctured a hole in his water pipe in order to prevent it from backing up. He knew that the garage into which the pipe leaked was unheated and that the water would freeze. Presumably he also knew that the garage employees and patrons would have to use more precaution to avoid slipping. The court held that punitive damages were appropriate." Mark F. Grady, "Punitive Damages and Subjective States of Mind: A Positive Economic Theory," 40 *Alabama Law Review* 1197, 1223 (1989).

20. In other words, an effort to make a plaintiff whole requires an estimate of only a single one of Patty's indifference curves. But estimating the counterfactual bargaining outcome would require an estimate of a substantial portion of both Patty's and Duke's utility functions. But even that would merely enable the court to recognize the infinity of points along the contract curve to which Patty and Duke could potentially have negotiated. The court would *still* have to guess which one of that infinity of points would ultimately have been agreed upon by Patty and Duke.

Imagining that court awards precisely restore anyone's pretaking utility is un-realistic, but it is credible that jury awards are often unbiased, low-variance estimates of the awards necessary to make one of the litigants whole. Litigants are often drawn randomly from the population. A jury is also selected more or less randomly. Hence, a juror's contemplation of an award that would make the juror whole under similar circumstances will lead to an unbiased estimate of appropriate compensation. Be-cause twelve independent estimates are averaged, unusually high or low ones will tend to offset each other in the jury consensus. But trying to imagine what deal would have resulted in a thin market, following a hypothetical negotiation between traders no juror knew well, would lead to estimates with a high variance around any potential real market outcome.

Clearly, if a litigant is not a natural person, or not a "peer" of the jurors, or committed his violation in an environment that few jurors have encountered, it is less likely that the jury will arrive at an award with the same desirable attributes.

21. If Duke anticipated paying compensation, the taking will have been only Et' so that the move to C is direct, because modest transaction costs are borne to reach C from R'.

22. Note that incentives for controlled opportunism will remain if the rule is not strict liability but negligence, unless it is possible to mold the legal standard of care in a way that renders all opportunism negligent.

23. In the corporate context, "public" refers to a relatively large number of shareholders, few of whom have any direct hand in the day-to-day operations of the corporation. Hence, the term "public corporation" does not imply—indeed, is inconsistent with—government ownership, but is in distinction to a "close" cor-poration, which typically has few shareholders, most or all of whom are directly involved in running the corporation.

24. For instances in which shareholders have attempted to profit individually by holding out under such circumstances, see *Stokes v. Continental Trust Co.*, 186 N.Y. 285, 78 N.E. 1090 (1906); *Matteson v. Ziebarth*, 40 Wash.2d 286, 242 P.2d 1025 (1952).

25. In the event that shareholders challenge management action as wrongful, corporate law typically assesses liability only when management has been negligent, that is, has not exercised the judgment of a reasonably prudent person in a similar

situation. This is the "business judgment rule." See Revised Model Business Corporation Act (RMBCA), sec. 8.30.

26. But if managers are discovered to have been behaving in a self-interested, opportunistic fashion, maximizing their own welfare at the expense of the welfare of the principals, the law will often impose extraordinary sanctions on them as well. That happens, for example, when managers attempt to exploit business opportunities for their personal profit when the opportunity belongs to the corporation. In that event, self-interested managers are made to return profits earned from the taken opportunity, and are thereby "made whole." That is, *Miller v. Miller*, 222 N.W.2d 71 (Minn. 1976).

27. Representation of the shareholders' interests by managers will also entail agency costs, of course, because nonowners will not act as vigorously as owners themselves would have. But in the ordinary course of affairs, those agency costs must be less than the transactions and holdout costs incurred if the principals insist on negotiating for themselves, given the ubiquity of nonowning managers in large corporations.

28. William J. Carney, "Shareholder Coordination Costs, Shark Repellents, and Takeout Mergers: The Case against Fiduciary Duties," *American Bar Foundation Research Journal* 341 (1983).

29. In a now famous pair of articles, Frank H. Easterbrook and Daniel J. Fischel argued that law should be changed to require that managers take no action that is primarily intended to alter the probability that an acquirer's efforts to take control of a firm succeed. See Frank H. Easterbrook and Daniel J. Fischel, "The Proper Role of a Target's Management in Responding to a Tender Offer," 94 *Harvard Law Review* 1161 (1981); idem, "Auctions and Sunk Costs in Tender Offers," 35 *Stanford Law Review* 1 (1982). Under present law, however, that is an option that shareholders can either elect or reject. Apparently to this point, no firm has elected such an option.

30. For further description of the tender offer as a prisoner's dilemma, see Jonathan R. Macey and Fred S. McChesney, "A Theoretical Analysis of Corporate Greenmail," 95 *Yale Law Journal* 13, 21–23 (1985).

31. The prisoner's dilemma is created by the offerer's willingness to pay a higher price to those who tender their shares in the first tier than the price that is to be paid when nontendering shareholders are merged ("squeezed") out subsequently. Theoretically, tender offers could be structured as any two-tier bid, as long as the second-tier price was substantially lower than the first. Hence, the second-tier price could theoretically be below the prebid market price. The prisoner's dilemma created by such a two-tier bid thus would result in expropriation of a portion of the current shareholder's wealth. The potential for expropriation is nullified, however, by state corporation statutes, which grant nontendering shareholders "appraisal rights." Appraisal rights guarantee all shareholders the right to receive at least the prebid market value of their shares. See RMBCA secs. 13.01–13.28.

32. Easterbrook and Fischel, *supra* note 29, focused solely on this "other side of the coin" and ignored both the concomitant benefits to shareholders of fine-tuning their entitlement protections and their abilities to optimize the level of permissible resistance *ex ante*.

33. See *Unocal Corp. v. Mesa Petroleum Co.*, 493 A.2d 946 (Del. 1985); *Paramount Communications, Inc. v. Time, Inc.*, 571 A.2d 1140 (Del. 1990).

34. These points are discussed further in David D. Haddock, Jonathan R. Macey, and Fred S. McChesney, "Property Rights in Assets and Resistance to Tender Offers," 73 *Virginia Law Review* 701 (1987).

35. Corporate reformers are fond of calling for greater shareholder approval *ex ante* for management actions that now are subject (as a legal default) to mere liability-rule protections, without recognizing the increased transactions costs that necessarily accompany strengthened property protection. See, for example, Melvin A. Eisenberg, "The Structure of Corporation Law," 89 *Columbia Law Review* 1461 (1989). But see Fred S. McChesney, "Law, Economics and Science: A Critique of Eisenberg," 89 *Columbia Law Review* 1530 (1989).

36. In view of much of the research of public choice theorists concerning demand-revealing tactics that might be used to bill individuals for their proportional share of the costs of public goods, it is unclear that the conventional public goods arguments apply to national defense. They are even less convincing with respect to highway construction. See Harold Demsetz, "The Private Production of Public Goods," 13 *Journal of Law and Economics* 293 (1970); Roland McKean and Jora Minasian, "On Achieving Pareto Optimality—Regardless of Cost!" 5 *Western Economics Journal* 14 (1966); Patricia Munch (Danzon), "An Economic Analysis of Eminent Domain," 84 *Journal of Political Economy* 473 (1976).

But this chapter is not addressed to that debate. So, for the sake of argument, the conventional analysis of public goods is adopted here to the extent that it concerns the desirability of using liability rules in the provision of public goods. A seminal work in the latter vein is Paul A. Samuelson, "The Pure Theory of Public Expenditure," 36 *Review of Economics & Statistics* 387 (1954).

37. The word "should," as used here, may be taken by some readers as a moral imperative, but it also possesses efficiency-based content; the optimal amount of a public good will not in general be forthcoming if the individual demands for it are not registered. Harold Demsetz, "Information and Efficiency: Another Viewpoint," 12 *Journal of Law & Economics* 1 (1969).

38. In line with the earlier discussion, one would hope that the legal process costs involved in acquiring the entitlements under a liability rule taking are not being ignored. If the lesser of transactions costs or legal process plus opportunism costs would still be greater than the net benefit of the asset once in place, even investments that otherwise would be extremely valuable ought not be made.

39. "Vermont City and Railroad Vie for Land," *New York Times* (National Edition), February 9, 1990, p. C6.

40. For an insightful discussion of this episode, see Steven M. Crafton (note), "Taking the Oakland Raiders: A Theoretical Reconsideration of the Concepts of Public Use and Just Compensation," 32 *Emory Law Journal* 857 (1983).

41. *City of Oakland v. Oakland Raiders, Ltd.*, 123 Cal.App.3d Supp. 422, 176 Cal. Rptr. 646 (Cal. App. Dep't Super. Ct. 1981), *rev'd*, 32 Cal.3d 60, 646 P.2d 835, 183 Cal. Rptr. 673 (1982).

42. To say that the city of Oakland was rightly denied the ability to condemn the Raiders says nothing about the desirability of allowing the NFL itself to insist that the Raiders remain in Oakland. We do not address the latter issue.

43. 348 U.S. 26 (1954).

44. 410 Mich. 616, 304 N.W.2d 455 (1981).

45. For a discussion of these and similar cases, see Richard A. Epstein, *Takings:*

Private Property and the Power of Eminent Domain (Cambridge, Mass.: Harvard University Press, 1985). See generally Terry L. Anderson and Peter J. Hill, *The Birth of a Transfer Society* (Stanford: Hoover Institution Press, 1980).

46. Walter Y. Oi, "The Economic Cost of the Draft," 57 *American Economic Review* 39, 59 (1967). For a discussion, see Mark V. Pauly and Thomas D. Willett, "Who Bears the Burden of National Defense," in *Why the Draft? The Case for a Volunteer Army*, ed. James C. Miller III (Baltimore: Perguin Books, 1968), pp. 53–57.

47. Epstein, *Takings*, *supra* note 45.

48. 28 U.S.C. sec. 2674.

49. Epstein, *Takings*, at 52.

50. See, for example, *Community Redevelopment Agency of Los Angeles v. Abrams*, 15 Cal.3d 813, 543 P.2d 905, 126 Cal. Rptr. 473 (1975).

51. Charles T. McCormick, *Damages* (St. Paul: West Publishing Co. 1935), p. 283. Some cases have resulted in punitive sanctions being imposed on principals. See McCormick at 284–85; Dan B. Dobbs, *Remedies* (St. Paul: West Publishing Co., 1973), p. 214. But that is desirable when the principal has been slovenly in instructing or controlling the predictable behavior of the agent.

52. In a very few exceptional situations, such as violations of federal civil rights statutes, government officials are personally liable for their torts. See Charles A. Wright, *Law of Federal Courts*, 4th ed. (St. Paul: West Publishing Co., 1983), pp. 119–26.

4

The Impact of Government Liability on Private Risk Avoidance

James L. Huffman

I. GOVERNMENT AND RISK

Modern governments affect risk in various ways. Through widespread and often large-scale activities, governments create risks. Through disaster planning and postdisaster response, governments seek to reduce risks and mitigate their consequences. Sometimes these risk-avoidance and mitigation efforts create new risks or substitute lesser for greater risks. Governments also establish and implement rules that influence risk-relevant private relationships and govern the assignment of liability where risks are realized in the form of injury. Governments also undertake social insurance and after-the-fact compensation measures designed to influence the distribution of losses.

In all risk-related activities, political agents generally seek to achieve some combination of allocational and distributional objectives.[1] Where the immediate policy concern is risk reduction or avoidance, government activities may be designed ostensibly to reduce the aggregate risk exposure of the members of society. Only occasionally, as in the case of rescue, has it been acceptable to reduce aggregate risk exposure by increasing the risks experienced by some individuals. Often, however, special interest groups will use the machinery of government to shift the distributional consequences of risks for their own benefit or for the benefit of those they purport to represent.

Where a government's immediate policy concern is other than risk avoidance—and thus the government action may create new risks without reducing existing risks[2]—the allocational and distributional consequences of the new risks will be only two among many factors that might influence the government's action. For example, where government's role is the creation and enforcement of rules for the resolution of disputes resulting from privately created risks, the government affects both risk-generating activity and the distribution of costs associated with the realization of risks. Because political action will have both allocational and distributional objectives, the development of risk policy is an unavoidably complicated matter.

The impact of government's liability for the consequences of risks on allocational and distributional objectives is an important aspect of risk policy. Although government liability can be conceived as a narrow question of tort liability, effective risk policy requires a much broader conception. Governments incur the costs of accidents and disasters in various ways. In addition to liability for damages in a tort action, government may influence cost assignment through direct subsidies (grants and low-interest loans) and indirect subsidies (public services, tax exemptions, and regulation). These subsidies may result from legislative and administrative programs established in anticipation of losses, from compensation schemes adopted after the occurrence of losses, and from government actions perceived to have no relation to risk management and avoidance. Whatever the form of government assumption of costs, it will serve to redistribute losses and, unless it is entirely random and thus unpredictable, will thus influence private behavior in the face of risks. A rational and effective risk policy must account for all of these forms of government liability.

This chapter addresses the impact of this broadly conceived government liability on private action in the face of risks. There is little reason to doubt that the law of government liability affects private decision making about risk. The costs borne by individuals in the event of an accident are affected by legal rules that assign liabilities and create immunities. As a consequence, individual perceptions of future accident costs will be significantly influenced by existing assignments of liability and immunity. The response to liability rules underlies deterrence theories of tort law. Even tort theories designed to achieve compensatory objectives cannot ignore the deterrent effect of liability assignment that eliminates the need to redistribute costs after accidents and avoids those injuries where compensation is difficult or impossible.

If the private actor believes that the government will be liable for certain costs in the event of an accident, that private actor will have no reason to account for those costs in deciding whether or not to undertake or avoid exposure to risk (assuming they are fully compensable and the government's liability is a certainty). On the other hand, if the government will be immune from liability for certain costs, even when caused by government action, the private actor will consider those costs in assessing the wisdom of risky action.

This assumption that government liabilities influence private decision making is valid notwithstanding the widely accepted proposition that liability assignments do not influence allocations of resources.[3] Liability assignments do not affect resource allocation where transactions costs are small. But liabilities and immunities can affect wealth distribution. This is particularly true where there is a large disparity in the wealth of the affected parties, the situation that normally exists in relationships between individuals and government. For most individuals, the prospect of liability will have significant implications for future wealth. Government, particularly big government, will be less influenced by the liability assignment, since the cost of an accident will generally be small in relation to the total governmental budget.

It should also be recognized that government liability provides an attractive opportunity for politicians to reward various interest groups by spreading costs across a large number of taxpayers. Government liability in many of its various forms involves wealth transfers from taxpayers to risktakers. When government compensates for injuries caused by its own actions, the compensation serves to avoid a redistribution of wealth from the injured party to the beneficiaries of the government's actions. However, whenever government compensates for injuries resulting from nongovernment-created risks, it subsidizes the risk taking of the party whose action created the risk.

II. GOVERNMENT LIABILITY LAW

Broadly conceived, government liability law involves traditional common law tort liabilities and immunities, statutory liabilities and immunities, statutorily established discretionary compensation programs, and the ad hoc compensation that politicians often provide in response to particular disasters and injuries.[4] The law of tort liabilities and immunities is a complex body of doctrine evolved over several decades of judicial and legislative action. This law applies broadly and has little special interest content. On the other hand, statutory compensation programs and ad hoc compensation are generally designed to serve a particular purpose or respond to a particular event.

Tort Liability

A common thread in the government liability laws of most nations is some formulation of sovereign immunity. In Anglo-American law the doctrine of sovereign immunity is described as originating in the divine right of kings. Whether for divine or secular reasons, with the rise of democratic government and the theoretical substitution of the people for the king as the source of sovereignty, the immunity of the sovereign was recognized "not because of any formal conception or absolute theory, but on the logical and practical ground that there can be no legal right as against the authority that makes the law on which the right depends."[5] Thus, "[w]hether sovereign power was exercised by Hobbes' Leviathan, or Rousseau's common will, the scope of that power was defined by the circumstances of government. The sovereign state, like the free individual, had those powers necessary to self-preservation."[6]

Civil law countries followed a very different historical path,[7] but they arrived at a similar legal doctrine under which the government was immune for harm resulting from the performance of governmental, as distinguished from nongovernmental, functions. Although for very different reasons, the law of most Communist states also provided for governmental immunity.[8]

In both civil and common law countries the doctrine of sovereign immunity began to come under attack in the late nineteenth and early twentieth centuries. To American commentators like Professor Edwin Borchard, it was "strange that authority from the fifteenth, sixteenth, and seventeenth centuries, intent on establishing the absolute supremacy of a secular king over a universal church, and of an absolute monarch as against popular government...should be invoked to support a legal doctrine for a 20th century democratic republic."[9] But the doctrine persisted with a tenacity that has allowed it to remain as the foundation of Anglo-American government liability law. Although the U.S. government, like the government of every other common law country, has significant liabilities under existing law, it is dependent upon statutory waivers of immunity. In theory at least, these waivers can be repealed and full sovereign immunity restored.

Statutory waivers of sovereign immunity have taken the form of crown proceedings acts in the British Commonwealth and tort claims acts in the United States. In some cases these acts purport to be total waivers of immunity, but they have seldom been interpreted that way.[10] The civil law distinction between governmental and nongovernmental functions has often served to preserve an area of immunity on the theory that immunity is necessary to the performance of basic government functions. Under the Federal Tort Claims Act,[11] injury resulting from discretionary acts,[12] misrepresentations,[13] and other specified types of acts are expressly excluded from those to which the waiver applies,[14] thus preserving immunity with respect to harm resulting from those acts. The most significant of these exceptions is for discretionary functions, which include planning, as distinguished from operational, activities of the government.[15] Although it is a theoretically defensible exception,[16] it has the potential of being very far-reaching. The misrepresentation exception preserves government immunity where harm results from reliance on a negligent assertion of incorrect information and has been held, for example, to bar claims based upon erroneous and nonexistent weather forecasts.[17]

To the extent that a government is liable because of a lack of immunity or because it has voluntarily waived its immunity, it is generally subject to the same standards of liability as any private entity would be under similar circumstances. Both the common law of torts and the civil law of obligations generally have imposed an ordinary care standard. This means that an actor, including the nonimmune government, is liable for harm caused by the actor's failure to exercise ordinary or reasonable care.[18] In the United States and elsewhere there has been a strong trend over the last two decades away from this negligence standard, which is rooted in determining the fault of the actor, and toward a strict liability standard, which is rooted in assuring the compensation of the victim. New Zealand became the international leader in this movement with the adoption of its Accident Compensation Act of 1972,[19] under which all personal injuries are compensated from a government fund without regard to fault or government involvement.

The fact of historic government immunity is largely responsible for the application of private liability standards to government and the reliance on private tort theory as an analogy in the development of government tort theory. The legitimacy of government immunity was most commonly challenged in circumstances where the uncompensated victim of government action would have been compensated had the actor been a private party. Waivers of immunity were enacted to permit recovery in precisely such situations. For example, the Federal Tort Claims Act permits lawsuits against the government "under circumstances where the United States, if a private person, would be liable to the claimant in accordance with the law of the place where the act or omission occurred."[20]

The application of private liability principles to injury-causing acts of government does eliminate some of the inequities inherent in government immunity, particularly where government is performing many of the same actions as are private parties. For example, equity surely requires that an individual injured by a negligent government truck driver have the same right to compensation as the individual injured by a negligent private truck driver. However, the private analogy has serious limits both with respect to fixing the standard of care and articulating a sound theory of government liability. Many acts performed by government have no private parallel and, in any event, government action is fundamentally different from private action in several respects. Government purports to act on behalf of the community as a whole, government officials may have different incentives than private actors, government can have access to resources well beyond those of any private actor, and most important, government has the power to change the rules governing its own liability and the liability of private parties. In analyzing government tort liability we deceive ourselves if we insist that government is just another actor in the world of modern risks.

The mistaken analogy of certain government action to private action is not peculiar to government liability law. In many areas of modern substantive law, a distinction between the proprietary and governmental functions of government is thought to justify distinct legal results. For example, the U.S. Supreme Court distinguishes between proprietary and governmental functions in its commerce clause analysis, thus permitting states to implement discriminatory legislation that would otherwise be violative of the

Constitution.[21] At the same time the Court imposes constitutional limits on private actors on the theory that their actions are of a governmental nature.[22] In these areas, as in government liability law, the distinction leads to peculiar results. Governments are fundamentally different from private actors in important respects, not the least of which is that government controls vast resources, has legitimate coercive powers, and has the authority to change the rules under which it and private actors conduct their affairs.

Statutory Compensation Programs

In addition to the general law of government liability and immunity, many countries have established compensation programs to deal with particular types of injuries or with injuries resulting from particular events or actions. These are liabilities voluntarily undertaken by government. They are often unrelated to the existence or quality of any prior governmental act. Pursuant to these laws, government compensation may be due to a victim of some third-party action, of an act of nature, or of the victim's own conduct. They are nonetheless government liabilities, which influence both private and public actions in the face of risk.

One example has already been mentioned: the New Zealand Accident Compensation Act, pursuant to which every victim of a personal injury is entitled to compensation based upon a statutorily defined schedule of benefits. New Zealand also has an Earthquake and War Damage Act that promises equitable compensation to all victims in the event of war or natural disaster.[23]

The United States has a complex array of laws relating to compensation of victims of natural and manmade disasters. Unlike the New Zealand legislation, however, the Disaster Relief Act of 1974,[24] which is the most recent federal version of comprehensive disaster assistance, does not guarantee compensation. Relief assistance is contingent on a variety of discretionary acts from the issuance of a presidential declaration, to the request for such a determination by a state governor, to local implementation by federal, state, and local officials. The Disaster Relief Act reflects the long-standing policy in the United States that disaster assistance should come first from private and local sources. This policy is also reflected in most other federal disaster legislation, which is directed at mitigation rather than compensation of disaster losses.

However, once a disaster occurs the victims and their affected local and state governments look to the federal government for compensation. As in all matters political, the federal response is dependent upon the influence of those seeking compensation. This means that the victims of large disasters, like hurricane Hugo and the San Francisco earthquake in 1989, have reasonably good prospects for federal resources, while the victims of small or personal disasters must fend for themselves or rely on the often sparse resources of local governments. This is true without regard to the predisaster precautions taken by the victims. Once a compensation program is in place, it tends to function as a no-fault system—magnitude of loss, rather than contribution to loss, becomes the basic measure of compensation.

However, not every victim is equal in the politics of disaster relief. In most cases federal compensation is channeled through state and local governments, which means that individual victims must be within the jurisdiction of a conduit government. Even when the benefits are administered directly by the federal government, the administering agencies often have limited jurisdictions that correspond to local political subdivisions. A result of this system of administering aid is that political influence is a key factor in determining whether victims in a particular locality will be eligible for compensation. This may lead to the perverse result that those in greatest need are least likely to recover since the disruption of their lives prevents political action until after available funds have been dispersed to less affected communities.

The United States also has legislation at both the federal and state levels for a coordinated workers' compensation program where qualifying workers recover for specified losses according to an established schedule of benefits. Like the more comprehensive New Zealand Accident Compensation Act, these workers compensation programs impose fixed liabilities on the government. Both the New Zealand and United States schemes are effectively self-financing so long as the taxes or premiums collected are proportionate to the compensation paid. However, both systems clearly have created expectations of compensation that the government must meet whether or not its insurance fund is adequate, and with little regard to the care exercised by the claimant.

Ad Hoc Compensation for Loss

A third significant way in which governments are liable when risks are realized is through ad hoc compensation in response to particular events or accidents. The appeals of human emotion and passion often lead to government compensation where neither tort law nor existing statutory obligations require it. For example, the government may have identified and perhaps zoned a particular area as a floodplain. The law may prohibit construction or permit people to build at their own risk. In the latter case the relevant regulations may be consciously based on a belief that individuals should be free to take risks if they are willing to bear the realized costs.

However, after a flood occurs and the voluntary risktakers, including those who acted in violation of the law, are financially and otherwise devastated, assistance is often forthcoming. This postdisaster change of heart may result from simple compassion or from the fact that the risktakers are often those who were attracted by lower land values and thus may be least prepared to bear the losses. It may also result from the political influence of those affected. Indeed, even a compassionate concern for all disaster victims or for those particularly in need will be sufficient to produce compensation only where the political rewards outweigh the political benefits of alternative uses of the resources. This will generally be the case since taxpayers seldom see any connection between their tax bills and particular expenditures of public monies. The result will be that those who choose to mitigate disaster losses in their personal lives will subsidize the risks taken by those who do not.

Seldom does any significant disaster occur without government assistance pursuant to an established assistance program or to a program established for the particular occasion. In some countries, like China, government response to particular disasters has often determined a government's future viability.[25] In other countries the political consequences may be less severe, but they are nevertheless very real. People come to expect these ad hoc responses, although the details of a particular response are difficult to predict. What is predictable, however, is that the victim of a private disaster has no reason to expect government compensation, while the victim of a major disaster is reasonably certain of some assistance. What is sometimes called the "big bang" event is the one that attracts government's attention, with the result that government compensation is significantly unrelated to the fault or the personal wealth of the accident victim.

Government compensation turns on both the magnitude and circumstances of the disaster. The victim of a large natural disaster is far more likely to be compensated than is the victim of a small natural disaster. Victims of "public" losses are far more likely to be compensated than victims of "private" losses. The homeowner who builds in the floodplain can expect to be subsidized by his fellow taxpayers when the waters rise. The homeowner whose pipes burst will need private insurance when his basement fills with water.

III. THE NEED FOR A THEORY OF GOVERNMENT TORT LIABILITY

If political leaders wish to deal rationally with the impacts of their liabilities on private risk decisions, and if they wish to manipulate public sector liabilities for coherent policy objectives, a sound theory of government liability law is necessary. As indicated previously, most governmental tort theory has depended upon analogy to private tort theory. Assumptions about private incentives have been applied to governments acting in similar situations. But there are many reasons to be skeptical about the relevance of these assumptions. Governments are clearly not individuals under another name, and those who work for government seldom have reason to view the government's liabilities in the same way they would view their personal liabilities or liabilities for a business. Even where the law permits tort actions against public officials, it is often possible for the public official to demand indemnification from the government.

Thus government liability theory must look elsewhere for its foundations. Those foundations are to be found in an understanding of political and bureaucratic behavior. The factors are historical, socioeconomic, and philosophic. To the extent that it is possible to predict human behavior, it will be possible to analyze the behavior of elected and appointed government officials. That behavior will be governed by circumstance and will thus vary from country to country and legal system to legal system.

The articulation of a theory of government liability will not be accomplished here, but recognition of the complexity of the task has implications for the specific policy problem raised in this essay. Policymakers can understand the impact of government liability laws on private risk decisions without fully understanding the impact of those laws on the government itself or its employees. Assuming that our private tort theories have validity, we can at least suggest how government liabilities will influence private risk taking.

Ultimately, of course, we will want to understand the impact of liability assignment on government action. Government will no doubt remain actively involved in risk creation and risk avoidance. How government's liabilities will influence its risk-creating and risk-avoiding actions is fundamentally important to the goal of optimizing individual exposure to risk. It is individuals, after all, who bear the costs and experience the benefits of risk exposure. But even for a government that places itself (or its functionaries) above the general population, a theory of government liability is essential to the achievement of governmental objectives. Policy goals cannot be intelligently pursued without an understanding or theory about the consequences of actions designed to implement those goals.

Individuals bear the costs and benefits of risk exposure, and individual actions are influenced by perceptions about the legal assignment of these costs and benefits. This basic premise is as valid for individuals acting within government as for individuals acting on their own or within private organizations. However, the private analogy breaks down at the point of relating the basic incentives of self-interest to the behavior of government officials. The incentives of government employees and politicians are different from those of people in private enterprise. They are defined by the structure of government and the political and cultural traditions of the society. The private person acts out of self-interest. The government, though comprised of individuals with self-interests, purports to act in the "public" interest. What incentives lead self-interested individuals to act in the interest of others? The answer to that question will lead us to an understanding of the impact of government liabilities on the actions of government.

IV. GOVERNMENT LIABILITY AS INSURANCE

Under circumstances germane to ordinary tort law, the liabilities of government are indistinguishable from those of a private tortfeasor from the point of view of a prospective victim. Exposure to risk is undertaken with an understanding of the prospective liabilities in the event of harm, and it is of no consequence, in terms of the nature of the risk, that the source of the harm may be governmental rather than private. However, even in those situations where government action is truly analogous to private action, the prospective victim may distinguish between the two on the basis of prospective compensation. Government, with its taxing powers, will generally be a more reliable provider of damages than will private parties, encouraging the prospective victim to take fewer precautions against risks posed by government than by private parties.

In the United States, where liability is determined increasingly with reference to compensation rather than fault, governments are good candidates for liability because they are good loss distributors; they have deep pockets, in the parlance of the plaintiff's lawyer. Like the large corporations whose loss-spreading abilities inspired the strict liability standards of modern products liability law, governments can compensate victims without imposing heavy burdens on any individuals. When corporations and governments are held liable on the basis of their loss-spreading capacities, they effectively become insurers rather than actors whose conduct is sought to be influenced by assignments of liability. Although corporate behavior may still be influenced, depending upon the magnitude of liability and the costs of risk avoidance, it is less likely that government behavior will be affected since the income and expenses of government are seldom related in a way that will affect management decisions.

Government liabilities that fall outside of the traditional domain of tort law, like statutory and ad hoc compensation schemes, are even more directly a form of insurance from the point of view of accident victims.[26] As insurance these government compensation systems are readily justified in the political arena. They promise compensation for future losses, with the costs distributed through, and concealed within, the general tax system. Rarely are the revenues for the compensation funds derived from special taxes that are properly analogous to insurance premiums.[27] In most cases the revenues come from general tax receipts. To the extent that taxpayers are equally exposed to the covered risks, which is seldom if ever the case in a large and diverse nation, general taxation will still not be a functional equivalent of insurance premiums because the payment will be buried in the taxpayers' general tax liabilities, and thus not linked to the insured risks.

To the extent that government compensation programs are a form of insurance, it may be argued that government compensation policy should be based on the same foundations as insurance policy generally. In his study of government compensation for losses resulting from changes in the law, Louis Kaplow points out that "[i]nsurance is one of the more common techniques for mitigating risk; government compensation has a similar effect." Although he goes on to recognize some differences, his central argument is that the risks of changes in the law, what he calls legal transitions, are no different than the risks of participation in the private market, and that insurance of those risks should be left to the market rather than the government. Government compensation for the risks of legal transitions will result in inefficient private conduct, concludes Kaplow,[28] unless that compensation is not different from what would be provided in the private insurance market.

Kaplow's argument is rooted in analogies he draws to market risks like changing demand, changing investment decisions by competitors, and natural risks like earthquakes and floods.[29] He contends that people will decide whether or not to insure against such risks depending upon the premiums, and that government compensation for these risks will distort the efficiencies of the insurance market.

Kaplow's analysis of these risks is sound, but his analogy to the risks of changes in the law is problematic. It is an analysis relevant to this chapter because what he identifies as the risks of legal transitions are the "incidental gains and losses" of changes in government policy,[30] precisely those risks created by government for which a liability will rest either with the government or the affected private parties. These gains and losses are among those for which a government's acceptance or rejection of liability will impact upon the risk-relevant decisions of private parties. Kaplow contends that these impacts on private action are indistinguishable from those associated with market risks, but there is a fundamental difference.

In the market, private actors proceed on the basis not only of predictions about the actions of other private actors, but also on the basis of predictions about the assignment of liability for harm resulting from their own and others' actions. They must make the same predictions about natural events and about the actions of government. If the private actor knows that the government will never be liable for the costs of legal transitions, the private actor can adjust to that liability rule. But this is not necessarily an efficient result. Government actions are not analogous to earthquakes and floods. Government actions are the actions of people who are as influenced by incentives as are private actors.

The conclusion that government should never compensate for the costs of legal change assumes that the actions of government cannot be influenced by liability assignment, or at least that government actions are somehow unrelated to efficiency. Either assumption is clearly incorrect. The flaw of the analysis rests in a failure to recognize that government action, like private action, has external costs that can be internalized by the assignment of liability to the party creating the costs. An efficient level of risk is dependent upon internalizing costs to both private and public actors, not in treating the external costs of government action as the equivalent of earthquake and flood damage.

As noted above, government liability law has distinguished between discretionary and nondiscretionary government actions, but that does not alter the fact that discretionary government actions have external or transitional costs that, if internalized, might influence discretionary action. Because the law applies traditional tort principles only to nondiscretionary actions, it is left for the government to resort to other systems of compensation if the external costs of discretionary actions are to be internalized. The insurance market will not result in efficient government actions unless there are assignments of rights on the basis of which market transactions can be made. The immunization of government for its discretionary actions, and the elimination of any basis for negotiation between private and public actors, places the private actor at the mercy of the public policymaker who has no obvious incentives to avoid risk except for the incentives provided through the political process. Those incentives will lead to anything but efficiency.

Thus, although many forms of government liability are analogous to insurance, there are also aspects of government liability that are quite different. This is so because of the existing law of government liability—law which economic theorists must recognize and understand if their prescriptions for efficiency are to prove valid. To the extent that the insurance analogy is valid, it is an important recognition since government compensation or liability in these contexts will share the advantages and shortcomings of insurance.

V. THE MORAL HAZARD PROBLEM

The assurance of compensation to victims may be seen as the principal advantage of government liability as insurance. However, unless compensation is limited in some way to those victims who have contributed to the compensation fund, contributors and noncontributors alike are entitled to compensation. This assured compensation without regard to contribution to the compensation fund leads potential victims to incur more exposure to risks, which is true of contributors as well, unless the amount of compensation is linked to the amount of contributions.

This induced behavior generates the moral hazard problem. While one may question the use of the term moral,[31] the "tendency of an insured party to exercise less care to minimize losses than he would exercise if he were uninsured,"[32] is nonetheless as real a problem when government is the insurer as when insurance is provided through private markets. Private parties who anticipate government compensation for future costs have reduced incentives to avoid those costs to the extent of the probability and magnitude of that future compensation. Indeed, the moral hazard problem will often be more serious for government compensation programs than for private insurance because of the manner in which such government programs are funded and the standards used in the distribution of benefits.

The funding for government compensation programs is normally derived from general tax revenues. There is no link between risk exposure and tax contributions. Those in high-risk areas or activities generally pay the same taxes as those with low-risk exposure. Because tax contributions are generally mandatory, government programs do avoid the adverse selection problem experienced by private insurers,[33] but the lack of any link between tax contributions and risk exposure exacerbates the moral hazard problem. No prospective recipient of compensation has an incentive to avoid the harm unless it is anticipated that the compensation will be less than for the full value of the loss. Government compensation programs generally promise to compensate the full loss. Thus both of the commonly proposed solutions to the moral hazard problem in private insurance—linking premiums to risk exposure and limiting payments to less than full compensation—are seldom a feature of government compensation programs.[34]

Government compensation programs have a moral hazard problem of their own, however, which relates to the prior point about the difference between government compensation and private insurance. Not only do the recipients of government compensation have little or no incentive to avoid harm, but the government actors who implement the risk-creating policies also lack incentives to avoid the harm. Rarely are government employees or officials personally responsible for harm their actions cause to others. Their incentives are dependent upon the organization of the bureaucracy, including such things as the factors that influence their promotion and compensation. To the extent that risk is inherent in a policy and not the product of negligent implementation, the risks are controllable only by high-level bureaucrats or politicians in policy-making positions. Politicians and bureaucrats are responsive to political incentives that reflect risk creation only if the risk is widespread or imposed upon politically influential people. Low-level bureaucrats seldom have any sense of personal control over risk-creating activities, and, even where they do, they have few incentives to take those risks into account.

These problems can be dealt with to some degree by building incentives into the organization of the bureaucracy that encourage policymakers to internalize the costs of risk creation. By imposing personal responsibility on low-level bureaucrats in the form of personal liability, advancement constraints, and other penalties, there could be incentives to avoid risk creation. However, the creation of such incentives would invite upper-level bureaucrats and legislators to avoid responsibility for risk-creating policies by attributing the risks to implementation by low-level bureaucrats. This prospect might be diminished by linking supervisory responsibilities of high-level bureaucrats to the risk-creating performance of their subordinates.

Perhaps the best incentive for upper-level bureaucrats will be to link compensation payments directly to agency budgets. To the extent that agencies have limited budgets, and to the extent that upper-level bureaucrats have incentives to maximize productivity within their budgets,[35] the moral hazard problem could be reduced in some measure by requiring compensation from the responsible agency's budget. Ultimately, however, government action is linked to legislative incentives that have far more to do with political risks than with the risks of accidents.

The development of solutions to the moral hazard problem faced by government officials may follow along the lines suggested. However, such solutions will finally depend upon an improved understanding of government behavior and the decision making of government officials. This is the same understanding necessary to the development of a sound theory of government liability. Indeed, given the broad definition of government liability adopted in this analysis, the solution of the moral hazard problem in government is part and parcel of the development of a theory of government liability. The objective of a theory of government liability is to understand how liability assignment influences government action so that liability assignment can serve to promote rather than deter the achievement of government policies. This is precisely what is at stake in dealing with the moral hazard problem in the context of government risk creation.

VI. GOVERNMENT LIABILITY AS COLLECTIVE RESPONSIBILITY

To the extent that we seek to deter governmental creation of risk, an understanding of how liability rules and compensation systems impact upon the actions of government officials and bureaucrats is essential. However, if our sole objective is compensation for losses, our liability policies must be based on other factors. There is much about both private and public liability law that suggests that compensation rather than deterrence is the fundamental objective of modern tort law. For example, products liability law has essentially abandoned fault as a basis of liability, and recent developments like market share, enterprise, and industry liability have weakened the traditional requirement of causation.[36] Both fault and causation are concepts rooted in individual responsibility as a key aspect of tort liability. By moving away from these concepts, and in the direction of liability based upon capacity to compensate and ability to distribute losses, we have shifted from a tort law rooted in individual responsibility to a tort law rooted in collective responsibility.

Government compensation programs are logical under a policy of loss compensation for precisely the same reasons that large corporations have been the principal targets of modern products liability law. Like large corporations, governments have considerable financial capacity and they are effective loss distributors. Indeed, governments are better loss distributors because they have coercive access to the resources of the citizenry and are thus not constrained by the need to market a product that consumers are willing to buy. Government is unaffected by elasticities of individual consumer demand because it can charge for its services and products whether or not taxpayers choose to consume.

Taxpayers do exercise some control over democratic government in their capacity as voters. However, democracy produces collective rather than individual choices. The choices made through the democracy are not the same choices that would be made through the market. The principal explanation for this disparity between democratic and market aggregations of individual choices is the usual separation in the political process between expressions of desire to consume and willingness to pay. The consumption of the benefits of specific governmental programs is seldom tied directly to the payment of the taxes that support those programs. Sometimes this leads voters to refuse to pay for the programs they claim to want. At other times it leads voters to approve expenditures because they are uncertain about the impact of a refusal to pay on the provision of services they desire. In the case of government compensation programs that promise full compensation for possible future losses, there will probably be strong popular support on the theory that the cost is a relatively small part of the total tax burden; the promise of full compensation eliminates the need to invest in personal precautions against the covered risks.

It is inherent in systems of collective responsibility that individual voters will be inclined to support the program, particularly if it promises to compensate in the event of major disasters, and that individuals will have diminished incentives to take personal precautions against the risk. If neither citizens nor government officials have any incentive to deter the covered risk, the prospective compensation burden of the government program can only grow with the growth in the risk. This is simply the moral hazard problem from another point of view. It is the tragedy of the commons, which is inherent in collective systems of resource ownership.[37] Liability for risk is not different from the assignment of property rights in terms of resource allocation. The collective assignment of those rights will lead individuals to overconsume. In the natural resource setting this means destruction of the resource.[38] In the liability setting, this means ever-expanding creation of risk.

If we are to deter losses—if we are to reduce exposure to risks including those risks generated by government action—we must rely on an individual responsibility system of compensation rather than the collective system, which is increasingly prevalent in American law. But the consequences of collective responsibility are not just the lack of incentive to avoid risk exposure and risk creation. Collective responsibility also will result in a corresponding increase in the compensation burden as incentives to deter risk are reduced and risk exposure is increased. In a system of government liability based upon collective compensation, there is an unavoidable government subsidy of private risk taking. Combined with the inherent difficulty in linking government action to its consequences, the result is unlikely to be either allocatively efficient or distributively fair.

VII. GOVERNMENT LIABILITY AND INDIVIDUAL PRODUCTIVITY

In the final analysis, our risk management and government liability policies reflect basic assumptions about the nature of our society. For much of the twentieth century the common law of tort reflected the individualist nature of American society, while the doctrine of sovereign immunity reminded us of past tyrannies. Rather than abandoning the doctrine along with the king, however, we devised a new justification rooted in the concept of popular sovereignty. The community became the beneficiary of the government's immunity, but from the point of view of the injured victim, little has changed.

Modern waivers of sovereign immunity in tort, and the many other forms which modern government liability has taken, reflect a continuing commitment to the individual. We are concerned that the individual be compensated for losses caused by others. But our enthusiasm for compensation has led to an expansive notion of government responsibility and the near abandonment of the concept of individual responsibility. We have moved in the direction of a liability law that is individualist in terms of entitlements and collectivist in terms of responsibilities. As Peter Huber has observed: "A legal system once concerned with individual justice is now a principal center of social engineering."[39]

Experience and logic suggest that this is an unworkable combination. For the collective to compensate, for the government to distribute the costs of risk, the government must have the wherewithal to fund the compensation. Governments have no difficulty acquiring the necessary funds so long as there are resources to tax. These resources will only be available if, on balance across all of our private and public risk taking, there are benefits in excess of costs. On average our risk taking must produce more gain than loss or we will not be able to compensate for all of the losses. By subsidizing private risk taking and by engaging in public risk taking without a good measure of costs and benefits, we are likely to undertake risks that in the aggregate will lead to a net reduction in the welfare of society, and that will, in any event, result in ethically questionable redistributions of wealth.

The collectivization of risk-taking decisions and loss compensation is no different from the collectivization of any other economic activity. It may be motivated by noble objectives, but it has seldom if ever worked to achieve those objectives. Private insurers have struggled to develop mechanisms for effective collectivization of risk with some successes and some failures. We need to recognize that much of what we describe as government liability functions as a form of insurance and faces most of the same problems as private insurance. But, in addition, government risk management through liability laws and subsidies faces all of the problems associated with public resource allocation. The arguments favoring privatization in many areas of government activity apply with equal strength to the privatization of risk taking. Informed and productive risk taking, which is at the heart of all economic activity, remains an essentially individualist enterprise. Our government liability laws must recognize this reality.

NOTES

1. Some writers object that the universe of policy options is not limited to allocational and distributional alternatives. See, for example, Mark Sagoff, "We Have Met the Enemy and He Is Us or Conflict and Contradiction in Environmental Law," 12 *Environmental Law* 283 (1982). As used here the term *allocational* is understood to encompass every manner of human preference, including what Sagoff describes as ethical values. The term *distributional* is understood to encompass the welfare of both current and future generations within the society regulated by the laws in question.

2. Government action can also incidentally reduce risks, although the experience of modern government action, like private action, suggests that most unintended impacts on risk operate to increase rather than decrease risks.

3. See Ronald Coase, "The Problem of Social Cost," 3 *Journal of Law & Economics* 1 (1960).

4. Contractual liabilities, although relevant to both government and private behavior in relation to risk, are not considered in this discussion. Although from the government's point of view both contract and tort liabilities inevitably reflect policy choices, from the private actor's perspective there is an essential difference between contract and tort. Contractual liabilities are self-imposed and determinant to the extent of the specificity of the terms of the contract. Tort liabilities are externally imposed and contingent upon legislative and judicial amendment.

5. J. Holmes, in *Kawananakoa v. Polyblank*, 205 U.S. 349, 353 (1907).

6. J. Huffman, *Government Liability and Disaster Mitigation: A Comparative Study* (Lanham, Md.: University Press of America, 1986), p. 509.

7. "During the Middle Ages, the continental conception was directly opposite to the Roman view which had influenced the common law. Continental theory... 'regarded the group as not a separate entity but merely as the collectivity of the individual members' (Edwin Borchard, "Governmental Responsibility in Tort," Part 4 *Yale Law Journal* 1 [1926]) and the groups could be liable for the acts of individual members. Roman law had its influences, however, and the result was a compromise which distinguished the acts done under the authority of the state from other governmental actions." Huffman, *supra* note 6 at 511.

8. In China the Communist government has always had de facto immunity. The Soviet Union adhered to the immunity of Russian law until 1961. Huffman, *supra* note 6 at 564–65.

9. Edwin Borchard, "Governmental Responsibility in Tort, Part II," 36 *Yale Law Journal* 757 (1927).

10. For example, the Washington Tort Claims Act provides that: "The State of Washington, whether acting in its governmental or proprietary capacity, shall be liable for damages arising out of its tortious conduct to the same extent as if it were a private person or corporation." Notwithstanding this apparently total waiver of immunity, the Washington Supreme Court has held that the state is immune for harm resulting from the performance of discretionary functions. See, for example, *Evangelical United Brethren Church of Adna v. State*, 407 P.2d 440 (1965).

11. 28 U.S.C. §§1291, 1346, 1402, 1504, 2110, 2401–2, 2411–12, 2671–80; 60 Stat. 812 title 4 (1946).

12. Id., at §2680(a).

13. Id., at §2680(h).

14. The other exceptions related to postal matters, collection of taxes and customs duties, admiralty, Trading with the Enemy Act, quarantines, vessels passing through the Panama Canal or in the Canal Zone waters, fiscal operations of the treasury or regulation of the monetary system, combatant activities during wartime, claims arising in a foreign country, activities of the Tennessee Valley Authority, and the activities of the Panama Railroad Company, 28 U.S.C. §2680.

15. For example, in *Dalehite v. United States*, 346 U.S. 15 (1953), the Supreme Court barred claims for the damages resulting from the explosion of fertilizer that was being shipped as part of the U.S. government's foreign aid program. The Court held that all levels of manufacture and shipping were controlled by a central plan, and therefore the discretionary function exception applied.

16. The theory, sometimes stated in separation-of-powers terms, is rooted in democracy and the need for government decisionmakers to make policy choices without being threatened by liability for harm resulting from the failure to invest more of the government's limited resources in one activity as opposed to another. If the government can be held liable on the basis of exercises of discretion, the courts necessarily become the ultimate policy-making entity.

17. *National Manufacturing Co. v. United States*, 210 F.2d 263 (9th Cir. 1954), *cert. denied*, 347 U.S. 967 (1954); *Bartie v. United States*, 216 F.Supp. 10 (W.D. La. 1963), *reh'g. denied*, 326 F. 754 (5th Cir. 1964), *cert. denied*, 379 U.S. 852 (1964).

18. In the common law the standard is the always evasive reasonable person. See W. P. Keeton, *Prosser and Keeton on Torts*, 5th ed. (St. Paul: West Publishing Co., 1984)., pp. 173–208.

19. Accident Compensation Act 1972. This legislation functions much like the workers' compensation system in the United States. Injured claimants are compensated according to a fixed schedule of benefits. See Huffman, *supra* note 6 at 325–30.

20. 28 U.S.C. §2672.

21. Under the dormant commerce clause doctrine, states are prohibited from regulating in a manner discriminating against interstate commerce. See *Pike v. Bruce Church, Inc.*, 397 U.S. 137 (1970). However, when the state is acting as a market participant (in a proprietary capacity), the state is exempt from the limits of the commerce clause. See *Reeves, Inc. v. Stake*, 447 U.S. 429 (1980).

22. See *Jackson v. Metropolitan Edison Co.*, 419 U.S. 345 (1974).

23. Earthquake and War Damage Act 1944. See Huffman, *supra* note 6 at 310–21.

24. 42 U.S.C. §§ 121 et seq., 42 U.S.C. §§ 3231 et seq.

25. See Huffman, *supra* note 6 at 23.

26. From the perspective of government these programs are like any other appropriation of taxpayers' monies. Unlike a private insurance company, the government has no *ex ante* premium schedule related to expected losses.

27. Exceptions are the New Zealand Earthquake and War Damage Act and the Accident Compensation Funds, which make some effort to link premiums to risks incurred by the insured.

28. Louis Kaplow, "An Economic Analysis of Legal Transitions," 99 *Harvard Law Review* 509, 528, 535, 541 (1986).

29. Id. at 530.

30. Id. at 519.

31. "[T]he response of seeking more medical care with insurance than in its absence is a result not of moral perfidy, but of rational economic behavior. Since the cost of the individual's excess usage is spread over all other purchasers of that insurance, the individual is not prompted to restrain his usage of care." Mark V. Pauly, "The Economics of Moral Hazard: Comment," 58 *American Economic Review* 531, 535 (1968).

Whether or not there are moral implications to the choice to consume insurance benefits as if the price were zero is an ethical, not an economic, question. An action can be economically rational and morally reprehensible, or economically irrational and morally correct. It all depends upon the operable definition of morality. It is true that insurance can tempt one to consume more than one has paid for, but giving in to temptation is not immoral in every conceivable context. Where the economically rational decision imposes external costs on third parties, it may be inefficient and it may be unethical, but there is not a necessary link. When morality and efficiency do coincide, ethical conduct, whether externally imposed or self-imposed, can contribute to efficiency. See Kenneth J. Arrow, "The Economics of Moral Hazard: Further Comment," 58 *American Economic Review* 537, 538 (1968).

32. Kenneth S. Abraham, "Individual Action and Collective Responsibility: The Dilemma of Mass Tort Reform," 73 *Virginia Law Review* 845, 903 (1987).

33. Adverse selection occurs when the probability of loss is known to the affected individuals but not to the insurer of those losses. Those at greater risk opt for the insurance while those at lower risk forgo the insurance, thus forcing the costs of providing benefits even higher. Private insurance companies are, of course, well aware of the problem and seek to discriminate among potential insurees.

34. The New Zealand accident compensation system does evidence that government compensation can use these solutions to some extent, by varying premiums among contributors and through a rigid schedule of benefits, but this is an exception among government compensation programs.

35. See W. Niskanen, *Bureaucracy and Representative Government* (Chicago: Aldine Publishing Co., 1971).

36. See Staaf, ch. 6, *infra*.

37. See Hardin, "The Tragedy of the Commons," 162 *Science* 1243 (1968).

38. See *supra* note 37 at 1243.

39. Peter W. Huber, *Liability: The Legal Revolution and Its Consequences* (New York: Basic Books, 1988) p. 82.

5

An Incentive to Avoid or Create
Risks: Market Share Liability

Robert J. Staaf and Bruce Yandle

I. INTRODUCTION

The landmark decision of *Sindell v. Abbott Laboratories*[1] created a novel
approach to the allocation of liability among firms within an industry. In
that decision, the court faced the difficult task of settling an action where
any one of a group of pharmaceutical product firms could have produced
and sold a drug that was later found to harm the offspring of drug consumers. The injured person could not identify the producer of the product.
To deal with the problem, the court developed the theory of enterprise or
market-share liability, which meant that all producers of the same product
would bear liability based on their share of the market during the time the
drug was taken.

The theory of market-share liability parallels other legal theories that
suggest producers are best equipped to bear and spread the cost of risks
across all consumers. Firms are seen as managers of an insurance pool. By
placing the burden of proof on producers to show they are not liable—in
this case just by virtue of being in a particular industry—producers and the
industry are given an incentive to minimize harm. It is argued that fewer
defective products will be forthcoming in future markets. An important
element of this chapter is a demonstration of the fallacy of the argument.

This chapter reviews the *Sindell* decision and the competing theories of
liability considered in and relevant to the case. Section II provides the legal
history and a review of the court's reasoning. Section III examines the
economics of product liability in the context of firm decision making. In
that section, market forces are shown to be the factor that determines the
amount of risk that is ultimately faced by consumers. The wealth-maximizing producer of risky products will combine insurance and avoidance
actions to minimize total liability costs generated by defective products. The

section also discusses problems of information asymmetries as between producers and consumers.

Section IV focuses on the effects of market-share liability on firm decision making. Using the elements of the model in the previous section, the discussion shows how market-share liability can increase the production of risky products by leading to an equilibrium level of more firms (decentralization) and fewer avoidance measures being undertaken in the industry. Section V considers some implications of market-share liability.

II. THE *SINDELL* DECISION AND THEORIES OF LIABILITY

Numerous commentaries on *Sindell*[2] and its implications for other areas have been written.[3] For our purposes, only a brief statement of the facts is necessary. DES (diethylstilbestral), a synthetic estrogen, was generally marketed and prescribed beginning in the late 1940s to prevent miscarriage. It was later linked to vaginal and uterine cancer in the daughters of mothers who ingested the drug. The claimed carcinogenic effect usually does not manifest itself until after adolescence. The prolonged delay in manifestation of injury, coupled with the fact that DES was not a patented drug (which led pharmacists to substitute among brands), created evidentiary problems for plaintiffs in that they were unable to identify the particular manufacturer. Over 200 drug companies produced DES.

In *Sindell*, Justice Mosk considered the present state of the law on causation, noting the difficulties with the existing theories in the DES context, before arriving at market-share liability. The *Sindell* court noted that the general rule was that the plaintiff must show her injuries were caused by the defendant's act or by an instrumentality under the defendant's control, neither of which could be demonstrated for any particular defendant. The exceptions to this general rule that were considered then were "alternative liability," "concerted action," and enterprise liability." The paradigm alternative liability case is *Summers v. Tice*,[4] where two hunters, both negligent, fired guns simultaneously. While only one of them injured the plaintiff, no one could determine which one. The Summers court held that, in such a situation, a showing of negligence on the part of both defendants would shift the burden of proof to each defendant to show that they did not cause the plaintiff's injury. Although dicta in *Summers* indicated that the defendant's superior access to information was important,[5] the *Sindell* court noted that superior access was not required by *Summers*' facts. The defendants did not know which of them caused the plaintiff's harm any better than the plaintiff.[6] However, unlike *Summers*, the plaintiff in *Sindell* had not brought all the potential tortfeasors before the court.[7] Consequently, the plaintiff could not show to a logical certainty that one of the defendants had caused her injury.

Another recognized exception to the causation requirement was a concert of action by the defendants. In *Sindell*, the plaintiff argued that the defendants had acted in concert by relying on each others' tests and using each others' marketing to their individual advantage. Furthermore, the plaintiff argued that the fixed formula established by the industry constituted joint action. The court said that because of the common nature of practices like industry acceptance of a standard and sharing in the benefits of others' marketing efforts, the liability that would result if it were used as an instance of joint action would be too broad. The fixed formula was the result of chemical requirements, not the choice of the manufacturers. The "concert of action" theory, according to the *Sindell* court, failed because no knowledge or encouragement among firms was shown and because there may be no such thing as liability for a tacit understanding to *fail* to do an act.[8]

The final exception accepted at the time was "enterprise liability," or, as the *Sindell* court preferred, "industry-wide liability."[9] Enterprise liability was recognized in *Hall v. E. I. Du Pont de Nemours & Co.*[10] In *Hall*, the court found that an industry standard, delegation of safety standards to a trade association, and industry cooperation demonstrated joint control of the risk and that, once the plaintiff showed that one of the defendants manufactured the product, the burden of proof on causation would shift to all of the defendants. The *Sindell* court found enterprise liability inapplicable because of the large number of manufacturers involved and the lack of delegation of safety functions to a trade association. The industry standards for DES were required by the government and simply indicated the unfairness of imposing liability on the manufacturers based on a government-set standard when the actual manufacturer whose product injured the plaintiff could not be identified.[11]

The "causation" issue of not being able to identify a particular manufacturer, the burden created on a firm if held jointly or severally liable, and the burden on a plaintiff to join all defendants combined to provide a rationale for a "market-share" approach. The market-share approach holds each firm liable for its "expected damage" by multiplying the plaintiff's damages by the market share of each firm at the time of injury. In essence, market-share liability is a mandated contribution rule.[12] The *Sindell* court, under its "expectancy" approach, held that the plaintiff need only join those firms whose combined output constituted a substantial share of the market.[13] Substantial market share was not defined.[14]

The *Sindell* court, in its holding, primarily followed Justice Traynor's policy argument that a firm is in a better position relative to the consumer to bear and spread the risk.[15] Because the firm could better bear and spread the risk, Traynor reasoned that, for public policy purposes, an individual manufacturer's responsibility for inflicting injury on the plaintiff was not important, where responsibility is viewed in the traditional sense of negligence by the manufacturer. According to Traynor, public policy demanded a new definition of responsibility—manufacturing the goods. Traynor therefore argued that the strict liability standard should be recognized generally for products liability. He noted that when certain standards of causation were used,[16] "the negligence rule approaches the rule of strict liability,"[17] and so he maintained that the courts should simply recognize what had already occurred with some causation standards. Traynor used the unimportance of individual manufacturer responsibility and causation standards to urge a different liability standard. *Sindell* built upon the *Escola* concurrence by using the unimportance of individual manufacturer responsibility and the strict liability standard to justify a different standard of causation that would lead to spreading the risk of injury in the market.

Despite the commentary it has generated, *Sindell* has not been widely followed.[18] Rather than market-share liability, *Abel v. Eli Lilly & Co.*[19] used a version of alternative liability, which the *Abel* court labeled "DES-modified alternative liability." DES-modified alternative liability differed from *Summers* in that plaintiffs would not be required to show that a particular defendant was negligent toward them. The plaintiffs would only need to show that the defendants acted tortiously, that the plaintiffs were harmed by one of the defendants, and that the plaintiffs could not identify which defendant caused their injury despite due diligence. The *Abel* court limited DES-modified alternative liability to negligence allegations.

The *Abel* court refused to consider market-share liability because the plaintiffs had not requested that it be adopted, but the court said it was not recognized in Michigan. The *Abel* court was able to avoid one of the most difficult points in *Sindell*—the absence of some potential tortfeasors as parties. The plaintiff claimed that the named defendants constituted all known manufacturers or distributors of DES, and since *Abel* was based on a motion for summary judgment, the claim had to be taken as true. However, in any subsequent litigation the presence of all potential tortfeasors is likely to be the most thorny issue.[20]

In *Collins v. Eli Lilly & Co.*,[21] the Wisconsin Supreme Court first found that the plaintiff was entitled to a remedy for her injury, then set about finding a basis for such a remedy. The *Collins* court rejected alternative liability, concert of action, enterprise liability, and civil conspiracy for practical reasons. Because market shares would be difficult to determine, the *Collins* court refused to make market share an exclusive basis of liability, but the court retained market shares as a factor to be considered by a jury using comparative negligence. Instead, the *Collins* court accepted a variant of the risk-contribution theory proposed by Professor Glen Robinson.[22] Robinson's risk-contribution theory imposed liability when a defendant creates an unreasonable risk of injury as well as when a defendant actually causes injury. The *Collins* court, however, would still require some showing that a defendant reasonably could have contributed to the actual injury.

To state a cause of action under the *Collins* risk-contribution theory, the plaintiff would need to sue only one defendant in negligence or strict liability and make the following allegations:

that the plaintiff's mother took DES; that DES caused the plaintiff's subsequent injuries; that the defendant produced or marketed the type of DES taken by the plaintiff's mother; and that the defendant's conduct in producing or marketing the DES constituted a breach of a legally recognized duty to the plaintiff.[23]

The plaintiff could sue more than one defendant if she chose. Defendants joined could then bring in others as third-party defendants when they produced or marketed the same type of DES taken by the plaintiff's mother. Others, including the note extensively cited in *Sindell*, have argued that market-share liability would create incentives for manufacturers to improve quality, design, formulation, and testing to lower the risk of product defects.[24]

We now turn to an analysis that shows how market-share liability, as a contribution rule, may actually lead firms to decrease expenditures on accident avoidance, with the result of an increase in defects relative to a rule such as joint and several liability. The economic analysis presented here indicates that the legal distinctions in the various market-share rules adopted by various courts are the same in their effects and are possibly perverse in their intent.

III. INSURING VERSUS AVOIDING WHEN CAUSATION IS NOT AN ISSUE

The Insurance/Avoidance Decision

Economists have generally argued that with damages restricted to a compensatory remedy, the standard of care undertaken by firms to avoid the risk of product defect or injury is determined by market forces rather than the legal standard imposed by the judicial or legislative process. The actual levels of care, as defined here, are actions undertaken by a firm (manufacturer, distributor, seller) such as quality control measures, design, and formulation and testing. These measures will be defined as risk-avoidance measures. Legal commentators and the courts have distinguished manufacturing defects from design defects. While this distinction is useful under certain circumstances, it is not important for our purposes.

A firm's actions with regard to products liability can be considered as a choice of a portfolio of avoidance or preventive expenditures *and* insurance expenditures. Whatever the liability standard, assuming no transactions costs, the absence of brand-name capital or reputation effects, risk neutrality of firms and consumers, and the absence of contributory negligence, the firm will undertake avoidance measures so long as the marginal cost of these measures is less than or equal to the marginal cost of insurance or the *expected* loss to the consumer. The choice of avoidance measures and insurance is simply a restatement of the profit- or wealth-maximizing hypothesis of firm behavior. Namely, the firm will choose to insure against (avoid) an expected loss whenever it is less costly relative to altering behavior to avoid the expected loss; that is, the firm will choose the least-cost alternative in order to survive in a competitive market. Under these conditions, the advent of strict products liability under either the *Greenman*[25] standard or the *Restatement of Torts*, Section 402A, standard has probably had little or no effect on the behavior of the firm in terms of avoidance expenditures. The negligence standard, or more specifically, the Learned Hand formulation, is a legal standard that approximates the behavior of the firm.

Strict liability has had its most significant impact in terms of who bears the risks that remain after avoidance expenditures are undertaken as discussed above. The risks that remain after avoidance actions are taken are defined as residual risks. A shift from a negligence standard to a strict liability standard shifts the residual risk from the consumer to the firm, which in turn is spread in the market.

For example, suppose there is a one in one hundred chance of a product defect with a resultant injury of $10,000. The expected loss is $100 for each of the one hundred items sold. If the avoidance cost per unit of reducing this probability from one in one hundred to one in one thousand (expected loss of $10) is $80, then the firm will have an incentive and consumers will demand the (higher quality) product with the avoidance measure. Market forces, even under *caveat emptor*, will provide the incentive for firms to undertake the measure because the expected loss decreases from $100 (borne by the consumer) to $10, while the avoidance cost, which is passed on in a higher price, is only $80. However, there remains a residual expected risk of $10 that either the firm or the consumer will bear (insure against) depending on the liability standard.

On the other hand, if the avoidance expenditure was $100, then firms would not undertake the expenditure nor would consumers demand the increased quality because the cost of avoidance ($100) exceeds the benefit of the reduced expected loss ($90). The residual risk is now $100. Under *caveat emptor* the consumer will bear the risk and either self- or market insure against the residual risk of $100. Under *caveat venditor*, the consumer will pay a higher price ($100) to compensate the firm for the cost of its insurance ($100). The choice of risk *avoidance* versus insurance, under these assumptions, is based on market forces rather than the legal standard.

Are There Asymmetries?

Professor Steven Shavell has argued that a rule of negligence relative to rule of strict liability is inefficient.[26] His argument is that there is a social cost (externality) that remains after all risk-avoidance measures are under-taken. If the consumer is not informed or aware of the risk of product defects that remain ($10 in the first example and $100 in the second ex-ample), the consumer will demand too much of the good relative to a situation where the consumer is fully aware of the total cost of the good, which is the sum of the direct costs (the price paid) and the indirect cost of injuries (residual risk).

At the margin, the consumer receives benefits that are less than the actual costs because of ignorance of the residual risk that remains. If the firm is liable for and aware of these indirect costs under strict liability, then these accident costs will be passed on to the consumer in the form of higher prices that will in turn lead to a decrease in the quantity demanded by the consumer and thus a decrease in injuries and risk. If the firm has a comparative advantage over the consumer/user in information about product risk, the price system will indirectly convey that information in the form of higher prices under strict liability. Thus, at the margin, the consumer's marginal value of the good will be equal to the total marginal cost including indirect cost.

Shavell presents an even stronger argument for strict liability (in the sense that it is not based on a comparative informational advantage) if the accidents involve third parties. Again, the firm has an incentive to undertake all avoidance measures as long as they are less than the cost of insurance. Moreover, even if the consumer is fully aware of third-party injuries from his use of the product, he may have no incentive to take them into account if he is not liable for such injuries. However, the residual risk to third parties from injuries that occur because of product defects is not knowingly assumed. The quantity demanded of a product or the level of use activity is reduced by a higher price to the consumer because the firm now passes the cost of liability on to the consumer, which in turn reduces demand and thereby reduces the risk of injury to third parties.

Shavell's argument turns on the point that injuries from product use are an external or social cost that needs to be internalized through the market to the demanders of the product. One means of internalizing this cost is to impose strict liability. Thus, the argument can be inter-preted as an argument for promoting safety, not through the actions of firms, but through the actions of consumers. Others have argued the op-posite result of strict liability because of the averaging (spreading) of in-surance premiums in the market.[27] Some consumers may demand more risky products because the average premium indirectly charged in the price may be lower than the individual premium if the consumers were liable. If there are information asymmetries that favor firms over con-sumers, the case for strict liability becomes a strong contender in the competition for liability rules.

IV. INSURING VERSUS AVOIDING UNDER MARKET-SHARE LIABILITY

Up to this point, it has been assumed that the firm that produces a defective product that causes injury can be identified and causation established. The transparent link between cause and effect magnifies potential losses associated with risky products and enables the firm to purchase liability insurance as opposed to self-insuring, if that is the least-cost action to take. Market-share liability is an attempt to overcome the identification problem of causation where the linkages are difficult to discern. Professor Robinson argues that market-share liability is not a radical change if the causation issue is related to risk exposure as opposed to actual causation.[28] In other words, the firm causes a certain amount of risk exposure to consumers simply by being a manufacturer in the industry.

Analysis of a Single Producer

To illustrate the general tendencies of market-share liability, assume a market-share approach is adopted despite the fact that a particular manufacturer could be identified as producing the item that caused the injury; that is, the industry is held liable because of causing risk exposure to consumers and the liability will be apportioned among the firms within the industry according to the market-share approach.

Assume initially that there is only one firm in the industry, and suppose that at current prices there is an annual market demand of 1 million units. Further, suppose there is a 1 percent defect rate and that each defect results in injuries of $10,000. Assume the firm is strictly liable for all injuries. Under these assumptions, the average expected loss or liability for each product is $100. This liability cost is a cost of production that can be self-insured or market insured. If no quality control or avoidance measures are undertaken, the firm will have 10,000 defects or a total liability of $100 million.

Now, assume the firm chooses to self-insure and establishes a reserve equal to the annual expected losses derived from the 10,000 defective units, or $100 million. The corpus of the reserve will be paid out annually. For simplicity's sake, assume that the firm earns a rate of return on the reserve equal to the return of other capital employed in the firm. In this case, the marginal cost of insurance is $10,000 per defective unit or $100 per unit of production when the cost is spread across the 1 million units produced. The firm has covered its expected losses, and no action has been taken to alter product features to reduce the risk of loss.

Suppose there are product changes available to the firm or other costly quality control actions that can be taken to reduce the number of defective products that enter the market. Suppose further that the alteration and

Figure 5.1
Avoidance/Insurance Analysis

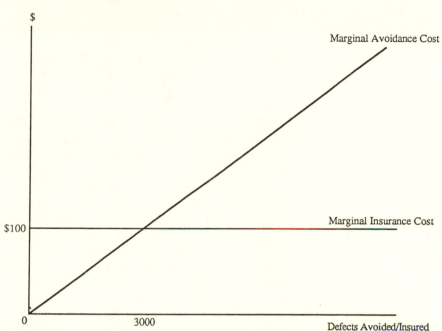

control costs rise as the share of defects removed increases. For example, one additional postproduction test may remove 20 percent of the defects at a cost of $10 for each production unit. Incremental reductions beyond that require engineering changes, and each change imposes increasingly higher costs on the firm.

Figure 5.1 illustrates the situation faced by the firm. The marginal cost of insurance, $100, is shown along with the rising marginal cost of avoiding a defect. The origin of the diagram is set at zero units. Movement along the horizontal axis implies defect reduction and insurance.

Since the marginal cost of avoidance lies below the marginal cost of insurance for part of the range, the firm will take some actions to avoid defects. When the marginal cost of insurance is less than the additional avoidance cost, the firm then insures. The result in the figure shows the firm avoiding 3,000 defects and insuring for the remaining 7,000 units. The insured units are the residual risk covered by insurance with the premium paid indirectly by consumers.

Two Firms with Market-Share Liability

Now suppose a second firm enters and captures one-fourth of the market served previously by the single producer. Total market output is the same,

1 million units. Both firms now face market-share liability because of informational problems. The larger firm is now liable for 75 percent of all defect-related liabilities without respect to which firm produces the product. The smaller firm bears a 25 percent liability. Each defective unit imposes a $10,000 claim for damages, which is paid by the two firms.

If each firm has identical production, insurance, and avoidance costs, and if each firm operates as if the other is not present, the outcome will be the same as for a single firm. Although the marginal cost of insurance for the individual firm's production has fallen, either by 75 or 25 percent, each firm is liable for the other firm's defects in proportion to its market share. At the end of the year, the larger firm will have produced 75 percent of the defects and paid 75 percent of the losses. The smaller firm will have covered the remainder.

But the inability of consumers (and judges) to identify producers leads to a market-share liability rule, which changes relative costs and may eliminate the economic viability of liability insurers, a point we will discuss later. There are incentives on the part of either or both firms to alter their avoidance/insurance actions and thereby affect the outcome. Given the market-share rule, either firm has an incentive to reduce the quality of its products (reduce avoidance measures such as inspections), which is to say that each firm will place more defects on the market.[29] The smaller firm has a greater incentive to do so, because 75 percent of the cost of defects is paid by its larger competitor.

Suppose total output remains constant as does market share, but that the smaller firm reduces avoidance costs and ships more defective products. The small firm will bear 25 percent of the increased losses. If the reduction in total avoidance costs exceeds the increased liability cost of the 25 percent share, the small firm will reduce product quality. Total defects rise, as do the profits of the smaller firm. The larger firm's profits fall, if it continues an unaltered flow of goods. The larger firm bears 75 percent of the increased losses from the smaller firm's increase in production of defective goods. The larger firm must reduce costs by more than 75 percent per unit as it seeks to gain from increasing the number of defective goods. This differential in marginal liability costs gives the smaller firm a relative advantage in producing defective products. In effect, the smaller firm can export a larger share of its liability costs to the larger firm, which may be able to export some of its liability costs to the smaller one.

The assumption that market shares will not be disturbed by the increased level of defective goods is important to the outcome. If consumers relate their demand for a particular firm's product to the average quality of the product and make proportional reductions in demand to proportional increases in defects, more or less may be gained by firms that increase production of defects. The firm's market share will fall for all its output, which reduces its liability cost. But total sales will also fall, which reduces total revenue. The final outcome depends on the marginal revenue effects of increasing the number of defects relative to the marginal cost of doing so. However, we note that if consumers can make the identification implied here, the problem of causation relied on in forming the market-share rule no longer applies.

The effect of market-share liability rules on commercial carriers of liability insurance is relatively straightforward. The economic purpose of insurance has to do with predicting expected damages for a pooled group of risk units. Uncertainty faced by each risk unit is substituted for the certain payment of the insurance premium. To be effective, the insurer must predict future claims with some competitive level of accuracy. A market-share rule is a substitute for insurance to the extent that future claims are based precisely on a known formula. Market-share liability does not forecast the level of total future claims confronted by an industry, but the rule does define the share paid by individual firms. Market-share liability weakens the market for liability insurance.

A Prisoners' Dilemma

In the case where identification of cause and effect is not a problem, each firm can be held accountable for its own defective goods. Two or more firms sharing a market will find a normal profit equilibrium. There are no distributional effects generated by the liability rule. However, in the absence of collusion or merger, the two producers of generic goods are caught in a classic prisoners' dilemma when a market-share liability rule is imposed and market share remains fixed after the rule is applied. Each has two courses of action available—produce higher or lower quality goods. The profits for the smaller firm rise when it reduces quality, while the larger one continues to maintain quality, assuming total demand remains constant. Profits for the larger firm decline. Conversely, profits for the larger firm rise when it produces defective units; profits for its smaller competitor decline. Absent collusion, the firms have an incentive to reduce product quality, with action and response leading to lower overall quality and possibly lower total profits than would be the case without market-share liability.

The elements of the dilemma shown in Figure 5.2 are based on assumptions regarding the shape of the function describing avoidance cost and a 75/25 percent market-share rule. The previously discussed production values are used. There are 7,000 defective units produced jointly (1 percent of 7 million) before the adoption of the sharing rule. The larger firm avoids the production of 2,250 defects, and the smaller firm avoids 750, giving 3,000 total defects avoided.

The northwest quadrant of the graph shows an initial state where both firms maintain quality (produce an unaltered stream of defective units) and pay their proportional shares of damages at the end of the period. There

Figure 5.2
Prisoners' Dilemma Analysis

LARGE FIRM

	High Quality	Low Quality
High	0 , 0	-.14 , +.14
Low	+.42 , -.42	+.98 , -.2

SMALL FIRM

are zero gains for each firm. The northeast quadrant depicts the case where the larger firm takes into account the reduction of liability costs (paying 75 percent instead of 100 percent of the $10,000 in claims per unit) and produces more defects, and the smaller firm continues to produce an unadjusted flow of goods. As indicated there, the larger firm gains $1.4 million and the smaller firm loses that amount. There is a direct transfer from the smaller to the larger firm. This gives the larger firm an incentive to reduce quality.

The southwest quadrant shows the result when the smaller firm expands production of defects based on the 75 percent reduction in marginal liability costs and the larger firm makes no adjustment in its production. In this case, the smaller firm gains $4.2 million and the larger firm loses that amount. When compared with the northeast quadrant the result here implies a larger incentive for the smaller firm to reduce quality. Finally, the southeast cell shows the result when both firms expand their production of defects after adjusting for the relative change in liability costs. Here, the smaller firm gains the $4.2 million but must subtract the $1.4 million in costs imposed on it by the larger firm, giving a net gain of $2.8 million. The larger firm bears the $4.2 million imposed by the smaller firm but externalizes $1.4 million, which gives it a net loss of $2.8 million. When compared with the northeast quadrant, the results here indicate a strong incentive for the smaller firm to reduce quality, while the larger one does the same to minimize the damage imposed. The implications of the dilemma predict that both firms will expand their production of defects, with the smaller firm being the protagonist in the process.

The situation here is described in the three quadrants of Figure 5.3. The northeast quadrant shows market demand and supply for the consumer good, where QE is the equilibrium level of industry (two-firm) output. The ray OR in the southeast quadrant measures the share of output that is defective and covered by market or self-insurance. The total number of defects is measured on the lower vertical axis. The ray OSS in the southwest quadrant measures the share of all defects for which the smaller firm is liable and converts total defects produced jointly to individual liability for the smaller firm. Total defects for the smaller firm are shown on the horizontal axis in the southeast quadrant at point A. The ray OSL is the share of defect costs borne by the larger firm under a fixed market-share rule, and the total number for which it is liable is shown at point B on the horizontal axis. Under a market-share rule with no strategic action by firms to export costs to their competitor, the smaller firm's liability will always lie along the ray OSS. Changes in demand or supply and corresponding increases or decreases in QE will lead to higher or lower points on OSS, always yielding the same share of liability for the smaller firm. The same holds for the larger firm along OSL.

When the smaller firm reduces avoidance measures and increases the number of defects on the market, it effectively rotates the ray OR to a position like OR'. The number of defects produced and the share of those produced by the smaller firm rises, but the smaller firm's share of costs is fixed by OSS, just as the larger firm's share is fixed by OSL. A reading from OR' yields a defect liability for the smaller firm at point B. The larger firm's defect liability is now at point C. Both firms' defect liability has changed, but the larger firm is now liable for a larger share of costs.

The dynamics of the prisoners' dilemma become more graphic when there are a larger number of smaller firms in an industry. Consider a case where there are fifty producers and the smallest twenty firms each produce 1 percent of industry output. Market-share liability implies they will be liable for 1 percent of damages. It costs can be reduced by less than 1 percent, they can gain by externalizing their liabilities to the remaining firms. Gains to be had by small firms diminish if they consolidate and become larger (relative to the largest firm in the industry).

In situations like *Sindell*, consumers cannot identify the particular producer of defective goods, which implies that market demand will decline with increases in the number of defective goods found in the market. As demand declines, all producers will reduce total production proportionately,

Figure 5.3
Defect Liability Analysis

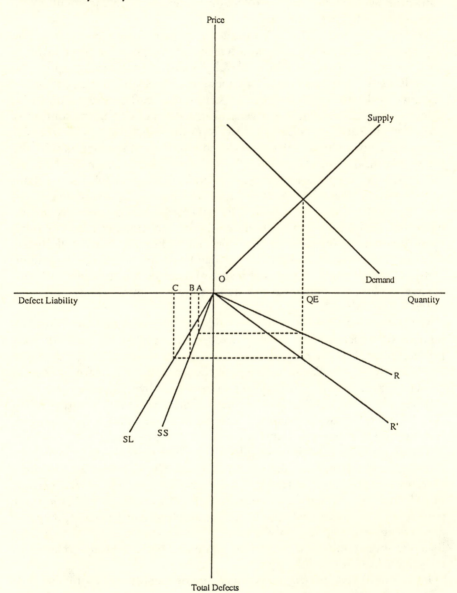

still maintaining their market share. However, the relative cost advantage enjoyed by smaller firms that produce defective goods will enable them to increase market share. Furthermore, any new entrants to the industry will build smaller rather than larger plants. As the industry expands market shares will change, as will the liability rule. So long as firms are not of the same size, smaller firms will have an advantage.

V. CONCLUSION

The introduction of product liability insurance in a strict liability-rule environment, where causation can be determined, will not change the distribution of liability losses across firms in the same industry. Each firm will have an incentive to consider the relative gains that obtain from substituting insurance for reductions in defect-avoidance costs. Where the per defect cost of insurance is less than the additional cost of avoiding a defect, firms will make economizing substitutions.

Since all costs are ultimately paid by consumers, the relative amount of risk borne by consumers from defective products will be determined by normal market forces. However, when the number of defective units produced increases as a result of smaller firms producing lower-quality goods in a market-share liability environment, total damage claims will increase. But the larger firm will pay a proportionately larger part of the increased premiums, even though it may have done nothing in an actuarial sense to increase its liability.

If continuing commercial insurers investigate and reassign risk to reflect the actuarial risk of the smaller firm that externalizes the majority of its defect costs to the larger firm, the smaller firm will simply self-insure and avoid the higher premiums.

The introduction of market-share liability in an existing industry environment is predicted to lead to structural changes in an industry so that eventually all firms will be equal in size. In that case, there can be no exporting of liability costs. If there are few economies of scale or low fixed costs, the industry will be composed of atomistic smaller firms. New firms will enter so long as the market share of the new firm is smaller than that of existing firms, which provides the opportunity for externalizing the cost of defects.

The induced changes do not end with structural adjustments across firms in an industry. While the adjustments are occurring product quality will decrease, and, as a result, demand will fall. Consumers overall are likely to be worse off because economies of scale in production and distribution may be lost. In addition, since the change in the relative cost of avoidance and insurance is the result of the market-share liability rule, and not underlying real factors, consumers would be willing to pay for more avoidance activity. In other words, market-share liability induces the production of defective products while introducing contrived incentives that reduce consumer welfare.

The introduction of market-share liability also affects liability insurers when they recognize that the production of defective units is increasing. Not knowing which firm produces defective units (the original *Sindell* problem), they will seek to raise premiums for firms that are not the chief source of the difficulty (large firms) while also raising premiums for small firms. As premiums rise, smaller firms will have an incentive to self-insure. The process leads to a shrinking market for liability insurance, as does the presence of the market-share rule itself.

Once an industry that produces generic goods equilibrates under a market-share liability rule, some of the distortions in the distribution of liability costs caused by the rule will be eliminated. At that point, losses to consumers are associated with lost economies of scale and the transactions costs generated by the induced adjustments in the size distribution of firms and at least one other lost opportunity to reduce risks.

Inspection firms provide quality assurance to buyers of commodities that are homogeneous. For example, an inspection firm will contract with buyers to inspect grains, chemicals, and other products purchased by buyers who convert the commodities to consumer goods and will guarantee a level of quality (number of defects). Market-share liability removes incentives for firms to employ inspection services, since liability is spread irrespective of actions taken to reduce defects.

There is one final prediction that comes from the analysis. Larger firms that find themselves bearing a disproportionate part of liability claims have an additional incentive to break out of the production of generic goods. Firms will devote resources to differentiate their product so as to identify a brand name or simply exit the troubled market. By establishing brand-name capital or exiting the market, the firm can avoid the market-share liability dilemma.

While the *Sindell* decision may appear to be narrowly focused in that it deals with producers of generic goods in circumstances where cause and effect cannot be determined, the logic of the ruling is found in another large category of cases. Environmental damage is frequently associated with multiple producers of emissions that cannot be linked to specific sources. There are also situations where long periods of time pass before damaged parties are aware of their harm.

The Superfund statute, in ways somewhat similar to *Sindell*, allows the U.S. Environmental Protection Agency to name potentially responsible parties when listing a hazardous waste site that was previously generated by chemical firms. The Department of Justice can then sue any one or all of the potentially responsible parties for all of the damages associated with the hazardous waste site. A rule of joint and several liability applies. Unlike *Sindell*, Superfund has no *ex ante* rule for sharing liability. That is determined on a case-by-case basis. Even so, there is an incentive for smaller firms to take on more risk when disposing of wastes at sites shared by larger firms, especially where the larger firm has brand-name capital at risk for other products.

Rules of liability that may appear to be logical in static situations, and may indeed be the only reasonable approach to take in particular cases, can induce unexpected and perverse effects in a dynamic setting. This chapter has focused on one such case—the case of market-share liability. In a static world where economic agents do not respond to changes in relative price, a market-share rule has no effects. In the real world, where such agents do respond to relative prices, the rule can readily lead to an increase, rather than a decrease, in the harm that caused the original action. Since there are predictable dynamic effects that work against the goal of reducing future risks, market-share liability must be viewed as a risky option. Care must be taken when the rule is applied, since the costs it induces may exceed the cost of the mischief the rule seeks to avoid.

NOTES

1. 26 Cal.3d 588, 607 P.2d 924, 163 Cal. Rptr. 132, *cert. denied*, 449 U.S. 912 (1980).

2. Abrahams and Musgrave, "DES Labyrinth," 33 *S C Law Review* 663 (1982); Fischer, "Products Liability—An Analysis of Market Share Liability," 34 *Vand Law Review* 1623 (1981); Robinson, "Multiple Causation in Tort Law: Reflections on the DES Cases," 68 *Va Law Review* 713 (1982); Zwier, "Cause in Fact in Tort Law—A Philosophical and Historical Examination," 31 *De Paul Law Review* 769 (1982); Note, "DES: Judicial Interest Balancing and Innovation," 22 *B C Law Review* 747 (1981); Note, "Sindell v. Abbott Laboratories: A Market Share Approach to DES Causation," 69 *California Law Review* 1179 (1981); Note, "Market Share Liability: A New Method of Recovery for D.E.S. Litigants," 30 *Catholic University Law Review* 551 (1981); Note, "DES and a Proposed Theory of Enterprise Liability," 46 *Fordham A Review* 963 (1978); Note, "Industry-Wide Liability and Market Share Allocation of Damages," 15 *Ga Law Review* 423 (1981); Note, "Market Share Liability: An Answer to the DES Causation Problem," 94 *Harvard Law Review* 668 (1981); Comment, "Beyond Enterprise Liability in DES Cases—Sindell," 14 *Ind Law Review* 695 (1981); Comment, "Overcoming the Identification Burden in DES Litigation: The Market Share Liability Theory," 65 *Marq Law Review* 609 (1982); Comment, "Market Share Liability for Defective Products: An Ill-Advised Remedy for the Problem of Identification," 76 *NW University Law Review* 300 (1981); Note, "Products Liability: Sindell v. Abbott Laboratories: Proportional Unidentifiable Fairness and the Oklahoma Perspective," 34 *Oklahoma Law Review* 843 (1981); Comment, "Refining Market Share Liability: Sindell v. Abbott Laboratories," 33 *Stanford Law Review* 937 (1981); Note, "Proof of Causation in Multiparty Drug Litigation," 56 *Texas Law Review* 125 (1977); Note, "Remedy for the 'DES Daughters': Products Liability without the Identification Requirements," 42 *University of Pittsburgh Law Review* 669 (1981); Note, "Emerg-

ing Theories of Proof in Products Liability: Resolving the Problem of Identifying DES Manufacturers," 26 *Villanova Law Review* 997 (1981); Note, "Market Share Liability Adopted to Overcome Defendant Identification Requirement in DES Litigation," 59 *Washington University Law Quarterly* 571 (1981).

3. Appleson, "Concert of Action Theory: Polluters Beware (Market Share Liability)," 68 *ABA Journal* 1209 (1982); Note, "The Causation Problem in Asbestos Litigation: Is There an Alternative Theory of Liability?" 15 *Indiana Law Review* 670 (1982).

4. 33 Cal.2d 80, 199 P.2d 1 (1944).

5. *Summers,* 199 P.2d at 4.

6. *Sindell,* 607 P.2d at 929.

7. Only 5 of approximately 200 manufacturers were before the court. *Sindell,* 607 P.2d at 931.

8. *Sindell,* 607 P.2d at 932, 933.

9. *Sindell,* 607 P.2d at 933.

10. 345 F.Supp. 353 (E.D.N.Y. 1972). *Hall* seems somewhat weak as authority. After the opinion the consolidated cases were severed and transferred. *Chance v. E. I. Du Pont de Nemours,* 371 F.Supp. 439 (E.D.N.Y. 1974). In other courts they were decided on entirely different, usually procedural, grounds. See *Hall v. E. I. Du Pont de Nemours & Co.,* 519 F.2d 715 (6th Cir. 1975); *Lehtonen v. E. I. Du Pont de Nemours,* 389 F.Supp. 633 (D. Mont. 1975); *Davis v. E. I. Du Pont de Nemours,* 400 F.Supp. 1347 (W.D.N.C. 1974).

11. *Sindell,* 607 P.2d at 935.

12. Note that any defendant could still escape liability if it could demonstrate that it did not cause the plaintiff's injury. *Sindell,* 607 P.2d at 937.

13. The plaintiff had joined only 5 of the approximately 200 DES producers, but those 5 were responsible for 90 percent of the DES produced. *Sindell,* 607 P.2d at 937.

14. The lack of definition of *substantial* has been criticized in *Martin v. Abbott Laboratories, Inc.,* 102 Wash.2d 581, 689, P.2d 368, 381 (1984) (en banc). See generally, Notes, 76 *Northwestern University Law Review* 300 (1981) and 94 *Harvard Law Review* 668 (1981).

15. *Escola v. Coca-Cola Bottling Co. of Fresno,* 24 Cal.2d 453, 150 P.2d 436, 440 (1944) (J. Traynor, concurring.)

16. Several devices can permit the plaintiff to raise an inference of negligence by the manufacturer when the actual cause is unknown. The most well known is *res ipsa loquitur.* When the cause of injury is unknown and the other necessary requirements are met, *res ipsa loquitur* raises an inference of negligence that, absent the sort of evidence unlikely to be available when the cause is unknown, is left to a jury decision. Prosser, *Handbook of the Law of Torts,* 4th ed. (1971): pp. 211–29.

17. *Abel v. Eli Lilly & Co.,* 94 Mich. App. 59, 289 N.W.2d 20 (1979).

18. For example, *Morton v. Abbott Laboratories,* 538 F.Supp. 593 (M.D. Fla. 1982); *Ryan v. Eli Lilly & Co.,* 514 F.Supp. 1004 (D.S.C. 1981); *Startling v. Seaboard Coast Line R. Co.,* 533 F.Supp. 183 (S.D. Ga. 1982); also see *Vigiolto v. Johns-Manville Corp.,* 643 F.Supp. 1454 (W.D. Pa. 1986), and *Celotex Corp. v. Copeland,* 471 S.2d 533 (Fla. 1989) for a discussion of why the *Sindell* approach has not been applied in asbestos cases.

19. *Abel v. Eli Lilly & Co.*, 94 Mich. App. 59, 289 N.W.2d 20 (1979).

20. *Prod Liab Rep* (CCH) 9943 (Mich. Sup. Ct. Feb. 6, 1984). Discussed in *National Law Journal* at 5, col. 1 (Feb. 20, 1984).

21. *Collins v. Eli Lilly Co.*, 116 Wis.2d 166, 342 N.W.2d 37 (1984), *cert. denied*, 469 U.S. 826, 105 S.Ct. 107, 83 L.Ed.2d 51 (1984).

22. The court refers with approval to Robinson, "Multiple Causation in Tort Law: Reflections on the DES Cases," 68 *Virginia Law Review* 713 (1982), 42 N.W.2d at 49 n. 10.

23. Id. at 51.

24. See Peter W. Huber, *Liability: The Legal Revolution and Its Consequences* (New York: Basic Books, 1988), esp. chs. 1, 2.

25. *Greenman v. Yuba Power Products*, 59 Cal.2d 57, 377 P.2d 897, 901, 27 Cal. Rptr. 697 (1963).

26. Steven Shavell, "Strict Liability versus Negligence," *Journal of Legal Studies* 1 (1980).

27. W. Y. Oi, "The Economics of Product Safety," 4 *Bell Journal of Economics* 3 (1973).

28. See *supra* note 22.

29. We note the effect here is similar to that described by Klein and Leffler in their discussion of production of higher quality goods when firms have brand-name capital at risk. At this point in our analysis, there is no brand-name capital at risk. See Benjamin Klein and Keith B. Leffler, "The Role of Market Forces in Assuring Contractual Performance," 89 *Journal of Political Economy* (1981) 615.

6

Deep Pockets, Insurance, and Taxes: The Implications of Uncertainty versus Risk for Product Liability Cases

Robert J. Staaf

I. INTRODUCTION

Liability and malpractice insurance premiums have increased in the last several years reflecting either (1) a broader scope of liability (e.g., strict liability), (2) higher frequency of lawsuits, or (3) higher damage awards. There have been massive tort litigation suits involving drugs (DES), medical devices (intrauterine birth control devices), and substances (asbestos). Several major corporations are in Chapter 11 bankruptcy because of tort liability. It has been argued that increased insurance premiums or the unavailability of insurance has forced firms to choose between closing down, going bare (self-insurance), or abandoning product lines.

Legislation has been enacted in some states and proposed in others and at the federal level to deal with what has been called the liability insurance crisis. Some states limit the amount of noneconomic damages awards (e.g., pain and suffering) and/or punitive damages. The Reagan and Bush administrations have pushed for restoration of the role of fault and causation, limiting noneconomic and punitive damages, periodic versus lump-sum payments, abolishing joint and several liability, reducing awards of plaintiffs who are covered by insurance, and limiting contingency fees.[1]

The Kasten Bill introduced in 1982 proposed a two-tier standard for products liability whereby *manufacturing defects* would fall under a strict liability standard while *design defects* would fall under a negligence standard.[2] President Bush briefly discussed proposing tort reform legislation in his State of the Union address. Finally, there have been a number of proposals aimed at specific relief for certain industries.[3] These proposals focus on industry-wide mandatory compensation funds (similar to workmans' compensation) that tax all manufacturers and place limits on damage awards.

The main purpose of this chapter is to examine the distributional and allocative effects of liability rules using a framework of risk and uncertainty. The courts' failure to distinguish between risk and uncertainty often creates a confusion as to the distributional and allocative effects that serve as a policy basis for advocating various liability standards. For example, proposals that provide a negligence standard for design defects and a strict liability standard for manufacturing defects often fail to distinguish between risk and uncertainty.

The second purpose of the chapter is to compare various proposals such as a return to a negligence standard, placing limits on recoveries, or creating a compensation pool to tax relief based on product liability losses. In particular, there is a neglected provision in the tax code that perhaps inadvertently provides a risk versus uncertainty distinction. The Tax Reform Act of 1984, Pub. L. 98–369, amended Internal Revenue Code (IRC) Section 172 to provide a ten-year net operating loss carryback for tort liabilities arising under federal or state laws. The normal period for net operating loss carryback is three years. To qualify, the liability must arise from an act or omission occurring at least three years before the current taxable year, and a tort must have occurred over an extended period, a substantial part of which elapsed at least three years before the current taxable year.[4] The amendment is designed primarily to provide relief for firms exposed to massive product liability actions where there is a delayed manifestation of injuries from the use of products such as drugs (e.g., DES), medical devices (e.g., IUDs), and exposure to substances (e.g., asbestos).[5]

Special legislation has been proposed to provide relief to firms exposed to liability in the asbestos industry. These proposals range from specialized acts such as establishing a compensation fund by taxing manufacturers, to general acts such as a national products liability law.[6] The proposals are directed at the so-called insurance crisis or bankruptcy crisis brought about by changes related to products liability. It will be argued that if delayed manifestation of injury cases are simply a question of risk allocation, then government intervention in the form of special tax provisions or other special proposals demanded by rent-seeking groups will have both redistribution and efficiency aspects.[7] On the other hand, if delayed manifestations of injury cases are the result of uncertainty, then a normative argument can be made that a tax proposal similar to IRC Section 172 (with modification) simply returns taxes on income that otherwise should not have been taxed. In this sense it is not a special interest redistribution scheme, such as limitations on damages or compensation funds.

II. RISK

Risk is associated with events that have a known probability distribution of occurrence. Consider the example in Table 6.1. Suppose product X is

Table 6.1
Product X

Alternative Outcomes	Probability of Outcome	X	Cost Under Alternative Outcomes	=	Expected Unit Cost
Defect/Injury: Type A	.3		$1166		$ 349.80
Defect/Injury: Type B	.4		$1156		$ 462.40
No Defects	.3		$1146		$ 343.80
TOTAL	1.0				$1156.00

manufactured at a direct cost of $1,146 per unit. Assume that testing and experience show that there is a 30 percent probability that X will have no defects. If a defect of Type B occurs, which has a 40 percent probability, an injury will result with an additional indirect cost of liability of $10 per unit, raising unit cost to $1,156 on these units. If a defect of Type A occurs, which has a 30 percent probability, then there is an additional $20 liability cost for a total unit cost of $1,166.

The expected per unit cost of product X is $1,156, which is derived by multiplying the probability of each outcome's occurrence by the associated costs. Or, alternatively, the expected cost consists of $1,146 in direct costs and $10 in indirect liability cost [(40% × $10) + (30% × $20) = $10]. The expected liability of $10 can be covered either by market insurance or self-insurance. In either case, it will be reflected in the product price as a cost of business.

Risk is commonly defined as the variance around some expected value given a probability distribution of events. The smaller the variance of outcomes around the expected value, the lower the risk. To illustrate, consider Y, a substitute for X, with the distribution listed in Table 6.2. Multiplying the probability of each outcome times the associated cost yields an expected cost of $1,156, the same as for X, but Y consists of $500 in direct costs and $656 in expected liability costs [(40% × $515) + (30% × $1500) = $656]. However, Y is associated with more risk even though both X and Y have the same expected costs of $1,156 and therefore the same price in a competitive market.[8] Y's actual cost can range anywhere from $500 to $2,000, whereas Product X's actual cost range is $1,146 to $1,166.

The policy arguments, as developed in *Henningsen v. Bloomfield Motors, Inc.*,[9] *Escola v. Coca Cola Bottling Co.*,[10] and *Greenman v. Yuba Power Products*,[11] for imposing strict liability is that the firm is in a better position to bear and spread the risk.[12] To understand this argument it is necessary

Table 6.2
Product Y

Alternative Outcomes	Probability of Outcome	X	Cost Under Alternative Outcomes	=	Expected Unit Cost
Defect/Injury Type A	.3		$2000		$ 600
Defect/Injury Type B	.4		$1015		$ 406
No Defects	.3		$ 500		$ 150
TOTAL	1.0				$1156

to understand when the firm will insure against the risk or undertake measures to avoid the risk.

When damages are restricted to a compensatory remedy, the standard of care undertaken by firms to avoid the risk of product defect or injury is determined by market forces rather than the legal standard imposed by the judicial or legislative process. The actual levels of care, as defined here, are actions undertaken by a firm (manufacturer, distributor, seller), such as quality control measures, design, and formulation and testing. These measures will be defined as risk-avoidance measures.[13]

The firm's actions in response to products liability can be considered as a choice of a portfolio of avoidance or preventative expenditures and insurance expenditures. Whatever the liability standard, assuming no transactions costs, risk neutrality of firms and consumers, and the absence of contributory negligence, the firm will undertake avoidance measures so long as the marginal cost of these measures is less than or equal to the marginal cost of insurance or the expected loss to the consumer. The choice of avoidance measures and insurance is simply a restatement of the profit- or wealth-maximizing hypothesis of firm behavior. Namely, the firm will choose to insure against (avoid) an expected loss whenever it is less costly relative to avoiding (insuring against) the expected loss. The firm will choose the least-cost alternative in order to survive in a competitive market.

The advent of strict products liability under the *Greenman* standard or the *Restatement of Torts*, Section 402A, standard has little or no effect on the behavior of the firm in terms of avoidance expenditures. The negligence standard, and more specifically the Learned Hand formulation, is a legal standard that approximates the behavior of the firm.

The strict liability standard's impact is in terms of who bears the risks that remain after avoidance expenditures are undertaken as discussed above. The remaining risks will be defined as residual risks. Strict liability shifts the residual risk from consumers to the firm, which in turn is spread in the market.

For example, suppose there is a 1 percent chance of a product defect with a resultant injury of $10,000. The expected loss is $100 for each of the one hundred items sold. If the avoidance cost per unit of reducing this probability from one in one hundred to one in one thousand (expected loss of $10) is $80, then the firm will have an incentive and the consumer will demand the (higher quality) product with the avoidance measure. Market forces, even under *caveat emptor*, will provide the incentive to firms because the expected loss decreases from $100 (borne by the consumer) to $10 or a savings of $90 while the avoidance cost is only $80 with a net benefit to the consumer of $10. However, there will remain a residual risk of $10.

On the other hand, if the avoidance expenditure was $100, then firms would not undertake the expenditure nor would consumers demand the increased quality because the cost of avoidance ($100) exceeds the benefit of the reduced expected loss ($90). The residual risk is now $100. Under *caveat emptor* the consumer will bear the risk and either self- or market insure against the residual risk of $100. Under *caveat venditor*, the consumer will pay a higher price ($100) to compensate the firm for the cost of its insurance ($100). The choice of risk *avoidance* versus insurance, under these assumptions, is based on market forces rather than the legal standard. Given the above assumptions, it would seem that product liability standards simply determine how the insurance premium for the residual risk is paid. Under the negligence standard, the consumers either self-insure or market insure. Under strict liability the consumer indirectly pays in the form of a higher price for the firm to self-insure or market insure.

The policy argument for strict liability based on the firm being in a better position to spread the risk has been discussed in chapter 5.[14] The argument is premised on an assumption that consumers, under a negligence rule, will purchase and use too much of the product because of ignorance of the full cost. Strict liability, on the other hand, will be efficient because the consumer/user will indirectly take into account the residual risk of injury by reducing the level of activity that influences the probability of injury. The reduced level of activity is brought about by the increased price of the product as a result of the firm either self-insuring or taking out market insurance. Because it is liable for the residual risk the externality is thereby internalized.[15]

Thus, the arguments for a rule of strict liability over other rules (e.g., negligence) is based on the assumptions that the manufacturer has a comparative advantage (that is, is in a better position) compared to the consumer in (1) assessing the risk of product defects, (2) assessing the damages that result from product defects, (3) insuring against such defects, and (4) spreading (diversifying) such risks in the market through higher prices. The argument also assumes that higher prices internalize the risk by providing that an efficient quantity of a product is demanded and produced. Under these assumptions, government intervention in the form of revisions to the tax code, mandating compensation pools, or limiting damage awards are either based on some normative distribution argument or are the result of special interest legislation (rent seeking). *Ex ante*, liability for various types of risk is a product cost and, like any other cost, will be incorporated in the product price and passed on to consumers.

Suppose the failure to insure adequately against liability causes firms such as Manville to file for bankruptcy. Consider the proposal to establish a victim compensation fund by taxing asbestos manufacturers. Such proposals will have distributional and allocative effects. First, the proposals are generally designed to place a cap on the amount of recovery, thereby redistributing income from victims to manufacturers. Second, as discussed, if damage awards are not compensatory, then prices will be too low with an overallocation of resources devoted to the defective product.

In the absence of a cap on damages, there would be little reason for firms to propose a scheme unless it is designed to restrict new entrants. For example, a firm may independently attempt to pass liability losses on to future consumers via higher prices. But new entrants, unencumbered with liability losses, will be at a cost advantage allowing them to decrease prices and capture the market. In the absence of some restriction on entry, liability costs that were not adequately insured against are a "sunk" cost.[16] If compensatory schemes are used to restrict entry by taxing all manufacturers, including new entrants, then the price will be too high, resulting in an underallocation of resources to the product.

In summary, bankruptcy proceedings can occur because the firm failed to market insure or self-insure adequately for risk.[17] There are no economic efficiency arguments under the risk assumption to "bail out" firms that inadequately insure.[18] Alternatively, a presumption can be made that the firm charged prices that included a "known" risk premium such that the cause of bankruptcy is the result of some other factors such as a change in the market. Compensation proposals in these circumstances are simply a subsidy in the form of a special limited liability.

III. UNCERTAINTY

The terms *risk* and *uncertainty* are often used interchangeably. Uncertainty has been discussed in the economic literature both formally and informally. Formal models that incorporate uncertainty usually let market demand or cost functions shift randomly but continuously through time according to a stochastic process that consists of utilizing an error term. There are unresolved issues as to whether the error term should be additive, multiplicative, or nonlinear.[19] For example, one article on uncertainty and the behavior of the firm concludes that long-run equilibrium or optimality conditions cannot be determined without imposing restrictive conditions.[20]

Uncertainty also exists in a dynamic, rather than a static, context. A firm that has low adjustment costs, such as short-term contracts and low specific capital investments, can more readily adapt once the random element or event becomes unknown. Many consumer goods manufacturers, as opposed to capital goods manufacturers, are likely to face less uncertainty simply because of the shorter time horizon of use or effects. In this sense, the delayed manifestation of injury cases such as drugs and asbestos are aligned with capital goods and long-term horizons. The fact that models incorporate a random element in some undetermined functional form suggests that a manufacturer may not adequately insure against these uncertain events. Of course, a manufacturer could take out a Lloyd's of London insurance policy that may cover an uncertain event. In such a case, the uncertainty is simply shifted from the insured to the insurer with unanticipated windfall gains or losses. This chapter uses the informal definition of uncertainty that follows.

The informal treatment of uncertainty is perhaps best exemplified by Frank Knight's treatise on *Risk, Uncertainty and Profit*.[21] Joseph Schumpeter,[22] Israel Kirzner,[23] and others have also examined uncertainty. Classical economics focused primarily on the equilibrium conditions of the firm and market under static conditions. By definition, no economic profits (or losses) are earned in a competitive equilibrium. All decisions are simply managerial and aimed at profit maximization, given a set of revenue and cost data and their probability distributions. Risks are also handled in a managerial sense by self-insurance or market insurance or risk diversification strategies.

Knight argued, however, that profits arise as a result of the constantly changing environment within which economic activity occurs and the associated uncertainty of the outcomes of alternative courses of action. Profit or loss is the residual left for the owners after the payment of all contractual obligations including risk premiums. The entrepreneur in control of a venture is responsible for all receipts and outlays and, thus, is subject to the uncertainty that surrounds the amount and sign of the difference between them. The entrepreneur is possible only in a world of costly information and transactions—a world of uncertainty. The profit-maximizing hypothesis in the static theory of the firm, it is argued, has nothing to do with the pure profits that are generated within the dynamic context of uncertainty and change. Profits (losses) under uncertainty cannot be deliberately maximized (minimized) *ex ante*.

Obviously, the uncertainty Knight and his followers perceived is quite different from the formal modeling of uncertainty discussed above. Knight and Kirzner would argue that to model uncertainty would be to contradict the very nature of uncertainty. What distinguishes entrepreneurs from nonentrepreneurs, other than luck, is not well defined and has been termed a special skill, ability, vision, or alertness to opportunities. Schumpeter argues that the entrepreneur is the spark that ignites the engine of economic growth;

Kirzner argues that entrepreneurs, operating in a state of disequilibrium, are forces that move the system toward, but never obtain, equilibrium. Buchanan and Faith have argued, in a slightly different vein from Schumpeter, that the entrepreneur is the optimist who creates change and growth.[24]

Therefore, to talk about the entrepreneur is to talk simultaneously about uncertainty. In fact, the entrepreneur must be defined in terms of the difference between risk and uncertainty. Decision making under risk involves a calculated choice based on given data. All individuals take or avoid risks. The insurance markets, gambling, stock markets, futures markets, indexed portfolios, and so forth, are institutional arrangements that permit specialization in risk or risk avoidance. But gains and losses through entrepreneurial decision making in the face of uncertainty are borne by shareholders or equity owners of the firm. The entrepreneur and owners do indeed anticipate and expect to gain from previously unforeseen opportunities; but this anticipation or expectation is not capable of being determined *ex ante* from objective data.

Entrepreneurship and uncertainty generally have been viewed as positive, dynamic influences giving rise to pure economic profits.[25] For example, Schumpeter's view of the entrepreneur as the catalyst for growth and Buchanan and Faith's view of the entrepreneur as the optimist are positive viewpoints leading to growth. However, entrepreneurship and uncertainty also lead to pure economic losses.

By definition, it is not possible to determine, *ex ante*, an insurance premium or cost that would pass uncertainty onto the market through higher prices. Therefore, the policy argument that the firm is in a better position to bear or spread risk, as elaborated in *Escola*, is applicable to risk and not uncertainty. Delayed manifestation of injuries and/or retroactive application of expanded products liability law can often be interpreted as uncertain events that by their very nature are on the negative side. Buchanan and Faith suggest that entrepreneurs in their optimism may underestimate the costs of their decisions.[26] The market, however, has a survival trait. The entrepreneur who earns profits will survive. The entrepreneur who suffers losses will fall by the wayside. Thus, in a dynamic sense, the market will correct for uncertainty, albeit at a cost in terms of a waste of resources viewed *ex post*.[27]

Although conceptually it is possible to distinguish between risk and uncertainty, as a practical matter it may be extremely difficult. The passage of time can turn uncertainty *ex ante* into risk *ex post*. For example, it can be argued that when DES was initially marketed, a state of uncertainty existed with respect to the carcinogenic effect of the drug on female offspring. But as time passed, as technology and knowledge changed, observations became available or feasible, and medical and statistical studies were undertaken, uncertainty evolved into risk with known probability distributions.

There are several areas of the law that border on the risk versus uncertainty distinction. One such distinction is illustrated by way of the unanticipated circumstances exception to the unenforceability of a modification to a contract without new consideration. Section 89D(a) of the *Second Restatement of Contracts* states that modifications are valid if "fair and equitable in view of circumstances not anticipated by the parties when the contract was made."[28] Comment (b) to the *Second Restatement* Section 89D states: "The reason for modification must rest in circumstances *not anticipated*...as part of the context in which the contract was made, but a frustrating event may be unanticipated...if it was not adequately covered, even though it was foreseen as a remote possibility [italics added]."

In the absence of new consideration, an attempted modification of a contract can be interpreted as opportunistic behavior or extortion. If the event is anticipated (i.e., risk), then the parties will have allocated the risk within the contract. For example, if a contractor "anticipates" there is some possibility that he will hit bedrock in an area that has been surveyed as consisting of sand, the contractor will incorporate a risk premium, albeit a small premium, in the contract price by multiplying the probability the event will occur times the additional cost to complete the contract. When the event becomes certain (*ex post*), the premium may not have been sufficient to cover the additional cost. If the contractor did not have a sufficient number of transactions to spread the risk, then bankruptcy may result. But this is simply a case of inadequate self-insurance. Absent bankruptcy, a modification of the contract by increasing the price under these circumstances is appropriately defined as opportunistic behavior.[29] On the other hand, if bankruptcy will result from performance, it may be argued that the nonbreaching party did not adequately insure by failing to select a highly solvent firm or requiring a performance bond. If there are, however, truly unanticipated circumstances, then the only issue becomes who bears the loss. There are other areas of the law that border on the risk versus uncertainty distinction such as "impossibility," "impracticability," and "frustration" that may operate to discharge a contract without consideration.[30]

While risk and uncertainty have been discussed in dichotomous ways, the more likely situation is a continuum of risk and uncertainty. As discussed, strict liability has not necessarily created a higher quality standard but rather rearranges liability for residual risk.[31] However, to the extent that a negligence standard is inextricably tied to some notion of forseeability, and therefore risk, it is difficult to reconcile the facts in delayed manifestation of injury cases such as DES and asbestos with foreseeable risks. Such cases would seem to be closer to uncertainty rather than risk.[32]

For example, in *Beshada v. Johns-Manville Products Corp.*,[33] the New Jersey Supreme Court held the asbestos manufacturer in breach of its duty to warn of product dangers even though conceding that the dangers could *not have been known* scientifically at the time of the breach. The risk-spreading rationale was used, regardless of the information available at the time of injury, because manufacturer liability will serve to distribute the risks of product injuries and their costs in the form of higher prices, which "is far preferable to imposing [these costs] on the innocent victims. The court went on to say . . . [t]he burden of illness from dangerous products such as asbestos should be placed upon those who profit from its production."[34] *Beshada* is an example of the court's failure to distinguish risk from uncertainty and its distributional consequences. Risk spreading is paid for by consumers, while placing the "burden" upon those who profit from its production is a "deep-pockets" argument and paid for by owners of the firm. Finally, uncertainty may not only be associated with unanticipated outcomes, but also unanticipated change in law.[35] It is assumed, at the margin, that some firms will be (and have been) liable for uncertain events. The following analysis is directed at the distributional consequences and alternative policies to deal with these losses.

For the purpose of this analysis, uncertainty is defined as an unforeseen accident that could not be purposively insured or avoided by actions of consumers, manufacturers, distributors, or sellers. Imposing liability on the manufacturer or seller for uncertain accidents will be borne by the owners or shareholders of the firm. Indeed, only if a state of uncertainty exists will the so called "deep-pocket" result obtain.[36] By definition, the costs of uncertainty cannot be insured against or spread in the market. If a firm attempts to pass the liability costs on to its future customers by increasing prices, firms who are not burdened with these fixed costs will enter the market and thereby bid the price down. This deep-pocket result is quite different from the risk-spreading argument presented for products liability in *Henningsen*, *Escola*, and *Greenman*. Moreover, given the above definition of uncertainty, there can be no efficiency argument *for* or *against* imposing strict liability. The only issue that remains is a distributional one of who bears the loss.

If the firm is liable, then shareholders will bear the loss. If the firm's assets are not sufficient to cover liability, then victims will bear, in part, the loss. From a normative standpoint, if shareholders claim the residual between revenues and costs when it is positive, then they ought to bear the liability when it is negative.[37] If equity shareholders receive the windfall gain from entrepreneurship in the face of uncertainty, then they should also bear the windfall loss of uncertainty regardless of whether it is in the form of market conditions or products liability.

To summarize, the effect of mandatory compensation proposals or ceilings on the amounts to be recovered serves to mitigate or eliminate the deep-pocket result by indirectly taxing consumers and victims. The net effect of taxing new consumers is inefficient in the sense that fewer resources are devoted to production than is efficient, because current and future consumers pay a price that includes a premium for past liability not associated with any direct or indirect cost of current and future production.

Table 6.3
Net Profits without Liability

Period	Revenues	Expenses	Gross Profits	Corp. Taxes	Net Profits
1	400,000	200,000	200,000	100,000	100,000
2	400,000	200,000	200,000	100,000	100,000
3	400,000	200,000	200,000	100,000	100,000
.	.	.	.	.	.
.	.	.	.	.	.
.	.	.	.	.	.
17	400,000	200,000	200,000	100,000	100,000
18	400,000	200,000	200,000	100,000	100,000
19	400,000	200,000	200,000	100,000	100,000
20	400,000	200,000	200,000	100,000	100,000
TOTAL	8,000,000	4,000,000	4,000,000	2,000,000	2,000,000

Compensation proposals generally involve a mandatory tax on all producers so that new entrants without past liability will not have a comparative advantage in entering the market.[38] Limits on the amount of recoveries are a redistribution away from victims in favor of shareholders, but will have future allocative effects because the prices will not include the full cost of production.

IV. TAXING UNCERTAINTY

Assume there is no Section 172 of the Internal Revenue Code and that firms are strictly liable for uncertain product defects. Uncertain events such as delayed manifestation of injury cases and a three-year carryback limitation on operating losses permit the government *ex post* to receive a windfall gain at the expense of shareholders.[39] It is not clear why the carryback provision is three years. Why should it not be five years, twenty years, or absent all together? As discussed above, by definition uncertainty cannot be purposively avoided or insured against. Accordingly, any losses resulting from uncertainty are by their very nature borne by owners of the firm.

However, a proposal to extend the loss carryback in cases of uncertainty can be defended on the grounds that it creates logic and symmetry in the tax code and minimizes or eliminates future allocative effects associated with other schemes that provide relief to owners of firms. Some sort of relief in massive tort cases is also likely to benefit victims because in the absence of some relief, the liability may be such as to cause firms to go bankrupt, thereby limiting victims' recovery of damages to the net assets of the firm.

Consider a version of Section 172[40] without limitation on the carryback period except the condition that losses must be carried back to the date when the victim consumed the product or was exposed to the substance.[41] Assume a firm with constant revenues and expenses for a twenty-year period as illustrated in Table 6.3. Gross profits are assumed to be $200,000 per year.[42] It is assumed that the corporate income tax rate is 50 percent. In

Table 6.4
Net Profits with Liability Spread over Time

Period	Revenues	Adjusted Expenses	Adjusted Gross Profits	Adjusted Corp. Taxes	Adjusted Net Profits
1	400,000	300,000	100,000	50,000	50,000
2	400,000	300,000	100,000	50,000	50,000
3	400,000	300,000	100,000	50,000	50,000
.	.	.	.	.	.
.	.	.	.	.	.
.	.	.	.	.	.
17	400,000	300,000	100,000	50,000	50,000
18	400,000	300,000	100,000	50,000	50,000
19	400,000	300,000	100,000	50,000	50,000
20	400,000	300,000	100,000	50,000	50,000
TOTAL	8,000,000	6,000,000	2,000,000	1,000,000	1,000,000

the last column, net profits are either retained or distributed as dividends. As illustrated, corporate taxes are $2 million and net profits are $2 million over the entire period. Now assume a scientific breakthrough reveals a causal relationship between an injury and the prior exposure of a material marketed throughout the period. Suppose further that twenty years lapse before the injury is revealed, and prior to that period there was complete uncertainty. Finally, assume that if the relationship had been known, *ex ante*, the firm would have insured against liability with premiums of $100,000 per year for the entire twenty-year period.[43] Assume a judgment is entered for $2 million (20 years × $100,000) in damages the day after the end of the twenty-year period. The value of the stock will fall by that amount or, if the net worth is less than $2 million, the firm will go into bankruptcy.

Table 6.4 reconstructs Table 6.3 *ex post* to incorporate an adjusted expense column for liability exposure. Each year's expenses are increased from $200,000 to $300,000 to reflect the $100,000 insurance premium. Adjusted net profits for the twenty-year period are $1 million rather than $2 million. Thus, if adjustments were permitted such that the damage award could be apportioned *ex post* as a self-insured risk, then this firm would be entitled to tax rebates of $50,000 each year for a total tax refund of $1 million. Note that shareholders still bear a portion of the loss ($1 million) because of the 50 percent marginal bracket.

Table 6.5 has the same result as Table 6.4 in that the $2 million judgment is carried through to the tenth period, thereby providing for full tax refunds of $100,000 per year for the first ten years. The tenth year represents the last year of the adjustment. The same result obtains in that the firm has a liability of $2 million that is partially offset by an asset in the form of a tax refund of $1 million with a net liability of $1 million.

On the other hand, if the conventional three-year limitation on carryback is in effect, only $300,000 ($100,000 per year) is refunded in taxes instead

Table 6.5
Net Profits with Liability Incurred in First Period (Figures in $ Thousands)

	Revenues	Expenses	Gross Acct'g Profits	Loss Adjustment	Adj. Gross Profits	Adj. Corp. Taxes	Profits
1	400	200	200	(2,000)	(1,800)	-0-	-0-
2	400	200	200	(1,800)	(1,600)	-0-	-0-
3	400	200	200	(1,600)	(1,400)	-0-	-0-
4	400	200	200	(1,400)	(1,200)	-0-	-0-
5	400	200	200	(1,200)	(1,000)	-0-	-0-
6	400	200	200	(1,000)	(800)	-0-	-0-
7	400	200	200	(800)	(600)	-0-	-0-
8	400	200	200	(600)	(400)	-0-	-0-
9	400	200	200	(400)	(200)	-0-	-0-
10	400	200	200	(200)	(200)	-0-	-0-
11	400	200	200	-0-	200	100	100
.	.	.	.	.	.	.	.
.	.	.	.	.	.	.	.
.	.	.	.	.	.	.	.
18	400	200	200	-0-	200	100	100
19	400	200	200	-0-	200	100	100
20	200	200	200	-0-	200	100	100
	8,000	4,000	2,000	1,000	1,000	1,000	1,000

of the $1 million with an extended carryback. Net liability in this case is $1.7 million. Of course, $1.4 million of the liability loss remains and can be carried forward to offset $1.4 million in profits yielding a potential $700,000 in future tax refunds. But the benefit, if any, of the forward carryover may be small for a firm faced with massive litigation and future claims that create liquidity problems.

For example, suppose a second judgment is awarded in the amount of $2 million associated with a product sold in the fifth period. As Table 6.5 illustrates, there would be no tax benefit for the fifth through the tenth period. However, in the eleventh through the twentieth period profits could be adjusted to offset the second claim. In this case, all prior income taxes amounting to $2 million would be refunded. Note, however, that shareholders still bear a $2 million dollar loss ($4 million liability minus $2 million refund). If a third judgment were awarded, the loss would be subject to existing carryover provisions without benefit of a carryback.[44]

The government can be viewed as a silent partner in businesses and entitled to a claim in residual profits. But symmetry would require that if the government claims part of the residual when it is positive, it should also bear the loss when the residual is negative. Under normal circumstances when events are confined within the carryback and carryover provisions this is indeed the case. But there is no a priori reason why past actions associated with liability and a temporal incidence that falls outside of arbitrary time limitations on carryback of operating losses should be a bar to receiving tax refunds. Unless there is some efficiency or equity reason for these limitations, the above analysis is consistent with general tax principles. For example, the federal tax code does not seem to contradict tax principles

Table 6.6
Gambling and Taxes

	Probability of Winning and Losing	Winnings and Losses	After-Tax Winnings and Losses	Expected After-Tax Winnings and Losses
Win	.50	$ 50	$25	$12.50
Lose	.50	[50]	[25]	[12.50]
Expected Value		0	0	$12.50

Novice Gambler

	Probability of Winning and Losing	Winnings and Losses	After-Tax Winnings and Losses	Expected After-Tax Winnings and Losses
Win	.50	$ 50	$25	$12.50
Lose	.50	[50]	[50]	[25.00]
Expected Value		0	[$25]	[$12.50]

such as equals should be treated as equal or that taxes should be based on the ability to pay.

A carryback limitation, such as three years or even ten years, truncates what might otherwise be a normal distribution of events associated with risk. To illustrate, consider a novice gambler (no carryback) and an experienced gambler (carryback). Suppose both are in a 50 percent marginal tax bracket. Consider Table 6.6 that illustrates a fair bet. There is a 50 percent chance of winning $50 and a 50 percent chance of losing (paying) $50 from a flip of a coin. Assume the established gambler has prior-year winnings of at least $50. After-tax earnings will be $25 if he wins. If he loses, then the $50 loss can be offset by a $25 tax refund of prior earnings for an after-tax loss of $25. Since there is a 50 percent chance of each event occurring, expected after-tax winnings ($12.50) equal expected after-tax losses ($12.50). Similarly, if the established gambler had prior-year losses instead of winnings, then the present year after-tax winnings would be $50 and the present year after-tax losses would be $50, resulting in tax neutrality with respect to the net expected gain (i.e., it would be a fair bet).[45] Now consider a novice gambler without prior-years winnings or losses. After-tax winnings will be $25 since there are no prior-year losses to offset current-year winnings. After-tax losses will be $50 as there are no prior-year winnings to offset current-year losses. The net effect of taxes in this case is to change the expected value of the bet from zero (fair bet) to ($12.50), an unfair bet.

Thus, limitations on carryback provisions impose a temporal bias in what would otherwise be a fair bet. In the above example, if the coin is flipped only once a year with a three-year limitation on carryback of losses, the expected value of the bet will also be negative because there is some probability that the government is able to retain some of the taxes that fall outside the carryback period.

The betting example is used to illustrate a principle of taxation based on taxing net income. Absent a limitation on carryback provisions, U.S. Treasury net tax receipts from gambling activity confined to fair bets should equal zero over the long run. Similarly, it can be argued that taxation of gambling in the form of business risk taking, where outcomes are temporally distributed around an expected value, should also be based on the net expected value without time limitations. Carryback limitations arbitrarily truncate the distribution, thereby lowering the after-tax expected value (net income). The net effect creates a bias against investments that are likely to have a large temporal variance (outcomes) and favor investments with less temporal variance. A priori, it is not clear that this is or should be a policy objective underlying carryback limitations.

V. THE INSURANCE BIAS

By definition, a firm that does not market insure against an event must either not anticipate the risk (uncertainty) or anticipate the risk and self-insure. Tables 6.4 and 6.5 in Part IV can be reinterpreted as a firm that self-insures. Suppose the firm fully anticipated the risks and established a reserve fund of $100,000 per year for twenty years as illustrated in Table 6.4. While the Internal Revenue Service will allow claims from a self-insurance reserve to be deducted, the deduction is conditional on the actual payment of the claim. Thus, the unclaimed reserve fund balance would be taxed throughout the twenty-year period. The firm pays income taxes of $50,000 a year on the reserve fund for a total of $1 million in taxes for the period. With a three-year carryback, it would receive a $150,000 refund, but the $850,000 in taxes paid for years one through seventeen are forfeited.

Now consider market insurance. Suppose insurance premiums are also $100,000 per year. Because insurance premiums are fully deductible, the net after-tax cost of market insurance is only $50,000, compared to $100,000 for self-insurance. Thus market insurance permits a result identical to that of self-insurance with a twenty-year carryback provision. $1,000,000 in taxes are saved by market insurance. This assumes that the insurance premium is the same as the self-insurance premium or actual risk. The reason that insurance companies have a comparative advantage over noninsurance companies is attributable to the tax code. Insurance companies are permitted to deduct reserves for future liabilities even though claims are not actually paid, whereas noninsurance companies are permitted deductions only when claims are naturally paid.[46]

There have been a number of articles dealing with the question of why corporations market insure.[47] The question arises because it would appear shareholders can eliminate insurance risks through diversification of their stock portfolio at minimal costs. Thus, the purchase of market insurance by corporations would appear to lower shareholder wealth by paying prices to insurance companies that must be actuarially unfair to cover insurance company costs.[48] There are several explanations offered, including tax savings, to answer this question. For example, D. Mayers and C. Smith briefly discuss carryback/carryforward provision and tax-rate progressivity as providing an incentive to market insure. Their analysis does not consider the temporal dispersion of risks and the effect of the three-year carryback provision as discussed above. There exists an incentive to market insure even if marginal tax rates are constant without advantages of bracket shifting when the insured events have a temporal variance that falls outside of the carryback limitation. The tax-code provisions of taxing noninsurance company reserves and permitting deduction for insurance company reserves encourage market transactions (purchase of insurance) rather than internal transactions (self-insurance).[49]

Because tax advantages of market insurance relative to self-insurance can be significant, there are strong incentives to market insure against liability associated with delayed manifestation of injury cases. Thus the circumstances leading to bankruptcy would seem to be based on uncertainty rather than inadequate self-insurance for known risks.

This analysis raises an issue of whether an extended carryback provision is a subsidy to a special interest group. As discussed, self-insurance with extended carryback of losses via Section 172 will have the same after-tax consequence to the government as market insurance.[50] Despite tax benefits that insurance companies enjoy, Section 172 provides an incentive for firms that are exposed to product liability to substitute self-insurance for market insurance. This substitution should not lead to lower tax revenues. However, in 1954 Congress allowed noninsurance companies to deduct self-insurance payments. It was argued that the treasury lost nearly $1 billion in less than a year. Congress repealed the legislation retroactively and recaptured the $1 billion.[51] To the extent that firms simply substituted market insurance for self-insurance, there should have been no loss in tax revenues. The loss to the treasury, if any, can probably be attributed to noninsurance companies overstating reserves in order to receive larger deductions. This bias may not exist with insurance firms because the market is competitive. Insurance firm premiums are competitively determined and approximate future claims.[52] Similarly, self-insurance by way of extended carryback does not have a bias of overstating reserves. Deductions are permitted only on the basis of *actual* claims paid. Thus there can be no overstatement. In summary, in the case of risk, the U.S. Treasury is not likely to lose from an extended carryover provision assuming firms simply substitute self-insurance for market insurance. There will, however, be a loss in treasury tax revenues from extended

Table 6.7
Insurance Reserves

Period	Liability in Twentieth Period Dollar	Insurance Reserve at 10% Interest Rate	Cumulative Earned Interest
1	$100,000	$14,864	$85,136
2	$100,000	$16,351	$83,649
3	$100,000	$17,986	$82,014
4	$100,000	$19,784	$80,216
5	$100,000	$21,763	$78,237
6	$100,000	$23,936	$76,061
7	$100,000	$26,333	$73,667
8	$100,000	$28,966	$71,034
9	$100,000	$31,863	$68,137
10	$100,000	$35,049	$64,951
11	$100,000	$38,554	$61,446
12	$100,000	$42,410	$57,590
13	$100,000	$46,651	$53,349
14	$100,000	$51,316	$48,684
15	$100,000	$56,447	$43,553
16	$100,000	$62,092	$37,908
17	$100,000	$68,301	$31,699
18	$100,000	$75,131	$24,869
19	$100,000	$82,645	$17,355
20	$100,000	$90,909	$ 9,091
	$2,000,000	$851,351	$1,148,646

carryover provisions in cases of uncertainty. By definition, market insurance based on actual premiums is not possible. In this sense, it can be said that an extended carryover provision for uncertain events spreads uncertainty to taxpayers relative to the current three-year limitation; that is, an extended carryover can be interpreted as partial social insurance for catastrophic massive tort liability such as drugs, medical devices, and substances.[53]

The above analysis did not consider interest rates or discounting. It may appear that there is a bias of being able to use liability losses expressed in today's dollars to offset profits expressed in prior-year dollars. In other words, is there a bias in terms of discounting? The following analysis illustrates that a positive interest rate does not affect the outcome. Consider Table 6.7. The second column, as in Table 6.4 in Part IV, indicates that there will be a $100,000 expected liability in each year's sales. The third column illustrates the amount necessary as an initial reserve for each period invested at a 10 percent (market) interest rate that would yield $100,000 to cover the expected liability in the twentieth period. In other words, if insurance companies had no costs, the figures in the third column would be the insurance premiums charged for a $100,000 expected payout twenty years from now. For example, $14,864 invested in the first period would, at a compounded 10 percent rate, yield a cumulative interest of $85,136 cover the twenty-year period, and combined with the initial investment of $14,864, yield the required $100,000 in twenty years.[54]

It has been assumed, however, that the $100,000 would be carried back at $100,000 with no adjustment; that is, the liability of $100,000 in the twentieth period is carried back to the first period at $100,000 and not discounted to $14,864. Moreover, it has been assumed that a $50,000 tax refund would be received from the first period. Such a refund would seem to overcompensate. But in fact there is no overcompensation. To illustrate, consider what amount would be necessary in twentieth-period dollars to compensate for the income that was taxed in the first period. If the firm is able to save $7,432 in income tax by being able to deduct a $14,864 premium in the first period, then that $7,432 would have increased to $50,000 in the twentieth period at a compounded interest rate of 10 percent.[55] With self-insurance, the government has the use of $7,432 in income taxes for a period of twenty years on income that was not earned *ex post*. Thus the carryback of $100,000 in liability expense for each of the twenty years is a carryback of $14,864 in first-period dollars, or the $50,000 refund is a return of $7,432 in first-period dollars in conjunction with tax-free accumulation of $85,132 in interest for the twenty-year period and so on for the second and third through twenty years.[56] This is a similar tax result to that afforded insurance companies under the IRC.

In summary, a tax proposal with an extended carryback of losses can be defended on the basis of tax principles. There is an indirect economic efficiency argument in that the tax proposal does not create inefficiencies that are associated with other proposals advanced. If liability is premised only on risk, and not uncertainty, then there are two consequences from extended carryback provisions. First, an extended carryback provision is likely to encourage self-insurance in the future.[57] It is interesting to note that the 1981 Risk Retention Act that permitted producers to form cooperative product liability insurance companies has led to few cooperatives. Second, because self-insurance is a substitute for market insurance, then there is no effect on tax revenues from extended carryback of losses. Under these assumptions, the only losers are insurance companies.

However, if liability is premised on uncertainty, then there will be a reduction in treasury tax revenues compared to a three-year limitation. But, an extended carryback can be interpreted as simply a return of taxes on profits that *ex post* were not earned. A three-year limitation on losses can be interpreted as a protectionist measure for insurance companies. Without limitations on carrybacks, profits can be interpreted as a reserve for risk or uncertainty. Inadequate reserves would only come about when *ex ante* profits are not sufficient to cover *ex post* liability costs. Inadequate reserves defined this way mean that the prices charged for the product were not sufficient to cover all costs including *ex post* liability costs. If *ex post* liability were known *ex ante*, the product would not have been produced. The resources used in production, including resources lost in product liability damages, have higher alternative use values. Inadequate reserves will only occur under uncertainty and not risk. The effect of a three-year limitation on carryback of losses will, at the margin, lead to bankruptcy or impose losses on victims for a failure to be able to recover tax refunds on profits that were not earned *ex post*.

VI. AN INTERPRETATION OF SECTION 172 AND CONCLUDING REMARKS

The above analysis is more general than the specific provisions of Section 172 of the Internal Revenue Code. First, Section 172 limits the carryback to ten years. The above analysis suggests that a carryback be permitted to the year in which the product was used or the year in which exposure occurred. There are, however, legal and practical arguments for a ten-year limitation.[58] Many states have statutes of repose whereby an action must be brought within a certain number of years from the date of manufacture or consumption of the defective product regardless of when the injury becomes known. These statutes act as an absolute bar similar to statutes of limitations. While states vary as to the number of years allowed, a common period is ten years. Thus, if manufacturers are not to be liable for delayed manifestation of injury cases after ten years, the carryback provision should be limited to that period.

Second, Section 172 does not require matching the year of consumption, use, or exposure with the tax years. The section reads:

(I) in the case of [a] liability arising out of a Federal or State law, the act (or failure to act) giving rise to such liability occurs at least 3 years before the beginning of such taxable year, or

(II) in the case of a liability arising out of a tort, such liability arises out of a series of actions (or failures to act) over an extended period of time a *substantial* portion of which occurs at least 3 years before the beginning of such taxable year [italics added].[59]

It would appear that liability associated with actions (or failure to act) four years ago could be extended beyond four years to permit recovery of taxes back to ten years under (I) or (II). There are several justifications for this. In cases such as asbestos, it may be difficult to pinpoint the year in which exposure caused the injury. The injury is also likely to be the result of cumulative exposure over a number of years. Thus, the ten-year period may be a practical measure to deal with what otherwise would result in litigation and/or information costs that exceed the benefits of having a more flexible rule that would allow carryback of losses beyond ten years.

The most important differences, however, are the conditions that permit a carryback. Under the IRC, the current-year liability loss must exceed the current year's profit (excluding liability loss) for there to be a loss to carry-back. Based on this analysis, the liability loss should be treated independently of the current year's profits or losses. Consider a provision that allows liability losses to be carried back even though there were net profits. The tax refund from carrybacks would equal the higher taxes paid by not using the liability losses in the current year.[60] The advantage of such a provision is that it matches the losses with prior earnings making explicit the self-insurance feature. Under current provisions, firms that are profitable in the year when the liability becomes an obligation forfeit the right of the extended ten-year period. Thus it penalizes successful firms and benefits unsuccessful firms. This may have been the intended effect in order to confine the application of Section 172 to massive tort liability resulting from delayed manifestations of injury cases, that is, firms on the verge of or in bankruptcy. However, such a restriction diminishes the self-insurance feature of an extended carryback.

NOTES

1. See, for example, "Causes, Extent and Policy Implications on the Current Crisis in Insurance Availability and Affordability" (Washington, D.C.: U.S. Justice Dept., February 1986).

2. Originally introduced as S.44, 97th Cong., 2d Sess. (1982), Senator Kasten's bill would also have established a national standard for all product liability actions and preempt state laws.

3. For example, see *Product Safety & Liability Reporter* (Bureau of National Affairs [BNA]) 49 (January 21, 1983).

4. [IRC Sec. 172(k)] (k) DEFINITIONS AND SPECIAL RULES RELATING TO DEFERRED STATUTORY OR TORT LIABILITY LOSSES.—For purposes of this section—

(1) DEFERRED STATUTORY OR TORT LIABILITY LOSS—The term "deferred statutory or tort liability loss" means, for any taxable year, the lesser of—

(A) the net operating loss for such taxable year, reduced by any portion thereof attributable to—

(i) a foreign expropriation loss, or

(ii) a product liability loss, or

(B) the sum of the amounts allowable as a deduction under this chapter (other than any deduction described in subsection (j)(1)(B) which—

(i) is taken into account in computing the net operating loss for such taxable year, and

(ii) is for an amount incurred with respect to a liability which arises under a Federal or State law or out of any tort of the taxpayer and—

(I) in the case of a liability arising out of a Federal or State law, the act (or failure to act) giving rise to such liability occurs at least 3 years before the beginning of such taxable year, or

(II) in the case of a liability arising out of a tort, such liability arises out of a series of actions (or failures to act) over an extended period of time a substantial portion of which occurs at least 3 years before the beginning of such taxable year.

A liability shall not be taken into account under the preceding sentence unless the taxpayer used an accrual method of accounting throughout the period or periods during which the acts or failures to act giving rise to such liability occurred.

5. The provision also would apply to liability from disposal of waste which may not technically be considered a product liability action. The focus of this chapter is on products liability. See the previous chapter for a detailed discussion of the DES cases.

6. For example, one bill was proposed to tax asbestos manufacturers and employers who use the substances. The fund would be administered by the Office of Workers Compensation Programs of the U.S. Department of Labor. *Product Safety & Liability Reporter* (BNA) 49 (January 21, 1983). A coalition of asbestos manufacturers has proposed a bill whereby half the money for a compensation fund would come from the U.S. Treasury based on the argument that the government mandated much of the use of asbestos during World War II. *The National Law Journal*, January 31, 1983, at 30.

7. To the extent that product liability judgments overcompensate for injuries, an efficiency argument can be made that there is an underallocation of resources devoted to products relative to, say, services where liability standards differ and thus damages should have limitations. The principal difficulty with limitations on damages is that there is no way to observe or measure the costs of pain and suffering externally (i.e., there is no market in pain and suffering). Tort injuries are generally the result of an involuntary exchange. Accordingly, this chapter avoids the compensatory issue. However, the issue of causation and standards is indirectly addressed by distinguishing between risk and uncertainty.

8. Note that while they are the same price, Y has a much higher risk premium incorporated into its price. Tables 6.1 and 6.2 illustrate the potential difficulties in distinguishing between a product defect related to quality control and a design defect. One might argue that Y is a design defect because of the availability of a lower risk substitute design such as X. But, suppose the total cost of X is significantly higher, then both X and Y might simply be classified as product defects with Y's defect cost a substitute for lower direct costs.

9. 32 N.J. 358, 161 A.2d 69 (1960).

10. 24 Cal.2d 453, 150 P.2d 436 (1944).

11. 59 Cal.2d 57, 377, P.2d 897, 27 Cal. Rptr. 697 (1963).

12. For an excellent history of the development of product (enterprise) liability law see G. Priest, "The Invention of Enterprise Liability: A Critical History of the Intellectual Foundations of Modern Tort Law," 14 *Journal of Legal Studies* 461 (1985). Priest traces the historical arguments of manufacturer power, manufacturer insurance, and internalization that form the basic arguments for present-day product liability. The focus of this chapter is on the latter two arguments. Moreover, the argument that strict liability may induce firms to take a higher level care is ignored. Rather the focus is on the residual risk that remains after feasible avoidance measures (design or quality control) have been undertaken; that is, where it is less costly to insure against the risk rather than prevent or eliminate the risk.

13. Legal commentators and the courts have distinguished manufacturing defects from design defects. While this distinction is useful under certain circumstances, it is not important for our purposes.

14. Steven Shavell, "Strict Liability versus Negligence," 9 *Journal of Legal Studies* 1 (1980). As Priest (1985), *supra* note 12, discusses in detail, there are legal predecessors to Shavell's formal analysis of internalization.

15. For example, Shavell considers a negligence versus strict liability rule for accidents from taxicabs. Strict liability, it is argued, will result in the correct "social price" (fare) by reducing the number of fares and therefore reducing the number of accidents; that is, the taxicab may take the proper level of care (that is, nonnegligent) under either rule, there will remain a residual risk of injury. Under a negligence rule, the taxicab would not be liable for the residual risk. Under strict liability, the taxicab, if liable, will find it less costly to insure against the risk rather than avoid the risk. There is no consensus to the limits on liability for the residual risk. Most commentators would agree that strict product liability is not absolute liability—the firm is not an insurer of *all* accidents or injuries.

16. Of course, these firms can compete if owners absorb the loss of inadequate insurance. However, to the extent that owners can turn to the political process, these costs may not be sunk.

17. It can be argued that the Johns-Manville bankruptcy may simply be a ploy to force consolidation of claims. The widely publicized $2 billion liability reflects the *ad damnum* provisions in the complaints. The actual claims will always be less than *ad damnum* provision as the recent settlement indicates.

18. Of course, the reason for such proposals may not be to bail out the manufacturers but a means to compensate victims because the firm has inadequate assets to cover damage awards. Such schemes are likely to be inefficient or at best simply have a distributional effect. Even if the proposals are allocatively neutral in the short run, the effect of a subsidy is likely to have long-run consequences in providing diminished incentives to insure adequately in the future. Therefore, it would appear that there is little, if any economic justification for any proposal, including a tax proposal, to modify the rules of game.

19. Donald Cox and Harry Miller, *The Theory of Stochastic Processes* (London: Chapman and Hall, 1965); David Baron, "Price Uncertainty, Utility and Industry Equilibrium in Pure Competition," 11 *International Economics Review* 463 (1970); Raveendra Batra and Aman Ullah, "Competitive Firm and the Theory of Input Demand under Price Uncertainty," 82 *Journal of Political Economy* 537 (1974); Robert Pendyck, "Adjustment Costs, Uncertainty, and the Behavior of the Firm," 72 *American Economic Review* 415 (1982).

20. Robert Pendyck, *supra* note 19 at 425.

21. F. Knight, *Risk, Uncertainty and Profit* (Chicago: University of Chicago Press, 1921).

22. Joseph A. Schumpeter, *The Theory of Economic Development* (Cambridge: Cambridge University Press, 1934).

23. Israel Kirzner, *Competition and Entrepreneurship* (Chicago: University of Chicago Press, 1973).

24. James Buchanan and Roger Faith, "Entrepreneurship and the Internalization of Externalities," 24 *Journal of Law & Economics* 95 (1981). But see Robert Staaf,

"Liability Rules, Property Rights and Taxes," 5 *Journal of Research in Law & Economics* 225 (1983).

25. But see Peter Greenwood and Charles Ingene, "Uncertain Externalities, Liability Rules and Resource Allocation," 68 *American Economic Review* 300 (1978).

26. Buchanan and Faith, *supra* note 24 at 106.

27. Bankruptcy is the result of the cost of information or uncertainty; its avoidance is possible only in a world of zero information costs and the absence of uncertainty. Thus, bankruptcy is not necessarily inefficient in the same sense that it is not inefficient to be rationally ignorant of many things. It is only with the advantage of hindsight that bankruptcy can be called a waste of resources.

28. *Second Restatement of Contracts*, Section 89D(a).

29. Timothy J. Muris, "Opportunistic Behavior and the Law of Contracts," 65 *Minnesota Law Review* 521 (1981).

30. But see R. Posner and A. Rosenfield, "Impossibility and Related Doctrines in Contract Law: An Economic Analysis," 6 *Journal of Legal Studies* 83 (1977). They analyze a number of cases in which they conclude that the law generally assigns the risk on the party who is the superior (that is, lower cost) risk-bearer. One can argue for such a rule even though the event was truly uncertain since the question is really one of the allocation of risk, *ex post*, which is a distributional question. To the extent that cases are within the gray area between risk and uncertainty, the rule would establish an efficient precedence for those cases where risk evolves out of uncertainty.

31. Strict liability may have simply lowered the plaintiff's burden of proof with the result that increased liability exposure is due to increased frequency of suits rather than a higher standard. For example, California, which has gone further than most courts in the direction of strict liability, has adopted a test for design defect that in significant part rests on negligence. A leading case is *Barker v. Lull Engineering Co., Inc.*, 20 Cal.3d 413, 513 F.2d 433 (1978). The two prong test is:

(1) . . . [I]f the plaintiff demonstrates that the product failed to perform as safely as an ordinary consumer would expect when used in an intended or reasonably foreseeable manner or (2) if the plaintiff proves that the product's design proximately caused his injury and the defendant fails to prove, in light of the relevant factors discussed above, then on balance the benefits on the challenged design outweigh the risk of danger inherent in such design. (At pp. 20–21)

The relevant factors are the gravity of the danger posed by the challenged design, the *likelihood* that such danger would occur, the mechanical feasibility of a safer alternative design, the financial cost of an improved design, and the adverse consequences to the product and to the consumer that would result from an alternative design (at p. 17). But note that this is a design standard. Most commentators would agree that a firm is liable for "defects" even though there is no negligence. But see Richard Willard, "Wheel of Fortune: Stopping Outrageous and Arbitrary Liability Verdicts," 11 *Policy Review* 40 (1986). Finally, uncertainty as defined creates a problem of how to define legal causation. If cause and effect are not known at the time of the act, can it be said that the act caused the injury or that it is not a negligent act?

32. Note that there is likely to be a time continuum where uncertainty turns into risk. Therefore, DES and asbestos cases taken as a whole are likely to involve cases

of uncertainty in the initial marketing of the product with later marketing involving risk.

33. 90 N.J. 191, 447 A.2d 539 (1982).

34. Ibid., at 206, 447 A.2d at 54.

35. See Senator Kasten's bill, *supra* note 2, which discusses three types of uncertainty associated with the tort system. The first is the uncertainty attributed to the evolution of product liability law from contract and tort law theories. In most states, a claim can be based on tort theories, such as fraud, negligence, and strict liability, *and/or* on contract theories, such as breach of warranty. The mixture of theories, it is argued, creates conceptual problems for both the parties and the trier of fact. The second source of uncertainty exists because product liability law is primarily common law, so that the rules vary from state to state and can be modified at any time by a court. This creates uncertainty for the national manufacturer, which often has little control over the final distribution and consumption of its products. Because the rules are judicially developed, they usually are applied *retroactively* to the case before the court.

Third, there are uncertainties in product liability law because there are conflicts among the philosophies underlying tort law. Negligence is based on traditional principles of fault. Strict liability theories have also been justified on the basis of traditional tort principles such as the "unreasonably dangerous requirement," of Section 402A of the Restatement. But other theories, such as the *Greenman* standard, which attempts to purge negligence or fault concepts, extend liability beyond traditional principles. The bill would have established a two-tier standard approach. Strict liability attaches to manufacturer or construction defects. On the other hand, a negligence- or fault-based standard attaches for injuries caused by defective design or formulation.

36. An exception may be with multiple defendants and joint and severable liability. But even here, if there is a known risk of being held jointly liable, the risk will be incorporated in the product price.

37. See Priest, *supra* note 12 (1985, Part 2A) for a discussion of Bohlen's benefit theory of torts. F. Bohlen, "The Basis of Affirmative Obligations in the Law of Torts," *American Law Reporter* 209 (1905).

38. See Roger E. Meiners and Bruce Yandle, chapter 10, *infra* for a discussion on how a portion of the savings and loan bailout is imposed on new, solvent savings and loan institutions that did not create past problems.

39. It is interesting to note that there are generally careful deliberations in many court decisions as to whether the decision is to apply prospectively only or retrospectively. In part, the decision to apply decisions prospectively may simply be to avoid a flood of litigation if applied retrospectively. Products liability law in cases of delayed manifestation of injury can be interpreted as being applied retrospectively.

40. See *supra* note 4.

41. In the case of DES, the time period would be when the mother took the drug or the date of birth of the female offspring. A more difficult issue in defining the period of carryback arises when the effects of exposure (e.g., asbestos) may be cumulative over a prolonged period.

42. Of course, accounting profits for tax purposes are different than economic profits. For the purpose of this discussion the difference is not crucial.

43. For the moment, ignore interest rates and issues of discounting. Insurance may be either a premium (market insurance) or a reserve (self-insurance).

44. The example illustrates that a priority problem may exist. Suppose the second and third judgments were awarded first, and then the first judgment. There would appear to be no a priori reason to change the priority rule of the first claim reduced to judgment so as to receive priority over a later claim. The priority issue would only arise in a case of bankruptcy and therefore be subject to bankruptcy rules.

45. It should be noted that the variance around the expected value of the bet (zero) decreases when there are prior-year earnings.

46. See L. Saunders, "Taxing Matters: With Liability Insurance Becoming Unavailable or Unaffordable, Why Aren't More Companies Self-Insuring?" *Fortune*, 1986. Insurance rates and reserves are regulated by the states. It is beyond the scope of this chapter to analyze these regulations, which vary by state. The IRC has extensive code sections and regulations on taxation of insurance companies.

47. See D. Mayers and C. Smith, Jr., "On the Corporate Demand for Insurance," 55 *Journal of Business 281 (1982)*, and L. De Alessi, *"Why Corporations Insure,"* 25 *Economic Inquiry* 429 (1987).

48. There are loading fees that cover the insurance companies' costs and return on capital independent of reserve requirements. Loading fees as a percent of the total premium are likely to be considerably lower than a corporation's marginal tax rate.

49. See R. Coase, "The Nature of the Firm," 4 *Economica* 386 (1937).

50. Because of insurance company loading fees, the consequences are not exactly the same. However, as long as loading fees as a percent of premiums are less than the marginal tax bracket, there is an incentive to market insure.

51. See *supra* note 46.

52. See *United States v. General Dynamics Corp.*, 481 U.S. 239 (1987) on the right of an accrual taxpayer to deduct self-insurance reserves. General Dynamics used insurers' own methods to calculate the proper reserve for a medical insurance plan. The deduction was not allowed under Sections 446(a) and 446(c)(2) of the Internal Revenue Code of 1954 because it failed the "events test." "Nor may a taxpayer deduct an estimate of an anticipated expense, no matter how statistically certain, if it is based on events that have not occurred by the close of the taxable year." At 243–44. But see Justice O'Conner *United States v. Hughes Properties, Inc.*, 476 U.S. 593 (1986), dissenting opinion.

It should also be noted that states vary as to how reserves are calculated, and for types of permissible investments and initial capital requirements of licensed insurance carriers. Usually a surplus is required over and above reserves required to fund future liability. It has been argued, however, that insurance companies are also overestimating reserves for tax advantages. Such a result may come about because of some market power by insurance companies. Because of extensive insurance regulation there may indeed be restrictions on entry that lead to market power (i.e., rate regulation controlled by insurance companies). The incentive to overstate may also come about from the investment side of insurance companies. If the return to their investment portfolio is increased dramatically because of unanticipated market charges, then there is an incentive to offset these profits with larger deductions such as reserves. Again, reserve requirements are regulated, and it is beyond the scope of this article.

53. Shareholders will *always* bear a portion of the liability loss even with an extended carryback provision.

54. Each year's taxes would be paid on the reserves contributed each year plus the annual interest earned on the cumulative reserve balance.

55. Note that *ex post*, the reserve plus interest buildup is tax free the same as for insurance companies except that taxes are paid and then fully refunded when the liability claim is paid.

56. There may be a net effect if corporate income taxes are progressive; that is, if $14,864 was deducted from income in the first period and accumulated interest each period from the $14,864 was deducted, then the marginal tax bracket throughout the period may be lower relative to carrying $100,000 back each period. This effect is likely for only the smallest firms given corporate tax rates. However, there may be a more pronounced effect even if marginal tax rates were constant at the margin. The carryback provision diminishes the effect of bracket creep associated with inflation: Real taxes increase with inflation and tax schedules expressed in nominal dollars. Thus, the carryback provision in essence bypasses the bracket shifting from inflation so that it has an effect on marginal tax rates by overstated deductions in early periods but understated deductions in later periods. This can be seen by looking at the earned interest column in Table 6.7. The $100,000 is carried back to period one, but only $14,864 plus one year's interest would be deducted under a self-insurance reserve. On the other hand, in the twentieth period, only $100,000 is deducted, but under a self-insurance reserve the accumulated interest on the reserve, $1,148,646 plus that year's payment would be deducted. The net effect of carryback is likely to be higher taxes. With income tax schedules currently indexed, there is no effect of bracket creep in the future. Finally, there is a loss of liquidity under the carryback provision. While the tax effect is the same, funds are not available until the twentieth period, whereas under market insurance the savings are available in each period. Thus, because liquidity has value, the carryback provision is less valuable than market insurance at the margin.

57. For small firms or firms that are not diversified there is likely to be a small number of events or pooling problems.

58. For example, a DES product liability suit has been filed against Eli Lilly by a granddaughter claiming an intergenerational injury resulting from her grandmother taking DES (*The Wall Street Journal*, March 13, 1990, B9).

59. Sec. 172(k).

60. The provision could be conditioned on receiving a tax refund no greater than the tax savings by including the loss in the current year.

7

Liability and Environmental Quality

Hugh H. Macaulay

I. INTRODUCTION

Origins of the Modern Debate

Ronald Coase opened the eyes of economists to the problem of social costs by observing that they are reciprocal.[1] What economists had previously seen as one-direction damages, whereby the smoke from a steel mill imposed an external cost on nearby residents, Coase argued was really a two-way cost. When the steel mill had its way and emitted smoke, its neighbors incurred costs due to this action. When the steel mill's neighbors had their way and were able to force a reduction in the output of smoke, the producers of steel incurred costs due to this action. Coase argued that the efficient economic solution to the problem of social cost required that both parties be subject to the same rules for determining costs and charges. Maximum total output of the two protagonists was the goal. Liability for environmental use is fundamental to the question: Who should pay?

William Baumol argued that while Coase's argument had much to commend it in cases involving only a few parties, the proper practical policy where large numbers were involved was to charge only the party emitting the smoke, for only it was imposing a cost on another producer.[2] In other words, the polluter should be held liable. Smoke creates an external cost; clean air does not. After a tax is imposed on the polluter, no other tax or subsidy should be paid, for that would produce an inefficient result.

These articles that reach conflicting conclusions are widely cited in the literature. The *Social Sciences Citation Index* for the five-year period 1976 to 1980 lists 314 articles citing the Coase article, which was published in 1960, and 74 articles citing Baumol's 1972 work. Despite the greater recognition given Coase's work, when economists and other policymakers propose ways to assign liability for pollution, almost universally they call for a charge on only the creator of the pollutant.[3] Indeed, the terminology used in the literature reflects this view and policy; effluent charges, emission fees, and taxes on pollution are proposed as solutions. Rarely, if ever, is there a parallel proposal calling for a cleanliness charge or a purity tax.[4] The problem is defined as pollution, and it is caused by smoke and its producers; clean air is not seen as pollution or a problem. One is forced to conclude that Coase won the battle, having garnered the most citations, while Baumol won the war, having seen support for his proposal for dealing with pollution.

Outline of the Chapter

This chapter argues that Coase should have won the war as well. The chapter is organized as follows: Section II restates the Coase argument. Because the Coase treatment has had little impact on policy, despite its widespread intellectual recognition, the case needs restating. Section III discusses Baumol's point that the laundry industry (a "nonpolluting" industry) does not damage the smoke-producing industry. Section IV examines the property rights associated with the problem of social cost. It is here that rules of liability surface, since liability is fundamental to ownership. Section V deals with the argument that the laundry is consuming a nonrival public good, clean air, and that the proper price for such a good is zero. Section VI is concerned with the argument that a lack of purity in the air will be a sufficient deterrent to other laundries to keep their number to an optimum level, and for this reason no charge need be levied on them. Section VII summarizes the case for and against charges on both parties concerned with the externality.

II. A COASIAN VIEW OF SOCIAL COST

Coase's major contribution to our understanding of spillover effects was the view that social costs are reciprocal. To illustrate, Coase notes that not only is cattle raising costly to neighboring farmers, but also farming can be costly to nearby cattle ranchers. To understand this principle, Coase recommended that we view social costs not as a case where A's actions hurt B, but as a problem where two parties, A and B, are competing for the use of a limited asset.[5] This recommendation has been widely ignored.

The Central Analytical Framework

Professors James Buchanan and Craig Stubblebine have expressed mathematically the bilateral nature of social cost. Many writers have cast it in graphic terms, as shown in Figure 7.1. Here the MB curve represents marginal benefits enjoyed by polluting firms (and consumers of its products) when they are permitted to discharge their wastes rather than be required to treat them or reduce output to avoid creating wastes. The MC curve represents the value of a net decline in utility or output that nearby residents would experience from an additional unit of waste being discharged.[6] At the optimal level of waste discharge, the gain to firms (consumers) discharging wastes is a + b + c and the net cost to those adversely affected is c. The marginal values are equal.

If the problem is viewed as involving two parties desiring to use an asset, say air quality, in mutually exclusive ways, then Figure 7.1 is just like the traditional graph showing two demanders wanting to use or own an asset that is finite in amount, but which is owned by neither of them. User 1, the party seeking to use air quality to carry away his waste product, smoke, has a demand curve sloping downward from the left Y axis. User 2, the party wanting to enjoy air with little or no smoke in it, has a demand curve sloping downward to the left from the right Y axis. For User 2 the activity measured on the X axis from its intersection with his Y axis is not smoke discharged but smoke removed, that is, the MC curve becomes an MB curve for User 2 as smoke is removed.

The costs, area c, borne by neighbors of the smoky industry when it emits smoke at the optimum level, are matched by the costs, area d, borne by the smoke-producing industry as it must pay for smoke removal, while those enjoying the cleaner air gain areas d + e + f.

Just as in other cases involving market-traded assets, each party gains by getting some of what he wants, and each party "suffers" by not getting all of what he would like if the prices were zero. Resources are scarce. Each party's liability is based on a common price for the amount of his preferred use, which is the cost imposed when the unnamed owner of the resource is unable to offer marginal units of the resource to the competing user. Coase's solution to the problem of social cost is the same.

III. SHOULD VICTIMS OF EXTERNALITIES BE TAXED OR SUBSIDIZED?

The title to this section is the same as the one used by Baumol for the second section of his classic article, where he concludes, "the solution calls for neither taxes upon x2, the neighboring laundry output, nor compensation to that industry for the damage it suffers." "Thus the obvious and apparently common interpretation of the Coase position is simply invalid."[7]

But the above title and Baumol's development depart from Coase's treatment of social cost and therefore quite logically arrive at conclusions inconsistent with Coase. Coase points out that externalities are reciprocal. Setting up his model, Baumol assumes "there is only one scarce resource, labor, and that the externality (smoke) only affects the cost of production of neighboring laundries." "Here x1 is an output whose production imposes external costs on the manufacture of x2 (say industry II is the oft-cited laundry industry whose costs are increased by I's smoke)." There is no mention of the laundry imposing an external cost on the smoke industry. Indeed, he notes that "the laundry whose output is damaged by smoky air does not, by an increase in its own output, make the air cleaner or dirtier for others."[8] This is physically correct but economically misleading.

Baumol defines the cost of producing the output of the smoky industry to be a function only of the labor used in that industry. Because the laundry does not produce smoke, it does not create an externality. The cost of producing clean linen in the laundry is, however, a function of the labor used in that industry plus the labor used in the smoky industry. It is not surprising, then, that efficiency requires that the price of the product of the smoky industry must cover the cost of labor in that industry plus the cost imposed on the laundry industry because of labor employed in, and the resulting higher output of, the smoky industry.

If the problem is analyzed in terms of Figure 7.1, the smoky industry and the laundry enjoy symmetrical benefits and suffer symmetrical costs. By getting cleaner air than it would if there were no taxes on pollution, the laundry enjoys benefits and imposes damages on the smoky industry. This can be incorporated in Baumol's model by observing that the cost of producing the product of the smoky industry depends on the labor employed in that industry plus the labor employed in the laundry. Alternatively, we might add environmental quality as an additional factor of production.

Another way to understand the effect of externalities is to consider how the two firms would operate if they were jointly owned by one person. With outputs sold in competitive markets, how would the owner decide on the output of each firm? The owner would do as Baumol suggests and take into account the effect of the smoke-producing firm, as a rise in its output increases the cost of operating the laundry. He would also do as Coase suggests and take into account the effect of the laundry, which increases the cost of operating the smoke-producing firm, because the value of clean air rises for the laundry. By not including this latter effect in the model, Baumol reaches his mathematically correct but economically erroneous conclusion that only one party should be charged for the externalities.[9]

IV. THE ROLE OF PROPERTY RIGHTS

Outcomes with Different Property Rights

Perhaps some of the confusion in the treatment of externalities arises because of the uncertain nature of the property rights involved.[10] Coase explains that if the farmer owns the property on which the cattle stray, the rancher is liable to the farmer for damages. If the rancher owns the land,

Figure 7.1
Analysis of Bilateral Effects

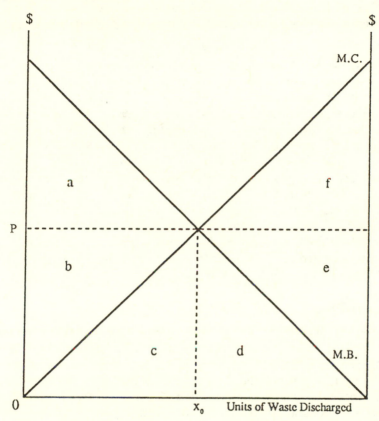

and the farmer wants to exclude cattle in order to grow crops, the farmer must pay the rancher. If no one owns the property, the use goes to the one favored by nature, or to the one able to force the other to pay. In the rancher-farmer case, the rancher is favored by nature for cattle roam and may destroy crops, but farm crops do not exclude cattle. A farmer with a gun may, however, shift the direction of payment.

If a third party owns the property, the case is similar to the one describing two demanders of one asset shown in Figure 7.1 above.[11] Each party who is permitted some of his preferred use at the expense of the other must pay for the benefit he receives and the cost he imposes. It is evidently this distinction that eluded Buchanan and led to his comment quoted in Baumol's article.

I did not ever think of this sort of [double] tax at all, and it would surely have seemed bizarre to me to suggest that taxes be levied on both the factory and the laundries. What we were proposing was the Wicksellian public-goods approach. Suppose that existing property rights allow the factory to put out the smoke.... There is a public goods problem here; the residents get together, impose a tax *on themselves* to subsidize the factory to install the smoke prevention device.[12]

Because Buchanan assumes that the factory owns the right to discharge smoke, it naturally would be bizarre to have it pay a third party for this activity. But if a third party were the owner of the right to use air quality, it would appear less unusual—indeed a normal market. The use of the word *tax* implies that government is the owner of these rights. The term *tax* helps disguise the true situation. A tax is a payment to government for the general services of government. It does not usually involve a quid pro quo return for payment. Some other payments to government, however, are made for particular services and are not called taxes. People pay tuition to state universities, pay tolls at bridges, and they buy postage stamps, license tags, fishing permits, and subway tokens. These are not considered taxes or payments to use the environment. Such payments are charges or fees that carry a right to a limited use of some asset or a right to receive a given service.

Pecuniary and Technical Externalities

Another issue derives from this nomenclature. Baumol asks if victims of externalities should be taxed or compensated. Rules of liability require that we compensate individuals not just because they are damaged but also because their property has been used. Damage may be a necessary, but not a sufficient, condition for compensation. A merchant may be damaged by competitors, domestic or foreign, who undersell him, but economists do not normally argue that this condition is grounds for compensation. A homeowner may be damaged if a neighbor builds an unattractive house or fails to maintain a decent lawn. These are usually called pecuniary externalities and are generally not recognized at law. The property owner is compensated for damages when someone attenuates one of the recognized rights to property; that is, technical externalities are often recognized at law—such as the negative effects of pollution. Thus, victims of all externalities are not automatically compensated.

If it is a true (technical) externality that occurs because no one owns the asset whose use is being contested, there is little or no economic logic in requiring that any one person be compensated, since no one person is the owner. Nor is there a reason to tax or charge a victim of an externality solely because he is damaged; he is already suffering some damage. If the victim is suffering because he does not enjoy the complete use of the asset he would like if it were free, but does enjoy some use of it at a cost to another party, he should pay a charge for the benefit he is enjoying and not be either charged or compensated for the use he is not enjoying.

An understanding of property rights can help clarify another problem Baumol encountered in his analysis of Coase. Coase argues that a failure to charge parties who gain from a cleaner environment will lead to too many such people moving into an area near the smoke-producing firm, thus raising to an inefficient level the costs to be paid by the smoke-producing firm.[13] Thus, they should be charged because they increase the costs of others. Baumol argues that this example "skates awfully close to an error analogous to the confusion between pecuniary and technological externalities."[14]

It is easy to fall into such errors of confusion because the two types of externalities are separated primarily by conditions associated with ownership of a factor of production. Consider an example. Firm A is established on a stream and uses labor and clean water as inputs to produce its output. It operates successfully for two years. Then Firm B moves in upstream, also using labor and clean water to produce its output, but it also discharges unclean water that affects Firm A downstream. A faces a rise in labor costs because B had bid away some workers; A can keep the wage rate where it was previously and use workers with lower qualifications, or it can raise its wage rate and command workers of the quality it formerly employed, or it may find most efficient a slightly higher wage for workers with slightly lower qualifications. This is a pecuniary externality at work.

The problem is similar for the use of water. Firm A can pay for water quality the same price as previously, zero, and receive, as it did with labor, water of a lower quality. Or it can pay to clean up the water it takes in and return water quality to its previous level, paying a higher price for water. If water quality is treated as a productive factor, as Coase recommended, and each user is charged for its use, the fall in quality and/or rise in the price of water would be only another pecuniary externality.

Baumol proposes a zero charge on Firm A for the water quality it receives. If the same rules were applied to the other scarce resource, labor, Firm B would have to pay the new higher price of labor and use the number of workers this higher wage would command, while Firm A would continue to pay the old wage rate, but be allocated the number and the quality of workers the new wage rate would have attracted to the firm.

Coase has not confused pecuniary and technological externalities nor has he made an error analogous to this confusion. Rather, the error is Baumol's when he says, "Like a price change, the variation in taxes constitutes a pecuniary externality,"[15] though he has proposed a zero tax on the laundry and no variation in this rate if more laundries move in. Coase, on the other hand, has recognized that one user of an asset, the laundry in Baumol's case, is not being charged, and argues that this will lead to a misallocation of resources.[16] The user will be charged not because he is damaging other users but because he is gaining from his preferred use of a scarce resource and is thereby depriving its owner of a less valuable use, which may be the sale of marginal units to another user.

Externalities and the Production Function

Another question that an emphasis on ownership of environmental factors may help resolve involves the relationship between pecuniary externalities, technological externalities, and the production function. It is usually argued that pecuniary externalities do not change the production function but involve only a change in prices and a movement along the production function. Conversely, it is often argued that technological externalities change the quality of inputs and so produce a shift of production functions. New inputs are needed because old ones are unavailable.

As the above example shows, what has changed is the price of the environmental input. These technological externalities could be treated the same as pecuniary externalities. In the case of a pecuniary externality, a price change may lead to a change in the quality of the input or the substitution of another input. In the case of a technological externality, the quality changes may lead to a change in the price of the input or the substitution of another input. The three dimensions of change, that is, price, quality, and quantity, apply in both cases. Along these lines, Francis Bator alerted us to the close relationship with the observation that "[t]he question of whether technological externalities involve shifts of each other's production functions, or mutually induced movements along such functions, is purely definitional."[17]

V. CLEAN AIR AS A PUBLIC GOOD

Is Air Quality a Public Good?

Baumol argues that a zero charge is justified for the laundry because clean air is a public good. A public good is defined as one that can simultaneously satisfy the consumption of an infinite number of users. Consumption or use by one party does not affect any other party's consumption, and there is no way to exclude consumers. Following this tack, Baumol states: "[W]here an externality is (like the usual pollution problem) of a public goods variety, neither compensation to nor taxation of those who are affected is compatible with optimal resource allocation." And, "[o]ne way to look at the reason [for a zero tax on laundries] is that our model (and the pollution model in general) refers to the important case of *public* externalities."[18]

Baumol then explains the rationale. "As with all public goods, an increase in one user's consumption does not reduce the available supply to others."[19]

The application of this principle to environmental quality is the result of a myopic view of the asset and its users. The asset is not clean air to be used by laundries but air quality that is desired by laundries and smoky factories.

If the asset is only clean air, Baumol can be correct. One laundry using the clean air does not reduce its cleanliness or its usefulness to other laundries. But if the asset is viewed as air quality, an increased use by the laundry results in a decreased amount, or quality, available to the smoky industry. In Figure 7.1, the addition of one more laundry will shift up the MC curve by an amount equal to the cost the new laundry incurs from each level of smoke being discharged. A new equilibrium position would call for a reduced level of smoke discharged. This means reduced use of air by the smoky industry and a higher price for the units it continues to use.

If all users of air quality are required to pay for the uses they enjoy, some interesting price relationships result from the change to a new equilibrium. The new user of clean air pays a price equal to the marginal value of the increased cleanliness. But the price to the smoky industry for smoke emitted goes up by less than this amount. Because the former users of clean air enjoy a greater level of cleanliness, its marginal value to them declines, as does the price they pay.

Nonrival or Rival Use?

The argument for a zero charge for users of a nonrival public good is fraught with problems. Thinking in terms of competition for the use of a scarce asset clarifies the issue. Arguments about the use of an uncongested asset often hinge on the good being already in existence. There is no obvious marginal cost for providing it. Some people see the environment this way. Environmental problems, however, are concerned with choosing the optimum level of environmental quality when there is competition regarding use. Even though the environment may be seen as existing without human effort, choosing to change the quality of the environment involves production costs. Thus, providing one group of users with an increase in the use they want will involve an immediate reduction in the availability of the good (and an increase in cost) to other prospective users. Rival use replaces nonrival use.

Unless a free good is involved, all cases of nonrival use involve rival use. The confusion often arises because initial production decisions are made independently of decisions to ration use. For example, a decision is made to build a bridge capable of carrying a given traffic load. Later, the bridge is operated well below its carrying capacity. There is no competition for particular traffic slots. As time passes, congestion may lead to rationing by toll or sticker. At that point, increased use by one party implies reduced use by another. In the case of environmental use, however, the two decisions are made concurrently, and the rival nature of the use should be just as obvious as with a congested bridge.

Polluters are often viewed as invading the property of purity lovers. In the absence of the polluter, laundries are viewed as nonrivalrous. Each laundry operator values clean air and does not degrade it when operating. However, given any level of smoke emission, each laundry that opens will impose potential costs on the polluter: Each laundry desires less smoke. In effect, the laundry competes with the polluter for the use of a scarce asset, which implies that all who use the asset should pay a market-determined price.

All of this helps justify the point that the only time we can say unequivocally that a public good should carry a zero price is when, in economic terms, it is a free good. If it is not a free good a zero price may still be justified, but not just because another user finds his preferred use reduced. There must be technical or institutional reasons that make the zero price more efficient than a positive price.

VI. PRICE AND THE OPTIMUM NUMBER OF USERS OF CLEAN AIR

Baumol next addresses the point made by Coase that those moving near the smoky factory will be inefficiently numerous unless they are charged. This, of course, contradicts Baumol's point that the proper charge on neighboring laundries is zero. If one assumes, as Baumol does, that the agency making the decision about the "tax" to be charged the smoky industry knows the marginal value that the smoky industry places on each unit of smoke discharged and knows the sum of the marginal values that each of the laundries places on each unit of smoke removed (or discharged), then the optimal level of smoke discharged (and removed) can be determined and the appropriate charge levied on the smoke-producing industry. This is the equilibrium point in Figure 7.1. The charge OP is the sum of the marginal values that all laundries place on this level of smoke removed, including even those laundries that find the marginal value of the final unit of smoke removed to be zero. While most, and perhaps all, of these users of this level of air quality would like the air to be even cleaner, those who would not move in unless the air were even cleaner are not considered. Hence, those who value this level of air quality would be willing to pay the sums attributed to them and still remain, and no more users would move in even if the charge were zero. Charge or no charge on the laundries, the result is the same.

This is a strange result. Both Baumol and Coase can be right, though they propose different solutions. Baumol is correct in stating that a zero charge on the laundries can produce an optimal result. Coase is correct in stating that a charge on each of the laundries that moves in can also produce an optimal result. But Baumol overdoes his position in declaring it is the only one admissible. "No tax on nearby residents is required or, taken in real terms, is even compatible with optimal resource allocation." And if laundries were given compensation for the damages they suffer, "the tax would be needed only to sop up the compensation payments which should never have been given in the first place."[20]

There is an additional difficulty with Baumol's position. Coase has provided an example that Baumol discusses in dealing with the question of determining the optimal number of laundries. Coase assumes a factory emits smoke that imposes damages of $100 a year on nearby residents. The factory could, however, at a cost of $90 a year install equipment that would remove the smoke. If the factory were charged an amount equal to the stated damage done by the smoke, it would avoid the $100 charge by spending $90 on the air cleaner. Given only these facts, that is an efficient result.

But there is more to the story. The nearby laundry could move to another location at a cost of $40 per year and avoid the damage done by the smoke. The optimal solution to the problem of who should use the air now changes; the residents should move. If the marginal cost to the residents from smoke emission is calculated on the basis of damage done to them, ignoring less expensive actions they might take to avoid this damage, the costs of pollution and the measure of damage will be overstated, and the solution with a zero charge on the laundries will not be optimal. Baumol recognizes that if the cost of moving is not taken into account in determining the optimum charge, the charge on the factory will be and could remain inefficiently high. This would not result under Coase's proposal to charge all parties equal prices.

The issue is further complicated by an example Baumol uses in corresponding with Coase. Baumol assumed that though the people who want cleaner air could get it at a cost of $40 by living elsewhere, some of them misguidedly move near the smoky industry and suffer costs of $50. Coase properly responds that the charge determined under the assumption of $40 for moving should not change. Coase continues, "[T]he tax system I was attacking was one which would in these circumstances, automatically lead to an increase in the tax as the damage increases."[21]

The lesson is a very valuable one. The definition of damage is most important. Just because someone is damaged by the action of another, a charge equal to that damage may not be efficient. The person adversely affected may be able to avoid the damage at a lower cost than the damage he suffers and the smoky industry pays. If he does not have to pay anything, he may stay and try to have the smoky industry clean the air. If he does have to pay a price equal to what the smoky firm is paying,[22] he will move. The question facing Baumol's environmental authority revolves around the definition of damage, and Coase makes clear that a broad definition is appropriate, taking into account all alternatives, including moving. The same concept guides participants in markets.

In determining the optimum number of nearby residents, Coase is more careful and recognizes that solutions other than his may exist.

If the factory owner is to be made to pay a tax equal to the damage caused, it would clearly be desirable to institute a double tax system and to make residents of the district pay an amount equal to the additional cost incurred by the factory owner (or the consumers of his products) in order to avoid the damage. In these conditions, people would not stay in the district or would take other measures to prevent the damage from occurring, when the costs of doing so were less than the costs that would be incurred by the producer to reduce the damage (the producer's object, of course, being not so much to reduce the damage as to reduce the tax payments). A tax system which was confined to a tax on the producer for damage caused would tend to lead to unduly high costs being incurred for the prevention of damage. Of course this could be avoided if it were possible to base the tax, not on the damage caused, but on the fall in the value of production (in its widest sense) resulting from the emission of smoke. But to do so would require a detailed knowledge of individual preferences and I am unable to imagine how the data needed for such a taxation system could be assembled.[23]

The Information Problem

There are several other problems with Baumol's call for a zero charge on the laundries. As noted above by Coase, a mandated charge on the smoky firms requires an amount and quality of information that would humble any reasonable citizen. The values assigned by the smoke-producing firms may be deduced based on their responses to the charges levied, for they are in effect participants in a market, buying a product at a price. The values assigned by the neighbors must be based on less tangible information.

Baumol implies that the value could be determined by trial and error. The regulator could raise the price to the smoke-producing firm and then observe the response. Baumol says the new higher price causes the smoke producer "to reduce his smoke, and so brings more laundries into the neighborhood. The tax is then readjusted to equal the new (higher) value of damage per puff of smoke, more laundries move in, and so on."[24] Equilibrium will continue to move up the smoky industry's MB curve, but this result is strange.

It is true that cleaner air has a greater total value to the laundries but it should also have a lower marginal value, and the price is based on marginal values. Existing laundries will find the cleaner air worth less at the margin, and the price to them should fall. New laundries may move in as the air becomes cleaner, but whether their addition to marginal value will offset the decline in marginal value of existing users is uncertain. Almost all presentations of the effect of pollution and of pollution abatement show a declining marginal value of cleanliness as its level rises. The MC curve in Figure 7.1 is an example.

A second result of Baumol's zero charge is that cleanliness is underpriced and overconsumed. Indeed, this is the criticism that for decades has been leveled on smoky firms, and the literature is rife with discussions of the need to make these perpetrators pay. It may be argued, of course, that the value of clean air to those who enjoy it is known to the agency levying the charge on the smoky industry, so only the optimum amount of pollution (and purity) will be produced. But those who prefer greater cleanliness as well as more of the tangible products made by the smoky industry will find that the purity they prefer costs less, relative to its cost of production. This gain will go to the consumers as higher income, for they now pay nothing for the cleanliness they get; or to producers, the laundries that use clean air to reduce costs; or as higher rent to owners of the sites with a favorable location that no longer suffers environmental pollution; or as a little of each. The result is subject to the same criticisms that attend a subsidy given for the purchase of any other good.

An analogous solution applied to land would be to decree that all businesses must pay a market equilibrium price for the land they use, but homeowners will be given, at a zero price, the land they would have bought if they had to pay the same market price. Further, if one follows Coase's argument that externalities are reciprocal, it would be equally valid to charge only those users who prefer clean air, for example, the laundries, thereby determining the optimal level of cleanliness, and then permit smoky firms the free discharge of the prescribed quantities of smoke.

Consuming the Environment to the Limit

Another difficulty with the Baumol solution is that since those who benefit from cleaner air pay a zero price for what they get, they will act to equate the ratio of prices paid to the ratio of marginal utilities enjoyed.[25] This is the efficient condition economists seek in all markets. However, with a zero price for clean air, consumers will want to consume increased quality until the final unit has zero marginal utility. This will occur at different levels for different consumers but will be at a zero level of waste discharged for some. So long as there are some consumers who prefer that level, they will press for that result. Since the good is provided by an all-knowing agency as a public good for the laundries and neighboring residents, they will press politically for perfection. There is certainly evidence of this in the push by environmentalists for extraordinarily tight pollution controls.

VII. CONCLUSION

The problem of social cost is pervasive. Despite Coase's clear analysis of the problem, it is still normal, even among economists, to see social costs as a one-directional problem. There are political reasons and forces of self-interest that lead us to see pollution this way. In addition, the solution to social costs as they apply to the environment is intuitively obvious: smoke pollutes but clean air does not; nonrival public goods, such as cleanliness, should be free; and the costs associated with a polluted environment will serve to keep down the number of users of clean air.

It has been argued above, however, that Baumol's support of a tax on environment users is less than convincing. It overlooks the opposite externality that flows from those who prefer cleanliness to those who would use the environment to help produce other goods. It uses a definition of public goods that is narrow and thereby overlooks the rival nature of the use of the environment. And the model and the policy that follow it are based on a level of knowledge that is impossible to attain.

It is true that the Coase solution, as presented here, has problems associated with it. It involves high transactions costs.[26] But so does the Baumol solution. To decree a solution by regulation, rather than rely on market transactions, may save participants from gathering large amounts of information and engaging in subsequent trading. But Baumol's solution requires expenditures to gather an impossible array of data and further expenditures to allocate, monitor, and enforce the use of the environment. These expenditures may well exceed the transactions costs of the market and arrive at equally, or even more, inefficient results. Government solutions also have transactions costs, and these may be much more than the costs of commercial assignation and trade.

There are lessons to be learned from the Baumol model, but they are not the ones Baumol proposes. The first lesson is that problems with the environment are problems of use, not problems of pollution. If use is the question, economic theory is well equipped to deal with the allocation of a scarce resource among competing users. A second lesson is that public goods involve problems of production and allocation among competing users, as well as allocation and pricing to a limited group of users. An examination of information and transactions costs, with existing price theory, may help us understand the problem better.

Indeed, the general lesson is the need to work into existing price theory the problems dealing with the allocation of the environment, rather than devise a separate theory to deal with pollution. This is what Coase tried to do. A common problem seems to be that smoke has gotten in our eyes to blind us to the proper treatment of what we call externalities.

Finally, we must ask how all this relates to questions of liability, a matter mentioned in passing throughout the chapter. Rationing environmental use implies ownership, and rules of liability rise in importance when someone's property has been damaged or used. In a broad sense, all market transactions involve forming liability and settling it. An ordinary purchase of a consumer good involves both steps. However, we generally do not think of market transactions in those terms. Liability is ordinarily thought of in association with nonvoluntary transactions.

The regulation of environmental use has emerged in the context of a nonvoluntary transaction, at least for some parties. Industrial firms and municipalities that discharge pollution are seen as forcing their use on a reluctant property owner. Recreationists and other consumers of environmental quality are seen in a more benign light. They are engaging in a voluntary transaction with nature. This popular line of thinking sees no need to impose liability on the latter group. Just as Baumol suggested, liability should fall on the polluter.

Environmental scarcity implies that ownership patterns must become more distinct. More certain rules of liability follow from that. If the government is the owner of the environment and acts with ownerlike concern, all parties who use scarce features of the environment should be liable for the costs they impose on others. The problem of social cost would then disappear. However, to think that government could act as a logical owner who allocates a valuable asset among competing users asks too much. Government is traditionally a redistributor of assets, not a market allocator.[27]

The Coasian solution urges us to consider how environmental assets, the right to use or conserve identified features of the environment, can be assigned to specific private citizens or groups. When that is done, liability will fall on those who use the asset without the permission of the owner. Payment or agreement will be required of those who use the asset in a voluntary setting.

NOTES

1. See Ronald H. Coase, "The Problem of Social Cost," *Journal of Law and Economics* 3 (October 1960): 1–44.

2. See William J. Baumol, "On Taxation and the Control of Externalities," *Quarterly Journal of Economics* 52 (June 1972): 351–79.

3. For example, see Richard A. Musgrave and Peggy B. Musgrave, *Public Finance in Theory and Practice*, 3d ed. (New York: McGraw-Hill Publishing Co., 1980), pp. 706–10. For a more recent statement calling for pollution charges, see "Environmental User Fees," *Regulation* 1 (1988): 4–5.

4. Notable exceptions are found in Herbert Mohring and J. Hayden Boyd, "Analyzing 'Externalities': 'Direct Interaction' vs. 'Asset Utilization' Frameworks," *Economica* 38 (August 1971): 347–61; Hugh H. Macaulay, "Environmental Quality, the Market, and Public Finance," in *Modern Fiscal Issues*, ed. Richard Bird and John G. Head (Toronto: University of Toronto Press, 1977), pp. 187–224; and J. H. Dales, *Pollution, Property and Prices: An Essay in Policy Making and Economics* (Toronto: University of Toronto Press, 1968).

5. See Coase, *supra* note 1 at 2, 44.

6. The MB curve represents a private good and is the horizontal summation of the individual MB curves of smoke-producing firms. The MC curve represents a public good, or in this case a public bad, to this group of users, and the curve is the vertical summation of the MC curves of nearby residents.

7. See Baumol, *supra* note 2 at 311, 309.

8. Ibid., 309, 310, 312–13.

9. Baumol has confined himself to the larger number case and may assume the

transactions costs of dealing with many laundries would outweigh the gains from reduced pollution. But transactions costs are a separate cost that can be worked into the model if needed. The model as written calls for a zero charge on each laundry even if transactions costs are zero.

10. Property rights to an economist are not the same as understood by lawyers in their strict meaning. See David D. Haddock and Fred S. McChesney, chapter 3, *infra*.

11. Actually, the figure is applicable and the allocation is the same regardless of who owns the asset, ignoring income effects. For example, one of the demanders may also be the owner. The source and receipt of payments depends on ownership.

12. See Baumol, *supra* note 2 at 304.

13. In fact, this happened in Chicago, where residents in the flight path of O'Hare Airport sued successfully to force flight pattern rotation. They thereby increased their property values by reducing an existing externality, dumping the cost on others.

14. See Baumol, *supra* note 2 at 312 n.8. Along these lines, Worcester states, "[t]he first satisfactory statement distinguishing between technological and pecuniary economies . . . seems to have been made by Baumol . . . although he does not claim originality." (See Dean Worcester, "Pecuniary and Technological Externalities, Factor Rents, and Social Costs," *American Economic Review* 59 [December 1969]: 873–75.)

15. See Baumol, *supra* note 2 at 312 n.8.

16. We shall see below that a zero charge may not lead to a misallocation of resources, but for this to hold the conditions are severe.

17. See Baumol, *supra* note 2 at 360 n.6.

18. Ibid., pp. 307, 311.

19. Ibid., p. 312.

20. Ibid., pp. 309, 313.

21. Ibid., p. 315.

22. As a consumer of a public good, the user pays a price that is his portion of the total price paid by all users for the marginal unit of emission removed.

23. See Coase, *supra* note 1 at 41.

24. See Baumol, *supra* note 2 at 315.

25. Ibid., p. 311.

26. On this, see Wallace E. Oates, "The Regulation of Externalities: Efficient Behavior of Source and Victim," *Public Finance* 38 (December 1983): 363–75.

27. This point is discussed at length in Bruce Yandle, *The Political Limits of Environmental Regulation* (Westport, Conn.: Quorum Books, 1989).

8

Rules of Liability and the Demise of Superfund

Bruce Yandle

I. INTRODUCTION

In 1980, on the heels of the Love Canal episode, which raised political passions regarding the hazards of abandoned chemical waste sites, Congress passed the Comprehensive Environmental Response, Compensation, and Liability Act (CERCLA).[1] The statute was designed specifically to deal with "orphan waste sites," where the identity of the previous operators and those whose waste products formed the site was known but divisible liability was difficult to determine.

To fund clean up operations, Congress initially established a $1.6 billion fund to receive the proceeds of a tax on chemical feedstocks and petroleum products. The fund, which subsequently was increased to $8.5 billion, was to be used by the U.S. Environmental Protection Agency (EPA) to mitigate hazardous sites selected by the agency, while the EPA simultaneously took legal action against one or all of the dischargers. A rule of strict and joint and several retroactive liability applied to the polluters, with the latter interpretation applying when it was impossible to divide liability. Proceeds from the suits were to replenish the fund.

The reach of Superfund liability does not end with those who might have operated waste sites, carried waste to them, or produced the waste ultimately located at the site. Banks and other lending institutions find themselves caught in the liability web when they repossess land containing a Superfund-designated site.[2]

Reviewers of the current status of Superfund agree at least on one thing: The program is hopelessly underfunded. One recent commentator put the matter this way: "Only 300 to 400 of the 951 sites on [EPA's] National Priority List (NPL) can be cleaned from the current fund."[3] The analyst noted that instead of the current funding level of $8.5 billion, Superfund needs at least $17 to $24 billion. Other reports suggest there may be as many as 425,000 potential sites to clean and estimate the cost to range as high as $700 billion.[4]

As of 1990 there were some 27,000 candidate sites listed for EPA to consider, and under the Superfund Amendments (SARA), which raised the tax and the level of funding, Congress has seen fit to fund citizen action to pressure EPA to act favorably when reviewing potential sites. It is obvious that EPA's Superfund program is seriously underfunded and inextricably bound by political pressures brought by interest groups who want their favorite waste site cleaned, without regard to how the riskiness of that particular site compares to others.

Besides being underfunded, the program's organic legislation established liability rules that give small producers who have no brand-name capital at risk an incentive to be less diligent in handling waste products, but more accepting of legal charges that signal their past environmental record to the public. In addition, the joint and several liability feature provides a costly environment for casualty underwriters who previously wrote liability insurance covering sudden and unexpected spills. The market for environmental insurance has been largely abandoned.

This chapter examines Superfund in the context of the liability rule that has contributed to its failure.[5] Using the logic of political economy, the chapter first develops a theoretical discussion of the efficient polluter. It then briefly outlines the history of Superfund, identifies the program's fatal flaws, and explains why the program is destined to fail. Proposals for modifying the program's flaws are included in the discussion.

II. LIABILITY AND THE EFFICIENT POLLUTER

The Static Analysis

Chemical producers and other firms use the environment along with labor, capital, and raw materials as inputs in the production of their final product. Some firms discharge wastes into rivers, streams, and municipal sewer lines for later treatment. Others emit gaseous wastes into the atmosphere. Still others arrange to haul away and bury solid waste products in underground storage locations and landfills. In many cases, polluters use all forms of environmental quality—water, air, and land—when disposing of wastes. Where property rights are established for these assets, individuals contract with polluters and require payment for the use of their environmental resources. Where private ownership is not established and the state is the manager of the resource, regulations and fees are used as rationing mechanisms. In all cases, the polluter is subject to suit when its use of the environment damages unwilling parties. The firm can be held liable and required to pay for those damages.

A polluting firm, aware of its legal environment, can take actions to minimize the total cost of using the natural environment. The firm can install pollution control equipment and treat wastes to reduce their hazardous nature. Where statutes require specific treatment techniques, which is the common approach taken under U.S. law, the firm can install the specified equipment and, having done so, purchase insurance to cover liabilities associated with equipment failure and other accidents that lead to unexpected pollution.

The level of control and insurance undertaken by the firm relates to the level of enforcement of property rights. When environmental regulation is strictly enforced or where class action suits or actions by individuals are readily brought against the firm, the firm moves to a higher level of environmental protection. Where no action is taken to enforce regulations and when no suits are brought for damages, the firm responds by reducing expenditures on pollution control and insurance. In this sense, the firm responds to market forces that are enriched by legal institutions. Given effective enforcement of laws and ready access by citizens to courts, polluting firms will balance their production of goods against the cost of using environmental and other inputs.

Does Pollution Impose Costs on Society?

Some analysts of polluting firms call attention to the external costs imposed on innocent parties when firms continue to discharge wastes after having met the expected costs of their actions, which include the purchase of insurance or allowance for the provision of self-insurance. However, the waste discharged after these steps are taken does not impose costs that are not accounted for. The prices of the firms' final product rise as insurance premiums and pollution control costs are paid and the expected costs of penalties are taken into account. Consumers of the final product are paying for the environmental use required in the production of the product, just as they pay for the cost of labor and other inputs.

When selecting the optimal combination of pollution control and insurance, the firm considers the incremental costs of each alternative. If it is cheaper to control a unit of pollution (avoid discharge of hazardous waste), the firm will treat that unit. If liability insurance is the cheaper alternative, the firm will insure against losses and discharge the unit of waste. All along, the firm will take avoidance and insurance actions so long as their expected costs are less than or no more than equal to the expected value of penalties and fines imposed when pollution exceeds the legally enforced maximum or damages a property owner. In other words, the firm's owners weigh the relative costs and benefits of treating, insuring, and discharging waste, and they minimize costs.

Some Dynamic Aspects of the Problem

There is more to consider and thus more to the story for firms that have invested in reputational capital. Multiproduct firms that produce polluting and nonpolluting products, as well as firms with brand-name recognition that simply produce environmentally intensive goods, consider another opportunity cost when choosing to pollute. Investment in brand-name capital assures quality to consumers and citizens. Negative publicity associated with suits and penalties can depreciate brand-name capital and raise marketing costs for all the products produced by the multiproduct firm.[6] Similar losses sustained by single-product firms make it more costly for the firms to build new plants and expand existing ones. The brand-name firm has to add this element of cost to other pollution control costs when determining how much pollution to discharge. All else being equal, the brand-name firm will pollute less than its generic competitor.

When Does Liability Insurance Work?

Pollution liability insurance and tort actions work effectively when the damaging effects of pollution can be traced to the polluter. In those situations, insurance contracts can specify the level of protection for each event, and insurance firms can protect themselves from claims that might be generated by sources other than their client. Those damaged by pollution have a cause of action against an identified tortfeasor, who must defend himself in court, perhaps calling on his insurer to indemnify the losses. Polluters failing to take appropriate control actions find themselves paying more claims and higher insurance premiums. The interaction of the insurer and the law forces firms to adjust behavior.

Problems arise when pollution cannot be traced to its source. Insurers have greater difficulty screening claims, and private parties seeking damages are hard pressed to specify the party to the controversy. For example, three paper mills under separate ownership that are located upstream from a community may each discharge similar wastes. One of the firms carelessly allows large amounts of toxic waste to enter the river, contaminating the community's water supply. It may be impossible to determine unambiguously which firm discharged the hazardous waste.

Since such risks are predicted in advance, insurers would not write contracts to indemnify individual firms without specifying rules of contribution that might apply in the event a claim is settled. Without insurance coverage, the firms would have to consider control costs alone when determining the appropriate level of control. In the absence of identifying which firm actually discharged the toxic waste, the court would allow the damaged citizens to bring actions against all three paper mills. Once damages were determined and awarded, the three mills could then settle their shares through litigation or negotiation.

The potential problems for producers of hazardous waste of the sort contemplated by Superfund are conceptually simpler to deal with, at least at the outset. Multiple producers of the same waste can contract with operators of waste disposal sites to handle their wastes and to be liable for future damages. Alternately, the individual polluters can keep records of their disposed waste products and purchase liability insurance to indemnify them from future claims. Cause and effect can be determined. Rules of strict liability will work effectively when citizens bring an action against particular (solvent) polluters.

Even under the best of circumstances, situations arise where safeguards fail. These can be termed social failures. Operators of hazardous waste disposal sites can go bankrupt, abandon sites, and leave no records. Firms that expected to be indemnified by operators can find the operator insolvent and without insurance. And firms that presumably kept good records of their disposal practices may find themselves bound to other firms at the same site who did not. As a result, new questions arise about liability and cause and effect. Polluters that continue in business must allow for these contingencies that spring from uncertainty.

III. CERCLA AND SUPERFUND

The Love Canal Episode

It is not possible to describe the evolution of CERCLA without touching on the event that galvanized the political forces that led to the passage of the statute. That event was Love Canal. Love Canal was an underground storage site in Niagara Falls, New York, developed and operated by Hooker Chemical Company for the disposal of hazardous chemical wastes.[7] According to public records, Hooker Chemical Company took prudent precautions when operating the storage facility and was fully aware of the risks associated with the waste products stored there. The facility was operated for a number of years, closed, and sealed. The canal, as it came to be called, was on company property. Unsuspecting individuals who might inadvertently contact the toxic wastes were guarded from doing so by the firm.

As the town of Niagara Falls expanded, the Niagara Falls School Board searched for land that could be used for the construction of a public school. Hooker Chemical was contacted by the board regarding the sale of land that contained the storage site. Hooker refused to sell the land, noting the presence of the hazardous waste site. The board persisted and indicated that the land would be condemned and taken under eminent domain proceedings if it were not sold. Hooker sold the land for a small fee in 1953 and wrote stipulations in the deed that indicated the land should not be used in ways that exposed people to the hazardous waste site.

Over the next twenty-five years, the land had been developed for homes and a public school. The stipulations had been disregarded, the storage site ruptured, and wastes seeped into homes. In August 1978, President Carter responded to the outcry that developed and named the Love Canal disaster a national emergency. The event provided the necessary momentum to pass CERCLA, which established Superfund.

Although no adverse health effects from the episode have been found, even after efforts to make a determination conducted by a panel of scientists assembled by Governor Hugh Carey, the New York State Department of Health, and the Center for Disease Control, high costs were suffered by homeowners. Hooker, the producer of the waste, was sued by the Department of Justice on behalf of EPA and by the affected property owners. Hooker settled the suit for $20 million.

Legislation for Dealing with Hazardous Waste

A review of the Hooker Chemical case leads to the conclusion that it represented a social failure, where legal and political institutions simply failed, not an accidental spill or failure by a firm to take normal precautions. In other words, Love Canal is an outlier, not an event that should form the basis for molding standard policy.

Even before Love Canal, political attention had addressed problems associated with waste management. Regulatory safeguards for current operators of landfills and waste sites had been included in the 1974 Resource Conservation and Recovery Act, which imposed cradle-to-grave rules on generators, carriers, and operators of disposal sites.[8] These rules were strengthened further by the 1984 Hazardous and Solid Waste Amendments, which banned outright the land disposal and underground injection of certain specified chemicals.

CERCLA (and Superfund) is intended to deal with problems where operators of waste sites are no longer on the scene. The legislation names 698 elements and substances as hazardous, with the categories including chemicals that are toxic, caustic, and flammable. The statute provides a Hazardous Response Fund to be used to pay the clean-up costs.[9] The fund was set at $1.6 billion and was to receive 87.5 percent of its revenues from taxes on petroleum and forty-two listed chemical feedstocks. The balance was provided from general tax revenues.[10]

The liability elements of CERCLA have to be among the most far-reaching in the legal system. Current owners of a Superfund site can be held strictly liable for the cost of cleaning it, even though they had no part in the contamination of the site. Those who transported the waste can be held liable, and all the producers of the waste can be held jointly and severally liable. The liability net is so large that it includes lending institutions that find themselves owning a site after foreclosure. Under the broadest interpretation of the statute, a lender who holds title to property during the time of a loan can be held liable for the cost of mitigating wastes. As one legal commentator puts it, the government agencies responsible for Superfund "are going beyond site owners and operators and transporting, turning to the parties with deeper pockets whose involvement...is tangential at best."[11]

Conceptual problems with CERCLA unavoidably led to difficulty. In the first place, the actors from the past may not have violated laws when storing hazardous wastes. There were no statutes to violate. Even so, the potential for damages was still present, and common law remedies were available in situations where producers were aware of the hazardous nature of their actions. Hazardous waste sites and landfills could contaminate groundwater sources of drinking water and impose other costs on unsuspecting citizens.

Individuals might bring an action against the damaging party, but there was no one to sue if the hazardous waste site was no longer managed. The firms that used the services of the waste site became the cause of damages, but their share in the liability may not have been easily identified. By establishing a fund to be nourished from taxes on existing waste producers, CERCLA provided the means to pay damages and correct problems, while EPA brought actions against the suspected dischargers on the basis of joint and several liability.

EPA has to deal with a difficult enforcement problem. As the typical Superfund process unfolds, EPA first identifies and notifies potentially responsible parties, informing each party of the other's position in the suit along with information on the waste products that had been assembled at the site.[12] Clean-up options are identified, and one is selected by EPA. The EPA then seeks to obtain settlements from the polluters, who have previously had an opportunity to negotiate and determine their individual liability. If settlements are not forthcoming, EPA commences the clean-up action or orders the polluters to do so. Negotiations then continue with the polluters, and cases are referred to the Justice Department to obtain court-ordered injunctions.

Suits are filed where the merits of the case suggest success, and those cases are usually directed toward the financially sound polluters. Elements in the decision to sue include information on the quantity of waste delivered to a site by each party; the kinds of wastes delivered, relative to their toxicity and potential damage; evidence on the sources of the wastes; and some estimate of the number of defendants that can be involved effectively in the suit.

A 1984 consent decree involving a recycling facility in Seattle illustrates the large number of defendants that can be involved in an EPA action.[13] In total, 198 waste producers and carriers participated in that site clean-up action. The possible number of suits that arise in Superfund litigation grows exponentially with the number of potentially responsible parties. If three parties are involved, it is possible for each party to sue the other two and in turn be sued by the others. That sets the limit of suits among the parties at six. If financial institutions become involved along with past and present insurance carriers, the number of potential litigants rises again. In an action like the Seattle case where 198 polluting firms became involved, it is theoretically possible for each firm to sue 197 others and be sued by that many, yielding thousands of suits. Of course, it is unlikely that the parties would want to incur the litigation costs or that any court would agree to hear that many suits on one such matter. Still, the point must be made that joint and several liability generates suits exponentially. Superfund's liability net is large.

The incentive to sue by larger firms is intensified by EPA's settlement strategy. EPA has chosen to go for 100 percent coverage of the cost of clean-up, refusing to use Superfund dollars in any situation where identifiable polluters could be expected to pay the full cost.[14] Larger polluting firms caught in clean-up situations involving smaller firms experienced a dilemma as EPA pushed toward 100 percent coverage. As a general rule, the larger firms (those with brand-name capital) wish to settle early. But as EPA pushes for 100 percent coverage, the larger firms resist covering the costs imposed by the nonsettlers. Resistance to settle delays the initiation of clean-up projects and causes litigation costs to rise. Facing delayed settlements on the one hand and pressure from concerned citizens to clean-up targeted sites on the other, EPA is pushed to use Superfund dollars to take action.

Superfund as an Insurance Pool

At first blush, Superfund has the appearances of an insurance fund. But insurance deals with identifiable risks associated with known hazards that impose costs on the insured in the normal course of doing business. By developing a pool of such exposure units, insurers can estimate the probability of damage occurring, set premiums, and fund losses for a large group of insured parties. The policy pays when an accident covered by the policy occurs. Competition among private insurance carriers promotes cost-effective controls, leads to the systematic collection of data on risks, and imposes risk-reducing management practices on insured parties.

Superfund violates insurance principles in several ways. First, the naming of a site by EPA is not a random event, nor is it related to an accident. EPA is under political pressure to identify sites and distribute funds where action is politically valuable. County-operated landfills along with abandoned chemical waste dumps can be candidates for action. A real insurer cannot estimate the expected value of damages in such an uncertain environment.

In truth, payments to Superfund are simply advances to be used in covering the unknown future cost of past actions that may never have involved the taxpayers. In contrast, liability insurance premiums are advances to cover future damages that arise after the insurance contract is written.

The joint and several liability feature of CERCLA also undermines the insurance concept. As it stands, one firm out of a large number can be found financially liable for the entire cost of cleaning a site, even if the firm contributed a small part of the waste. The generic nature of the waste and the difficulty of determining cause and effect weaken the prospects for a rule of strict liability. Liability insurers cannot operate rationally in such environments. Even so, insurance underwriters that had provided past coverage to firms that later found themselves being sued by EPA are being held liable for the firm's actions. Even worse, individual polluters have been allowed to recover from their liability insurance for damages to their own property.

The Demise of Private Pollution Liability Insurance

Problems with interpretation of insurance contract language expanded with Superfund litigation. One category of problems related to standard language limiting insured claims to damages associated with sudden and accidental spills. In a number of instances insurers were forced to pay for damages caused by slow seepage and poorly managed facilities.[15] The unexpected interpretations of contract language imposed more costs on insurance firms than their premium reserves would cover. By 1987 only one insurance company actively marketed pollution liability insurance in the United States.[16] In the same year, EPA estimated there were 100,000 firms generating hazardous wastes, and all are required to meet financial responsibility guidelines that require either insurance or a showing of financial strength for meeting potential pollution liabilities.

The problem with pollution exclusions in insurance contracts is illustrated in a New Jersey landfill case where a municipality was alleged to have erred in selecting and operating the site.[17] As a result, pollution seeped into an underground aquifer and polluted ninety-seven privately owned wells. The city sued its insurer for recovery of costs, but the insurance contract had the standard language. It provided coverage for accidental spills only. However, the court ruled in favor of the municipality, stating that the exclusion was clear but that the damage was not expected, which meant it was accidental.

That same case illustrates how insurance firms can face a multiplier effect when their contract language is disregarded. The standard policy limits the total damages to be paid for each occurrence covered by the policy. The court first required the insurance firm to pay for an event it intended to exclude from the contract and then interpreted the policy's occurrence limitation to mean per claim, not per occurrence. In other words, numerous parties can claim damage from one occurrence, and the limits will be applied to each party, not to the total of all claims.

The ninety-seven well owners were initially awarded a total of $15.9 million for their losses, including $2.1 million for emotional distress for the knowledge that their wells were contaminated. A total of $5.4 million was paid for the deterioration of quality of life for the twenty months when the plaintiffs were deprived of running water. An award of $8.2 million was made to cover medical surveillance activities for those thought to be harmed. On appeal, the higher court upheld the interpretation of the contract but reduced the total damages to $5.4 million, noting there was no evidence of any harmful health effects.[18]

In another New Jersey case, a firm leased land on the Hackensack River where it maintained storage tanks containing asphaltic oil.[19] A vandal opened the valve on one of the tanks and 14,000 gallons of oil leaked into the Hackensack River. Having cleaned up the mess, the firm filed a claim with its insurance carrier to recover costs. The insurance firm rejected the claim, citing the fact that the loss was caused by vandalism and was not an accidental spill, which the contract specified. In court, the judge sided with the firm, noting that from the firm's standpoint the loss was sudden and unexpected.

In other cases involving attempts by firms to recover the costs of environmental clean-ups from their insurance companies, courts further weakened the meaning of contract exclusions. Eventually, exclusions for all events that were not accidental, sudden, and unexpected were translated to mean a lack of intent on the part of the polluters. Any pollution, even that associated with leaking pipes and tanks that occurred over a period of years, was defined to fall within the bounds of "sudden and unexpected," so long as the polluter was not shown to have intended to pollute.

Superfund sites are often the result of decades of waste disposal, which means that many firms and many insurers and lenders can become potentially liable. Settlement negotiations can involve hundreds of firms and as many or more insurers. In one case, a polluting firm is suing 240 insurers who provided liability coverage over a thirty-seven-year period.[20] In another, some 370 insurance companies are involved. The avalanche of cases and associated litigation costs can hardly be justified if the end purpose of CERCLA is to protect citizens from the damages caused by hazardous waste.

IV. THE INDUCED BEHAVIOR OF POLLUTING FIRMS

The effects of Superfund and the demise of private insurance can now be examined in light of the theoretical discussion that spoke to the incentives faced by firms when making decisions about insurance and avoidance. In the absence of Superfund and the problem of generic waste where cause-and-effect linkages are blurred, each polluter has incentives to minimize the costs of its environmental use. A combination of insurance, avoidance actions, and protection of brand-name capital causes the firm to manage environmental inputs in ways similar to the management of other inputs. Superfund changes the incentive structure.

Imagine a situation where two firms have participated in shipping solid waste to a particular site where a waste disposal firm manages the site and insures against damages that might be imposed on unsuspecting parties. The interaction of market forces within the legal environment leads to some optimal combination of actions taken to minimize damages. Now, suppose the site is closed and the operator goes out of business. Later, the waste disposal location is defined as a Superfund site. EPA identifies the two waste shippers as potentially responsible parties and brings a suit against them to cover the cost of correcting the site. The two firms bring their insurance firms into the litigation, hoping to be indemnified for some if not all of the potential damages.

Under Superfund either or both firms can be found liable for the damages. However, the insurance contracts are written to meet a strict liability standard and to cover accidental spills and damages. If both firms are identical with respect to financial strength and brand-name capital, both will litigate the action hoping to avoid costs. They will argue that they met their legal duties at the time they participated in the waste site and that the site operator is accountable. Recognizing that the operator no longer exists and that someone will be held liable, the two operators will each attempt to avoid costs. There is an incentive for each firm to use litigation resources up to the expected value of claims brought against them.

The insurer will argue that its policy does not cover the event. Recognizing that past court decisions have given alternate interpretation of contracts holding insurers liable, the insurance firms will tend to use litigation resources up to the expected value of the liability they may face. The sum of litigation costs can be quite large as each party works to avoid clean-up costs. In the absence of perfect forecasts regarding the outcome, and assuming risk aversion on the part of each litigant, the total resources expended in fighting the suit may exceed the value of the claims that might be avoided.

Now assume that the two firms are different. One firm has national brand-name capital at risk and the other firm does not. The firm with the reputation will spend more to defend itself, if it decides to litigate. More likely, the brand-name firm will seek to avoid litigation that advertises a questionable environmental record. It will have a greater incentive to settle without litigation and sue its insurance firm.

As experience with Superfund developed, the American Insurance Association retained a consulting firm to estimate the expected cost of litigation for Superfund activities alone.[21] The consultants assumed that 1,800 sites would eventually be placed on the Superfund list and that the average clean-up cost would run to $8.1 million, giving a total of $14.9 billion. Drawing on recorded litigation costs per site, the consultants found that total litigation expenditures would run to at least $8 billion, or 55 percent of the direct cost of cleaning the sites. Of the $8 billion, 79 percent would be paid by private parties. Elimination of litigation would release enough resources to clean more than 400 additional sites.

The insurance industry is now largely out of the picture. They have generally abandoned the market. Large firms can self-insure, which has the effect of limiting competition from the more vulnerable small firms. Smaller firms, particularly those lacking brand-name capital, can gain by delaying the settlement process, thereby externalizing their costs to larger firms that self-insure. Meanwhile, Superfund sites await action, and litigation costs consume resources that might be used for some beneficial purpose.

EPA's failure to deliver the expected level of clean sites surfaced when Congress evaluated EPA's Superfund record. Disappointed with progress under the original Superfund legislation, Congress was made aware of the insurance demise and related issues when Superfund reauthorization was debated in 1985–1986, but none of the insurance-crippling features was changed. Instead, Congress took the regulatory burden on itself, tightened timetables, increased appropriations and Superfund taxes, and opened the door wider for the inclusion of additional sites.[22] Under the Superfund Amendments and Reauthorization Act of 1986 (SARA), EPA was required to begin remedial work at a rate of not less than 175 sites annually through 1989. (By 1990, the agency was again behind schedule.) The agency was mandated to speed up its internal review of candidate sites, without considering the relative risks across sites. Reaching further to please members of the electorate who may have been unsuccessful in getting a particular site targeted for clean-up, SARA assures a long life to Superfund by authorizing private parties to petition EPA to perform risk assessments on any site, whether or not the site has been placed on the national priority listing. Further controversy is assured by SARA requirements that Superfund site communities be given grants for the purpose of contesting EPA's selected clean-up remedies.

V. CONCLUSION AND RECOMMENDATIONS

As currently constituted, Superfund and CERCLA offer few incentives for efficient action by polluters. Smaller firms have an incentive to avoid clean-up costs, while larger ones have an incentive to settle early. EPA has an incentive to conserve Superfund dollars by bringing more suits and extending the settlement period, and communities have an incentive to join the Superfund gravy train.

The words *hazardous waste* are emotionally laden. When a community learns that an old waste site, even a landfill previously operated by the community itself, may be risky, they naturally seek to do something about it. When the community learns that federal funds can be tapped to clear away old eyesores, they demand even more action. Superfund has evolved to a pork barrel.

Politicians naturally find Superfund an attractive process. They can promise assistance to communities, pressure EPA, and condemn polluters while urging communities in their districts to push for action. Excess demand for political favors of the sort promised by Superfund makes politicians all the more valuable to constituents.

The liability rule in Superfund is logical on its face. If cause and effect cannot be identified, it makes sense to bring actions against all parties who might have damaged others by their environmental use. However, Superfund has to do with actions taken in the past, actions that were generally legal at the time and, more often than not, generate little in the way of harm to exposed citizens. According to EPA's own reviews, most Superfund sites rank low on the list of environmental hazards that should be corrected. Put another way, there are far more serious environmental hazards that deserve attention long before the typical Superfund site is cleaned.[23]

Even though damages are not proved, and need not be, polluting firms must defend themselves against the possibility of paying more than their share of the costs of correcting a Superfund site. The resulting dynamics generate a costly process that yields little in the way of measurable ecological benefits for the nation but much in the way of benefits for selected communities.

What are the potential remedies for Superfund? A review of experience with the current procedure suggests going back to the drawing boards. What is the problem to be addressed? It is generally agreed that the problem relates to current desires to improve a situation that was generated innocently, for the most part, by actors now difficult to identify, costly to find, and judgment-proof in many cases. Who benefits from actions taken to clean up old landfills and waste sites? Communities and landowners in close proximity to the site. Who should pay for such improvements? The benefit principle of public finance theory suggests that those who gain from having a cleaner environment should pay.

Since it is costly to identify and prosecute firms that contributed to old waste sites, and since the beneficiaries are generally located near the site, logic suggests that Superfund should be "decriminalized." The entire notion of fault and liability rests on the political need to obtain revenues at a time when the federal government is strapped to fund the current budget. If fault and liability are removed from the problem, Superfund becomes a standard government pork-barrel program. Just as the Corps of Engineers is funded with taxpayer dollars to dredge harbors and rivers that have become silted by the actions of upstream users who are difficult to track down, EPA could be funded to oversee the clean-up of abandoned waste sites. Appropriations from general revenue would identify the amount to be spent, and communities would have to struggle to obtain government funds in the political marketplace. Taking that approach would cap the expenditures to be obligated in a given period, eliminate litigation costs, and force communities to define priorities when going after federal funds.

A related proposal calls for establishment of a National Environmental Trust Fund, like the federal highway trust fund.[24] Under that proposal, a fee would be attached to all commercial/industrial property-casualty insurance premiums paid in the United States. A similar fee would be developed for firms that self-insure. Proceeds from the fee would then be dedicated to clean-up activities. The notion of liability would be erased from the law.

Another alternative is to eliminate Superfund as a federally operated program. Since the benefits and costs of hazardous waste sites are local in nature, there is little reason to have a federal program. It is possible that EPA has expertise not generally available to state and local governments, but that expertise can be purchased with local funds. If the problem were left to state and local governments, the linkages between benefits and costs would be made clear. Local citizens who will bear the costs of their actions would be much more careful when "demanding" public action to clean an old landfill or waste site. They would also tend to stop far short of perfection when mitigating the effects of past polluters.

While these policy options may provide the basis for debating the relative merits of the current program and its liability rules, what are the prospects for change? The history of federal government efforts to control the use of the environment suggests there is little prospect for change. Even though Superfund is currently underfunded and unlikely to produce large numbers of improved sites, the program itself is exceedingly valuable to elected officials. Programs operated by local and state governments provide no benefits to federal politicians. Their political capital is enhanced when they deliver tax funds paid by other people to the constituents in their states and districts. Since redistribution of income is the political game being played, Superfund will likely continue to operate with little in the way of substantive change.

NOTES

1. For background discussion, see Robert E. Litan and Clifford Winston, eds., *Liability Perspective and Policy* (Washington, D.C.: The Brookings Institution, 1988), pp. 128–54; Raymond A. Rea, "Hazardous Waste Pollution: The Need for a Different Approach," *Environmental Law* 12 (1982): 443–67; and for a discussion of CERCLA, see *Environmental Law Handbook*, 8th ed. (Rockville, Md.: Government Institute, Inc., 1985), p. 61.

2. On this, see "Waste Site Cleanup Liability May Be Hazardous to Lenders," *Insight* (November 13, 1989): 42–44.

3. Thomas P. Grumbly, "Voluntary Cleanup: The Key to Maximizing Superfund Resources," *National Environmental Enforcement Journal* 3, 5 (June 1988): 12–16. The number of Superfund sites recognized by the EPA was over 1,200 in 1990.

4. See Mautice R. Greenberg, "Financing the Clean-up of Hazardous Waste: The National Environmental Trust Fund," (New York: American International Group, Inc., March 2, 1989).

5. See Bruce Yandle, "Environmental Policy in the Next Decade," (Washington, D.C.: Manufacturers' Alliance for Productivity Improvement, 1988).

6. For related literature on this point, see Mark L. Mitchell and Michael T. Maloney, "Crisis in the Cockpit? The Role of Market Forces in Promoting Air Travel Safety," *Journal of Law and Economics* 32, 2 (October 1989): 329–55.

7. This discussion draws on Peter Huber, "Environmental Hazards and Liability Law," in *Liability Perspectives and Policy*, ed. Robert E. Litan and Clifford Winston (Washington, D.C.: The Brookings Institution, 1988), pp. 128–54; Eric Zuesse, "Love Canal: The Truth Seeps Out," *Reason*, (February 1981), pp. 17–33; and Raymond A. Rea, "Hazardous Waste Pollution: The Need for a Different Statutory Approach," *Environmental Law*, 12 (1982): 443–67.

8. For discussion, see *Environmental Law Handbook*, p. 61.

9. See "Superfund: A Game of Chance," *Natural Resources and Environment* 1, 3 (Fall 1985), a symposium issue.

10. See *Environmental Law Handbook*, p. 134.

11. See "Waste Site Cleanup Liability," pp. 42–43.

12. For more discussion on this, see F. Henry Habicht II, "Encouraging Settlements under Superfund," *Natural Resources & Environment* 1, 3 (Fall 1985): 3–6.

13. Ibid., p. 6.

14. On this, see Richard G. Stoll and David B. Graham, "Need for Changes in EPA's Settlement Policy," *Natural Resources & Environment* 1, 3 (Fall 1985): 7–9.

15. See Peter Huber, "The Environmental Liability Dilemma," *CPCU Journal*, (December 1987), pp. 206–16.

16. U.S. General Accounting Office, "Hazardous Waste: Issues Surrounding Insurance Availability," GAP/RCED–88–2 (Washington, D.C.: U.S. General Accounting Office, October 1987).

17. See Bradford W. Rich, "Environmental Litigation and the Insurance Dilemma," *Risk Management* (December 1985), pp. 34–41.

18. Such court actions obviously contribute to underwriting problems and the exiting of underwriters from the environmental hazards market. However, before exiting the insurance firms must still bear the cost of litigating suits brought against them when past policies were in force, as well as the cost of awards won by damaged parties.

19. For details see Eugene R. Anderson and Abraham C. Moskowitz, "How Much Does the CGL Pollution Exclusion Really Exclude?" *Risk Management* (April 1984), pp. 29–34.

20. See "Financing the Clean-up of Hazardous Waste."

21. Ibid., p. 41.

22. See James J. Florio, "Congress as Reluctant Regulators: Hazardous Waste Policy in the 1980s," *Yale Journal on Regulation* 3, 2 (Spring 1986): 351–82.

23. See "Unfinished Business: A Comparative Assessment of Environmental Problems: Overview Report," (Washington, D.C.: U.S. Environmental Protection

Agency, February 1987). Also see Paul R. Portney, "Reforming Environmental Regulation: Three Modest Proposals," *Issues in Science and Technology*, 4, 2 (Winter 1988): 74–81.

   24: See "Financing the Clean-up of Hazardous Waste," *supra* note 4.

9

Consumer Protection, Government Liability, and the Flammability Rule

Gordon Shuford and Bruce Yandle

I. INTRODUCTION

If only by its sheer volume, federal regulation in the 1970s was marked by efforts to rearrange the burden of risk in consumer markets. Where risk could not be reduced, liability for harm was shifted from consumers and workers to producers, retailers, and manufacturers. Following congressional guidance, the Federal Trade Commission embarked on an effort to become the nation's largest consumer law firm. The Department of Transportation unveiled its new National Highway Traffic Safety Administration. Occupational safety and health became a major area of regulatory concern in the Department of Labor, and the Environmental Protection Agency became the largest civilian agency in the federal government. Each of these agencies had a specific focus, and each one was involved in shifting rules of liability among participants in various markets.

In 1972, the Consumer Product Safety Commission (CPSC) joined the growing list of regulatory agencies and, as its name implies, focused its efforts on consumer goods not already regulated by other agencies such as the Food and Drug Administration and the Department of Agriculture. In line with its work, the new CPSC set out to develop product standards to be followed by all manufacturers in its purview.[1] Like the EPA, which was formed from parts of preexisting agencies, the CPSC received elements from older agencies that had struggled to regulate consumer goods.

In a sense, the expansion of the market for consumer protection brought regulatory specialization. Activities housed previously in larger multiproduct agencies were transferred to the new agency.[2] Enforcement of the Federal Hazardous Substances Act and the Poison Prevention Packaging Act was transferred to the CPSC from the Department of Health, Education, and Welfare. Responsibilities for the Refrigerator Safety Act came from the

Commerce Department and the Federal Trade Commission (FTC). And of key importance to this chapter, enforcement responsibilities for the Flammable Fabrics Act of 1953 were transferred from the Department of Commerce.

Since 1972, economists and others have examined the CPSC record in an effort to assess its effectiveness in meeting its legislative mandate. The investigators have sought to answer one principal question: Did CPSC actions actually reduce the riskiness of the products it chose to regulate? Or did the agency's actions simply rearrange rules of liability in consumer markets while simultaneously redistributing incomes and costs?

Two major studies conclude that the CPSC has not benefited consumers by reducing death rates associated with several hazardous products. Linneman (1980) found no significant beneficial effect from the CPSC 1973 standards for mattress flammability. Viscusi's (1985) study of three major areas of CPSC activity—fire and burns, poisoning, and ingestions—also found no significant beneficial effect from CPSC regulations. These studies suggest that the CPSC Act generated few benefits that accrued to the large mass of American consumers. However, that conclusion does not necessarily mean that no one or group of consumers and producers benefited. Put differently, instead of being efficiency enhancing, which means they provide widespread gains across the economy, the CPSC enforcement actions may have been largely redistributional—some gained, but others lost.

The Coase Theorem implies that generally there are no efficiency gains generated when liability is shifted from buyers to sellers.[3] To illustrate, a move from *caveat emptor* to *caveat venditor* may reduce consumer search costs when they seek to determine which product is least risky. At the same time, specification of how products will be produced while shifting liability can raise production costs, cause consumers to believe that all products are safer than they really are, and give producers who happen already to meet the new standard opportunities to drive competitors from the market.

In this chapter, we focus on distributional effects generated by changes in producer liability and the implementation of rules that derived from one major CPSC rule. However, the regulatory story does not end with that focus. As the story unfolds, the federal government becomes involved in a struggle regarding its own liability when regulatory actions impose high costs on producers and produce hardly any benefits for the consuming public. The struggle over liability—private versus public—becomes a major element in the story.

Our analysis addresses the application of the Flammable Fabric Act to children's sleepwear, a regulatory episode later aborted when the chief flame-retarding chemical used—Tris—was found to be a carcinogen. In our review of the record, we describe the candidates for redistribution through regulation. These include public interest groups who lobbied for safety, the producers of fiber used in the production of fabric sold to apparel manufacturers, the producers of fabric, the apparel industry itself, and the producers of flame retardants for the textile/apparel industry used in the production of children's sleepwear.[4]

The chapter is organized as follows: The next section describes events and institutional facts associated with the passage of the flammability standards ultimately enforced by the CPSC. The following part discusses elements of a special interest theory used to explain the behavior of the apparel, cotton and synthetic fiber, textile, and chemical manufacturers as they participated in the development of the flammability regulations. That section offers testable hypotheses regarding the regulation-induced import restrictions and the distributional effects of the rule. We describe a coalition that formed within an apparel trade association that included synethetic fiber, fabric, and apparel producers. The members of the coalition, who arguably sought to influence the form and effects of the final regulation, become elements in a separate empirical test of the effects generated in production channels by the regulatory episode. The fourth section reports empirical findings of those tests.

The question of government liability is the key element in section five of the chapter, which examines the postban events—the adjustment period—and deals with the question of government liability as it surfaced in the legislative debates. Key events involving court and legislative actions are identified and become the focus of a final battery of financial market tests using the three industry portfolios examined in Section IV. The last section gives a few final thoughts on the research.

II. BACKGROUND: THE PARTICIPANTS IN THE STRUGGLE

How the Rule Developed

The story of CPSC flammability regulation begins on June 30, 1953, when the Flammable Fabric Act (FFA) was enacted by Congress. After that and until 1972, the act was under the jurisdiction of the Department of Commerce (Commerce). The wording of the law left little doubt about liability for producers of clothing. The act overrode common law remedies and shifted liability from consumers, who could no longer contract around a rule of liability, to producers. The statute made unlawful the manufacture or sale of any wearing apparel or item so highly flammable as to be dangerous when worn. The FFA was amended in 1967 to include all textile apparel and household furnishings. The 1967 act also empowered the Secretary of Commerce to promulgate standards without having the prior approval of Congress.[5] On January 21, 1970, Commerce gave notice that a flammability standard might be required for children's wearing apparel. The notice stated that evidence indicated high risk for young children. Commerce data showed that children under nine years of age were 1.5 times more likely to be burned than those in other age groups.

Commerce announced the first children's sleepwear standard on July 27, 1971, to be effective twelve months later. The regulation recognized the possibility that some firms might not be able to meet the regulation by allowing products to be sold at retail for twenty-four months if they were labeled to show the products were not in compliance with the standard, FF 3-71. A similar regulation (standard FF 5-74) for older children's sleepwear was proposed by Commerce on March 6, 1973. The final rule for those size categories was promulgated by the CPSC on May 1, 1974, with all products to be in full compliance by May 1975.[6]

Once the flammability standards were in place, producers struggled to find a treatment that would satisfy the standard. Tris (2,3-Dibromoprophyl Phosphate) became the chief treatment used by sleepwear producers. However, after a brief time, Tris was found to be a carcinogen. Efforts to reduce risk or shift liability in one dimension of consumer activity generated new risks and liabilities in another. The carcinogenic possibility was first raised in 1975, and on April 8, 1977, Tris was banned from use in children's sleepwear.[7] The ban was all-encompassing. All affected products in process, in shipments, on display for sale, or already sold, were ordered by the CPSC to be repurchased by the garment manufacturers.

Cotton Producers and Apparel Manufacturers

Like many regulations before and since, the CPSC regulation drew fire from the affected industry. Rules of logic and American politics predict that trade associations will come to the fore. The flammability standards were no exception. Attacks came from the American Apparel Manufacturers Association (AAMA), Cotton, Inc., and others who argued the rule was neither reasonable nor technologically practical, which was another way of saying there was no known method for meeting the standard without disrupting the sleepwear industry. Since the standard was to be met in one year, existing treatments offered the only means for meeting the standard. Most firms met the regulation by treating fabric with Tris, a chemical already used in the foam plastic industry as a flame retardant for auto seat cushions and produced by five chemical companies under a license held by Michigan Chemical Company.[8]

Looking back at the episode, we can clearly see that cotton producers had an interest in the flammability standard, one interest that became more intense as time passed. But while the facts support this view, there is only weak evidence of lobbying at the time of the rule making and ban.[9] Why would cotton producers have such a stake in the outcome? And why might such a vulnerable interest group not seek to influence the rules? Before the standard, 85 percent of domestically consumed sleepwear contained 100 percent cotton fabric. That share was destined to fall to zero, since cotton could not survive the requirement for continued protection after fifty washings. Sleepwear made from blends of cotton, polyester, rayon, and nylon fell to zero. By the time the episode reached its peak, the regulation had induced a shift to 100 percent Tris-treated polyester and acetate fabric, favoring specialized producers of synthetic fibers and licensed flame-retarding chemical producers.

Our efforts to explain the rather nonchalant attitude taken by cotton producers led us to three possible explanations. First, in 1972 the affected children's sleepwear producers consumed 34.9 million square yards of cotton fabric out of a total cotton fabric consumption of 10 billion square yards, slightly more than 0.3 percent of total consumption.[10] Since World War II, apparel producers had increasingly substituted away from cotton fabric as they responded to consumer preferences for low-care synthetics. The loss of the sleepwear market represented another defeat, albeit a very small one.

Second, the flammability standard was long expected, though its details were not, and the cotton industry knew that cotton could not be treated in ways that maintained consumer acceptance of the finished product. At the time, however, cotton producers may have had a greater regulatory concern than the flammability standard. The Occupational Safety and Health Administration was in the process of developing a cotton dust standard that would affect every stage of cotton processing for all fabric, no matter what the product destination. That rule would raise the cost of the natural fibers relative to synthetics.[11]

Third, unlike the chemical, synthetic fiber, and apparel producers, cotton producers were already cartelized by the U.S. Department of Agriculture. A rich program of government price supports and income maintenance offered a potential buffer to external forces that might adversely affect the industry. To the extent that rent-seeking, or rent-preserving, strategies explain partly the demand for the flammability regulation, the associated motivation to resist the regulation was relatively weak for cotton interests. Our preliminary search for changes in cotton prices and production in association with the flammability regulations gave no encouragement for productive statistical testing. While cotton producers may have sustained wealth losses from the Tris episode, we found no way to estimate them.

The Sleepwear Industry

Perhaps recognizing that the CPSC standard would somehow be met, but not knowing how, the apparel industry had other reasons to be concerned about a costly regulation. Typical of the industry's modern history, apparel producers were caught up in a global struggle for the U.S. sleepwear market.

Any increase in production costs that cut disproportionately across domestic firms would push marginal firms out of the market.

Import penetration had been increasing in the United States and United Kingdom from 1963 until the 1970s, when both countries adopted flammability standards. Asian imports continued to penetrate the Canadian and European markets through the decade of the 1970s.[12] Like the entire apparel market, imports as a percentage of U.S. domestic production of children's sleepwear showed a large increase from 1967 to 1972, before the flammability standard, even though for demographic reasons the domestic market was declining. In 1967 there were 1,025 U.S. firms that manufactured products in the women's underwear and children's sleepwear category. By 1972 the number had fallen 20 percent.

Global struggles over the U.S. market were nothing new to the American apparel industry, which periodically called on politicians to come to its aid. Imports had been regulated since 1962 by the Long-Term Arrangement Regarding International Trade in Cotton Textiles, which limited growth of imports of cotton goods in domestic markets. After several renewals, the Arrangement expired in December 1973, and a new multifiber agreement, more desirable from the domestic industry's point of view, took effect on January 1, 1974. The new agreement covered more products and fibers than the older one. However, even that protection was not firm enough to offset the effects of differential costs and losses in demand that follow from higher prices.

The Fiber/Fabric/Apparel Coalition

Unlike the cotton producers, the apparel industry rose to meet the regulatory challenge, calling on its chief trade association to organize and lead the battle. A committee was formed in the industry's trade group, the American Apparel Manufacturers Association (AAMA), to study, monitor, and advise the organization in its lobbying efforts. Committee members included twenty New York Stock Exchange-listed producers of synthetic fibers, fabric, and apparel. Membership on the Apparel Products Safety Committee revealed interest in the rule and indicated the potential effects the rules might have across firms that provide apparel to consumers. The affected industries were large and, with the exception of the producers of synthetic fibers, involved a large number of firms. The fiber producers, which included American Enka, Eastman Chemicals, Celanese, and Du Pont, provided an inelastically supplied product at the origin of the apparel production channel. The producers of the flame-retarding chemical were similarly situated.

The Chemical Treatment Industry

There was a small number of chemical firms that produced Tris, and the production of flame-retarding chemicals was a very small part of the total sales of the domestic chemical firms in the 1970s. But in the period between 1969 and 1977, the outlook became far more promising. Regulation was the driving force, as mentioned in a 1970 trade magazine article:

Commerce has taken the first steps under the FFA ... including a recent proposed flammability standard for carpets and rugs, expected issuance in the near future of notices that new flammability standards may be needed for bedding and for general wearing apparel. The steps taken and planned also indicate greater growth for flame-retardant finishing compounds used on fabrics.[13]

Later that year, the president of Stauffer Chemical Company reported that he saw a "healthy future for flame-retardant additives that go into textiles."[14] A comprehensive estimate of the growth of flame-retardant chemical output publicized the next year by Stauffer Chemical Company indicated that new and proposed government regulations would increase industry sales of those chemicals from 150 to 193 million pounds in 1971 to as much as 851 pounds in 1975 for apparel production alone. The report estimated that flame retardants for nonapparel uses would reach a total volume of 3.5 to 4.5 billion pounds by 1975.[15]

Enforcement and Monitoring

The predicted growth in demand for flame-retardant chemicals was increased further by the enforcement policies of the FTC and CPSC. In 1970, FTC Chairman Caspar W. Weinberger announced that his agency would issue cease-and-desist orders for all firms that produced noncomplying fabrics detected in U.S. retail markets.[16] Relying on an old FTC regulatory instrument that dated back to the agency's founding, Weinberger indicated that the FTC would impose high costs on noncomplying firms by immediately publicizing the identification of untreated products rather than quietly negotiating a settlement.[17] By June 1970, 106 such FTC press releases had been distributed.

FTC and CPSC labeling and record-keeping requirements compelled all manufacturers and importers of regulated sleepwear to maintain written records of date of manufacture, source and quantity of input materials, description of fiber content, and the kind of flame retardant applied to all fabric. The record-keeping requirement simplified regulatory monitoring of compliance by producers of synthetic fibers as well as for the producers of flame retardants.

Furthermore, the regulations required premarket certification by all garment producers. Domestic manufacturers were required to use statistically based sampling techniques to exclude substandard items from the market. Importers were required to apply the same techniques after foreign-produced sleepwear arrived at U.S. ports. Importers faced additional warehousing and

shipping costs not felt by domestic producers, and foreign producers incurred the additional cost of shipping flame-retardant chemicals to and from
the point of manufacture, or finding an approved alternative for satisfying
the standard. For these reasons, coupled with the short time allowed for
meeting the standards, U.S.–produced Tris became a higher cost hurdle
faced by foreign apparel producers.

III. WHAT ECONOMIC THEORY TELLS US

Rent Seeking and the Demand for Standards

The institutional story of the CPSC's flammability standard presents a
picture of shifting liability, emerging regulatory standards, output restrictions, and mandatory demand for new chemical treatments that could affect
synthetic fiber producers, textile fabric firms, specialty chemical producers,
and the import-sensitive apparel industries. The short time allowed for
meeting the CPSC standard predicted the adoption of an existing chemical
treatment in the short run as opposed to a longer-run development of new
flame-resisting fibers. Both the short- and long-run prospects implied that
owners of existing synthetic fiber-production capital might gain since it was
clear that cotton fibers could not be treated adequately for flammability.
The pressure of time also led to the use of Tris. Availability of the chemical
additive and the enforcement and monitoring requirements of the regulation
imposed differential costs on the producers of imported sleepwear.

All these considerations lead us to argue that Tris—the ultimate flame
retardant—became the key element in a regulatory episode that favored the
licensed Tris producers and domestic sleepwear and fabric producers over
foreign ones. Not knowing that Tris would be banned, these economic
agents saw potential gain in the regulation.

The possibilities that Tris might link together a loose regulatory cartel
are fortified by several institutional facts. There were a small number of
synthetic fiber producers and a few licensed firms that produced and marketed the flame retardant, the assistance of the FTC and CPSC was available
in monitoring and enforcing the regulation, record-keeping requirements
revealed the sources of the chemical retardant, and costly publicity was used
for punishing noncomplying producers of sleepwear.[18]

Along with these relatively well-defined interests, one must consider a
second element that enters a theory of regulatory demand for consumer
protection. That element relates to stories of sharply different interest groups
that coalesce in political struggles to accomplish the same end. Sometimes
labeled the theory of bootleggers and Baptists, the theory suggests that the
"Baptist" element in regulatory struggles is often crucial to the bootleggers.
Bootleggers like laws that limit the sale of alcoholic beverages through
legitimate outlets. Baptists like those laws also. By having one group that

appeals to higher moral standards, the other group gains economic rents.[19] In the flammability episode, some parents and other special interest groups raised the issue of burned children in their call for a government regulation that might reduce risks. Interestingly, earlier efforts by retailers to market higher-priced flame-resistant sleepwear had been unsuccessful. The mass market simply did not support the product. Quite possibly, an industry-wide regulation would spread the cost of the desired product across the entire population. In any case, the addition of the resources of the special interest groups arguably reduced the lobbying costs of those who simply wanted to conserve profits.[20]

The potential bootlegger-Baptist result was mentioned in a 1971 magazine article. Discussing the flammability episode, the article stated that "an unlikely coalition of mothers and some chemical companies is pleased with the newly promulgated standard." The article went on to explain that mothers liked the standard for the protection of their children, and certain chemical firms stood to profit from increased demand for flame retardants.[21]

Finally, there is a third element to the theory we draw on. McChesney has argued that regulatory threats can be used politically to expropriate quasi-rents from firms that employ specialized factors.[22] The threat of costly regulation elicits efforts by a targeted industry to deflect the regulatory action. In this case, the textile/apparel industry was in a peculiar position. The industry stood to gain protection from imports, but would sustain the increased costs of flammability treatment and possible revenue losses due to higher prices. Further, lacking legal barriers that might delay expansion of output, any net gain from the restrictions could quickly be dissipated by increased domestic production. Alternately, expected rents would provide the funds to be used to lobby for particular features in the flammability rules. In this sense, the flammability regulation was a two-edged sword. If the apparel/textile industry was engaged in a regulatory struggle for either retention or expansion of profits, rentless rent seeking would likely be the final result.

Three Propositions

This summary of theories and the situation existing in the children's sleepwear industry during the early 1970s leads us to state three propositions that can be tested statistically.

1. The U.S. domestic sleepwear producers gained an import restriction. Consumer protection was converted to industry protection.
2. Owners of firms engaged in the production of apparel, fabric, and synthetic fibers gained positive abnormal returns in association with the flammability regulations and suffered abnormal negative returns when Tris was banned.
3. The owners of U.S. producers of Tris gained wealth from the regulation-induced

cartel that managed the sale of Tris during the period Tris was applied to sleepwear.

The three propositions are stated in terms of abnormal returns, which are unexpected gains and losses generated by the Tris episode. Modern financial markets analysis allows us to estimate those effects and draw inferences about the episode's effects.

While abnormal returns might accrue to the owners of the affected industries, there is another financial market effect that also can be isolated. Over long periods of time, the shares of particular firms and industries are driven by investor buying and selling to assume a relative relationship with respect to the shares of all other firms and industries traded in the market. When that relationship becomes stable, one can predict movements of particular stocks when the overall market moves. For example, a 1 percent increase in the all-stock average of the New York Stock Exchange might predict a 1 percent change in a particular stock. In that case, the stock is said to be no more risky than the market in total. Larger or smaller proportional movements imply that a stock is more or less risky than the market.

The relationship between a particular stock's movement and the market's movements is termed systematic risk. It is possible that regulatory events such as Tris destabilize investor perceptions of the riskiness of a stock so that systematic risk changes. For example, an industry's returns relative to the market could shift to a lower (or higher) level, if the regulation had permanent effects that made the industry more (or less) like all firms in the market. Being more specific, the Tris regulation could stabilize fibermakers' profits due to the elimination of cotton competition. On the other hand, higher profits induced by the regulations, and related abnormal returns, would be reduced through industry expansion. The regulations could also destabilize earnings relative to the market in the apparel industry, while reductions in profitability might be observed in financial markets due to the quick adjustments expected for the industry. Our statistical tests were organized to isolate both abnormal returns and changes in systematic risk for the industry segments.

IV. THE FIRST STATISTICAL TESTS

Our first set of statistical tests focused on the three propositions stated in the last section, with the first having to do with international competition. Once these tests are presented, discussion of government liability enters the story, and that generates a second set of empirical tests.

A Model of Imported Children's Sleepwear

Empirical support for the first proposition must show that the CPSC regulation is significantly associated with a reduction in imported children's sleepwear. To test this hypothesis, we developed an import penetration model that stated:

$$IMP = f(INC, PRICE, DUM\ 72, DUM\ 75, BAN)$$

The dependent variable (IMP) is the total quantity of imported sleepwear divided by the quantity produced domestically, INC is real total disposable income, PRICE is the apparel consumer price index (ACPI) divided by the all-items CPI, and DUM 72 marks the data for the first regulation (Commerce FF 3-71), promulgated in July 1971, and is set equal to one for the years between 1972 and 1984. DUM 75 marks the data for a second rule (Commerce FF 5-74), promulgated in June 1972 and is set equal to one for the years between 1975 and 1984. The second rule extended coverage of the flammability standard to larger sizes of sleepwear. Finally, BAN indicates the period affected by the ban on Tris and is set equal to one for the period between 1977 and 1984. The three dummy variables are layered to reflect the fact that none of the regulations was rescinded even though Tris was banned. The data set used annual observations for all variables for the years 1967 to 1984.[23] We had no well-developed prediction for the effect of INCOME. Even though we expected sleepwear imports to increase with income, we had no way to argue that imports would increase more than domestic shipments, which are also income sensitive. Recall, our dependent variable measures penetration, not shipments.

Competing theoretical explanations of the relationship between import penetration and the relative consumer price index for apparel made it difficult to predict the effects of that variable. Given the construction of the variable, if the change in the relative price was driven more heavily by relative price increases on imported goods, import penetration will fall, which is what our discussion suggests. However, if the relative price index is driven upward because of relative increases in domestic prices, import penetration will increase.

The import penetration proposition argues that the two regulatory events, DUM 72 and DUM 75, will have a negative effect, which is to say importers will suffer relative to domestic producers. Cutting the other way, the ban on Tris, which weakens the effects of the regulation yet also brings confusion into markets, was predicted to have a positive effect on import penetration.

After compiling data for each of the variables, we made an ordinary least squares regression estimate of the model.[24] The statistical results showed that the two regulatory events identified by DUM 72 and DUM 75 had negative effects on import penetration. Those effects were approximately three times larger in 1972 than in 1975. The effect of the ban was also negative and highly significant. In fact, its effect was larger than the combined effects of the two regulatory variables. What might explain this result?

On thinking about the finding, we concluded that the import market bore the major brunt of the episode because of confusion that entered consumer markets. Apparently, U.S. consumers moved to brand-name merchandise and sellers who offered greater assurances than foreign producers. Given the somewhat hysterical nature of the situation, which was abetted by news stories about cancer as well as the riskiness of flaming sleepwear, it may be understandable that consumers would be willing to pay a premium for U.S. goods.

All of the other variables in the model were also significant. The sign on the coefficient of INCOME was positive, indicating that import penetration increases with adjusted real disposable income. The effect of the relative price index was negative, which supports the notion that higher relative prices for U.S. apparel leads to less import penetration.

Financial Market Tests of Fiber/Textile/Apparel Producers

The second proposition states that the flammability episode initially increased the wealth of the owners of firms engaged in the production of apparel, fabric, and synthetic fibers. To investigate that proposition, we developed a portfolio of firms from the affected industries. Viewing membership on the apparel trade association's flammability subcommittee as an indication of deeper interest in the problem, we scanned that membership list and selected firms whose stock was traded on the New York exchange.

Taking the committee membership listing, we formed three equally weighted portfolios based on product categories that carry production from basic fibers to fabric producers and on to producers of apparel.[25] We then undertook event analyses to test for wealth effects. The composition of each of the portfolios tested is shown in Table 9.1. The first portfolio, labeled "fiber," included producers of synthetic fibers, which we predicted would gain from the substitution away from cotton fibers.

A second portfolio, labeled "fabric," was composed of firms that chiefly produce fabric, as opposed to finished consumer goods. There was no apparent restriction on fabric output associated with the regulation, but firms in the industry incurred the cost of applying flame-retarding chemicals, a cost that competitive forces passed to apparel producers. We expected no unusual gains or losses for the fabric portfolio.

The last portfolio formed from the committee membership included producers of apparel and bears that name. We make very tentative predictions for this portfolio for two reasons. First, none of the listed firms specialized in sleepwear, although there could have been expectations of an expansion of the regulation to include a wider range of garments. (None of the typically small, specialized sleepwear producers is listed on the NYSE.) Second, we had observed a decline in import penetration in the first model, but believed that any resulting rents would be dissipated quickly. We expected to observe weak positive returns in association with the two regulations and weak negative returns in conjunction with the ban.

Table 9.1
American Apparel Manufacturers Association Members, Included in Portfolio Analyses

---

FIBER

American Enka
Celanese
Du Pont
Eastman Chemical

FABRIC

Beaunit
Champion Products
Duplan
M. Lowenstein
Reeves Brothers
J. P. Stevens
Wayne Knitting

APPAREL

Blue Bell
Cluett Peabody
Farah
Genesco
Kayser Julius
Kellwood
Manhattan
Phillips Van Heusen

The apparel portfolio contains firms that could be viewed as competitors to the smaller fringe firms not included in the financial market test. That raises the possibility of observing what appear to be perverse outcomes. Expected losses for the smaller firms could register positive returns for the larger ones in the portfolio.[26]

We employed a modified market model approach in our study of the flammability episode that states:

$$R_{it} = a + B_1R_{mt} + B_2D_t + B_3(D_tR_{mt}) + e_{it}$$

where R, the dividend-adjusted return to the portfolio at time t, is a function of a constant, the market return (R_{mt}), the event dummy (D_t), a slope-shift dummy variable (D_tR_{mt}) to test for the stability of B_2, and a random error term (e_{it}). Any significant changes registered in the slope-shift variable indicate changes in systematic risk that are associated with the event being considered.

The effect of the first flammability regulation (Commerce FF 3-71) was ex-

Table 9.2
Summary of Fiber, Fabric, Apparel Portfolio Estimates

Event	Abnormal Returns	Change in Systematic Risk
FIBER		
First Regulation	No Effect	Reduction
Second Regulation	No Effect	No Effect
Ban	Negative	No Effect
FABRIC		
First Regulation	No Effect	Reduction
Second Regulation	No Effect	No Effect
Ban	No Effect	No Effect
APPAREL		
First Regulation	No Effect	Increase
Second Regulation	No Effect	Increase
Ban	No Effect	No Effect

amined by assigning the dummy variable a value of one for a nineteen-month period that begins with the January 1970 notice of a finding that a flammability standard may be issued. The dummy variable continues in the one position through July 1971, when Commerce issued a notice of standard FF 3-71.

The expansion of FF 3-71 by Commerce FF 5-74 is the second regulatory event we examined. We set a ten-month event dummy that takes on a value of one on June 1972 when a notice of a second standard was released and ends with March 1973 when the proposed standard was announced. The 1977 ban on the use of Tris was the last event we examined. In this case, March 1976, the date of an Environmental Defense Fund petition, initiated the event dummy variable, which ends with April 1977, the date of the official CPSC ban of the chemical.

Estimates of abnormal returns relative to the total NYSE were made for each of the three portfolios for each of the three regulatory events: (1) the first regulation, (2) its extension to include larger-size sleepwear, and (3) the ban. We give a summary of the statistical findings in Table 9.2, which reports significant abnormal returns (at the 10 percent level of significance, two-tailed test) and systematic risk (the slope-shift control variable).

As indicated there, the fiber portfolio experienced a reduction in systematic risk in association with the first regulation, which is to say its stability relative to the market changed in a negative direction—systematic risk went down. We concluded that the elimination of cotton fiber competition in the sleepwear product market reduced risk for the owners of synthetic fiber producers without imparting positive abnormal returns. We found that the second regulatory event had no identifiable effects on fiber. However, the ban generated negative abnormal returns for the producers of synthetic fibers, which is consistent with our proposition.[27]

Turning to the fabric portfolio, we found a decrease in systematic risk in association with the first regulatory event, but found no effects for either the second regulation or the ban. Quite possibly, the regulation reduced variations in the production of domestic fabric, since foreign producers of fabric were placed at a disadvantage. Finding no abnormal returns, positive or negative, we infer that the regulatory episode produced no rents for the domestic fabric industry.

The apparel portfolio registered an increase in systematic risk in association with the first and second regulations, but showed no abnormal returns. Although the evidence is weak, since the portfolio is hardly ideal for testing for the effects of the events on sleepwear producers, we infer that future profits in the apparel industry became more volatile in association with rules that could be expanded across other apparel products and that the new higher level of risk was not changed when Tris was banned. The finding also supports the notion that output expansion dissipated all rents generated from the import restriction. Our weak prediction that owners of firms in the apparel industry gained abnormal positive returns is not supported.

By way of summary, we found that the firms that made up the Apparel Products Safety Committee of the American Apparel Manufacturers Association experienced little in the way of gains or losses from the flammability regulatory episode, but that the events destabilized investor perceptions of the riskiness of those industries. Of the twenty firm members analyzed, those producing synthetic fibers experienced a reduction in systematic risk and then sustained abnormal losses from the ban, which suggests they may have expanded plant capacity to accommodate the increase in demand for fibers that replaced the displaced cotton input. Firms in the apparel industry sustained increases in systematic risk in association with both stages of the regulation, but experienced no abnormal returns relative to the total financial market.

While we found the changes in systematic risk to be interesting and of value to our research, we concluded that since none of the committee-member firms gained abnormal positive returns in conjunction with the three episodes, either one of two explanations was in order. First, the regulatory event did not provide a profit-making restriction on output for the firms in the portfolios. Second, the regulations did provide rent-generating opportunities, but the rents were dissipated through lobbying and other expenses related to the rules themselves, an example of rentless rent seeking. We know of no way to distinguish between these competing hypotheses.

Financial Market Tests of Tris Producers

Our third proposition stated that the regulations and ban initially increased the wealth of owners of firms producing Tris, the principal flame retardant used to meet the regulation. The test of this hypothesis required us to construct a financial markets test using a portfolio consisting of the five chemical companies that produced Tris. Two firms, Great Lakes and Michigan, were not listed on the NYSE, so the three remaining firms (Dow, Stauffer, and Tenneco) formed the portfolio we tested.

Using the same logic and model described for the estimation of gains and losses to the fiber/fabric/apparel portfolios, as well as the same event windows, we estimated abnormal returns for each of the three regulatory events.[28] The results of the three estimates indicate the event dummy variables are significant and positive for the two regulatory events and negative for the ban.

Our estimates of the first event's effect indicated that a 1.8 percent abnormal gain is earned by the portfolio for each month during the nineteen-month period. The second estimate shows a 2.7 percent abnormal gain for a ten-month period. The last estimate indicates a 2.9 percent loss each month for a fourteen-month period. We estimated the cumulative average gains and losses for each of the three models to make a determination of overall wealth effects relative to what a simple market model, without the events, would have predicted. Using data 105 months prior to the first event, we found the event to be associated with a 32.7 percent cumulative gain. On the same relative basis, the second event generated an 18.9 percent cumulative gain. Using data for seventy months prior to the ban, we found the portfolio suffered a 38.8 percent cumulative loss.[29] Our financial markets tests support the hypothesis that the shareholders of Dow, Stauffer, and Tenneco, three of the five Tris producers, gained and then lost wealth in association with the flammability episode.

V. THE LIABILITY DEBATE AFTER THE BAN

The April 1977 ban on Tris ended one chapter of the regulatory episode but served as an introduction to the second and last chapter. Because of the ban, and the fact that it came without notice, substantial inventory losses hung in the balance. It was not clear just how many industries in the channel of production leading to sleepwear might bear losses from the CPSC-required repurchase of treated sleepwear, fabric, and fiber.[30] However, the air was cleared on April 13, 1977, when the CPSC ruled that the sleepwear producers alone were the responsible "manufacturer" as defined in the Federal Hazardous Substances Act, which contains the repurchase requirement relied on by the CPSC.

In just seven days after that announcement, the American Apparel Manufacturers Association (AAMA) filed suit (April 20, 1977) on behalf of its members, asking that the financial impact of the ban be spread across the producer pipeline and include chemical, fiber, and fabric producers. On May 3, 1977, the D.C. federal court issued the order. With that, fiber and fabric producers became more deeply involved.

With an announced expansion of the repurchase requirements, Springs Mills of South Carolina, a major apparel fabric producer, filed suit against the CPSC in the federal district court of South Carolina, arguing among other things that due process had not been followed by the CPSC in issuing the ban and asking for a stay of the ruling. On May 24, 1977, the district court issued a temporary restraining order against the CPSC, stopping CPSC enforcement of the repurchase agreement for the fabric industry. Judge Robert Chapman's final opinion stated:

Tris was the only flame retardant to effectively treat polyester, acetate, and triacetate fabrics used in children's sleepwear, which would enable the sleepwear to comply with the (Commerce) Secretary's ... standard. This had the practical effect of Government ordering Tris to be used. Now another department of the same government has not only banned Tris, but ordered the repurchase of articles containing it.[31]

On appeal of the district court's ruling by the CPSC, the U.S. Court of Appeals refused to reinstate the ban, but indicated that the CPSC could accomplish its intended goal through enforcement actions taken on a case-by-case basis.

In the midst of these proceedings, Senator Thurmond of South Carolina introduced legislation on May 12, 1977, for the federal government to reimburse the affected members of the apparel/textile industry for their Tris-related losses. Precedent for reimbursement was suggested by language in the Federal Insecticide, Rodenticide, and Pesticide Act, which provides for an indemnification for persons suffering losses by reason of the suspension or registration of a pesticide that has been found to present an imminent hazard.[32] Without debate, the bill was passed on January 20, 1978, by the Senate and sent to the House of Representatives. The law was passed by both houses on October 12, 1978. On November 8, 1978, President Carter allowed the reimbursement law to die by pocket veto. In a letter explaining his action, the president indicated that the matter was simply a business bailout. Since most of the affected apparel producers were small firms, he suggested that they seek help from the Small Business Administration.

The election of Ronald Reagan provided Senator Thurmond with another opportunity for government reimbursement for firms that claimed to be adversely affected by the Tris episode. Joining ranks with Senator Edward Kennedy of Massachusetts and South Carolina Senator Ernest Hollings, Senator Thurmond had introduced a second bill on March 1, 1979. A new version of the bill was proposed on February 21, 1981. Finally, the law was passed and signed by President Reagan on December 30, 1982.

The Reimbursement Theories

Two competing theories of liability were presented in the reimbursement hearings. The theory offered by the sponsoring and sympathetic congressmen is summarized by Senator John C. East in a final hearing on the proposal.

[T]his bill requires that an individual or firm claiming injury must prove the extent of the damages sustained before (gaining compensation) for claims against the government. It is a principle of American law that even the Government is not entirely immune from responsibility for the consequences of its conduct when that conduct injures private parties.[33]

Congressman Herbert E. Harris III gave further elaboration on the point and added a theory of negligence when he stated: "[I]t seems to me the only time we can really in this area step in and say we use taxpayers' money for indemnification is where there is a clear act of government that has caused the situation either through neglect or improper type of government action."[34] Congressman Harris emphasized causation, but then added traditional points about negligence and fault.

The Department of Justice, represented in the hearings by James F. Merow, Chief of the U.S. Court of Claims, argued a purer negligence theory of liability.[35] It was the position of the department that the government should not accept liability unless the government was proved to be at fault in developing the flammability regulations and in banning Tris. In other words, the Federal Torts Claim Action provided the appropriate vehicle for dealing with the issue. Merow also expressed the view that providing indemnification for one narrow interest group would open the door even wider for a host of other efforts to obtain special favors from Congress. Related to this, he saw no problem in government's authority to regulate safe consumer products and the procedures followed and felt it legitimate for government to ban hazardous products.

Merow pointed out that Tris, the sore spot of the controversy, was chosen voluntarily by industry to meet a performance standard. Selection of Tris sprang from consumer choice, not government mandate. He also argued that economic damage to the industry occurred when the consuming public became aware of the risky nature of Tris through media notices, and that the government ban simply ratified inevitable market forces.[36] He noted that distinguishing government's action from simple market action would be extraordinarily difficult, if government chose to indemnify firms for its actions. Merow said that industry had the option of not putting a product on the market at all, which is to say the industry would have sustained substantial capital losses due to the government rule.

Merow also described a moral hazard problem in government's *ex post* indemnification efforts. Firms in the future might be less cautious in developing consumer products, and indeed continue to produce and sell them after becoming aware of a hazard, if they could assign a positive probability to gaining reimbursement for inventories of banned products. Of course, Merow's concern would only apply if consumers either assigned no relative cost to the government-identified hazard, were barred from bringing private actions against firms that persisted in producing hazardous products, and if firms could gain a return on capital when obtaining reimbursements for banned goods.

David H. Moulton, a representative of Public Citizen Congress Watch, addressed one of these points: "This is crucial to the issue, whether or not in fact when the Government steps in and regulates that all common law liability and court liability prances out the window."[37] Moulton expressed deep concern that government assumption of liability in the Tris case would signal firms that government rules were maximum standards, bringing an end to tort liability actions brought by aggrieved consumers in those markets.

The Causality Theory

In a way, the causality theory of liability articulated by Richard Epstein for private action settings describes the position taken by Congress. The deeper issue of whether or not government should be viewed as a private party was never debated.[38] What appeared to be needed was a basis for Congress to make adjustments for an unintended redistribution of wealth.

Epstein describes a situation where A causes B to harm himself, a case where "the plaintiff assumes the risk because the defendant has forced him either to take the risk of harm or to abandon the enjoyment of his property."[39] Epstein's argument addresses the presumed government defense mentioned by Claims Court Chief Merow when he suggested that the affected firms had voluntarily assumed governmental and other risks upon continuing in the business of manufacturing sleepwear.

In the Tris case, the causality theory sees government compelling firms to meet a standard that ultimately leads to the loss of their property. Whether or not any part of the flammability episode satisfies the point relates arguably to the magnitude of risk imposed when regulatory institutions are changed. On the other hand, the flammability standard could be thought of as a normal risk. There was notice and warning. However, the interaction of the regulations and ban with its repurchase requirements and ban on export sales arguably formed an unpredictable amount of risk for the firms. Firms in the industry had produced revenue-generating products and inventory assets that suddenly had negative and zero values. The theoretical argument points out that property having a demonstrable market value was taken.[40] Epstein suggests that a causality theory is operative in such private settings, that party B is in position to obtain damages from A. Of course, the plaintiff's ability to deflect the effects of the compulsory action are surely relevant.

The focus on private actions parallels in the congressional debate is interesting in a broad constitutional sense. Fundamental questions simply were not debated. For example, the argument that property was taken through a regulatory process applies to many government regulations.[41] There are also strong arguments that government regulation redistributes wealth, making some better off while all taken together are worse off. The regulation of fares, granting permission to enter or exit an industry or occupation, altering advertising language, and imposing emission standards can each affect the wealth of individuals and owners of firms. If asset values are altered, property rights are arguably rearranged.

In a constitutional sense, the use of due process in making such determinations may be what distinguishes one set of property takings from another. However, Congress did not focus on due process failure, though Judge Chapman of the South Carolina district court did. Instead, Congress appears to have imposed a private action rule on itself, without either debating the fundamental role of government in enhancing markets in the economy or considering the question of adequate due process and whether or not CPSC, let alone other regulatory agencies, provided adequate property safeguards. The process was driven more by redistribution than by legal principles.

The Final Law

The signing of Pub. L. 97-395 on December 30, 1982, set in motion the claims process that gave standing for fabric, yarn, and fiber producers to file claims for losses in the U.S. Court of Claims.[42] The law established a filter that emphasized the availability of Tris substitutes to particular parties, tested efforts by each party to obtain substitutes, and assessed before-ban levels of knowledge of the riskiness of Tris. The law also screened claimants on their cooperation with the ban and later prohibition on the export of Tris products. In other words, the law established a method for determining that government was the responsible party.

Prior to the passage of Pub. L. 97-395, estimates of the potential taxpayer reimbursement costs had been repeatedly set at $50 million.[43] As of February 29, 1988, sixty-seven firms had made claims for losses under the 1982 legislation that totaled $39 million. Slightly more than $19 million had been awarded to them, with the average award being $292,000 and the largest settlement being $3.8 million.[44] Practically all of the petitioning firms were small, unlisted apparel firms.

Other Theoretical Considerations

We considered the competing theories of liability presented in the legislative debates and then found it instructive to contemplate what might have happened had government not entered the flammability arena at all. Previous private sector efforts to produce and sell flame-resistant sleepwear had not been commercially successful, which suggests there was insufficient consumer demand for those first treated products.

Had demand increased and technological innovations followed, we can argue that some firms would have provided flame-retarding sleepwear to those domestic consumers who valued the reduced risk. Suppose, for the sake of argument, that many of the free-market firms selected Tris as the preferred treatment, while others found alternative approaches for satisfying demand for the safer product. Later, just as in the actual episode, Tris is found to be a carcinogen. If consumers viewed the risk of cancer to be more costly than the reduction in risk of burning, demand for Tris-treated sleepwear would fall to zero. Market shares in the sleepwear industry would shift as the sale of nontreated sleepwear increased.

The effects of the injection of government regulation in the story seem to be twofold. First, treated sleepwear arrived prematurely on the market, and consumer demand for untreated products was eliminated by the regulation that required uniformity across firms and markets. Our results on import penetration support the argument. Although theory suggests there would be losses in consumer surplus in the truncated markets, which we cannot measure, we find no abnormal gains or losses for the sleepwear industry. Only the producers of Tris are the net gainers at that point.

Because the regulation encompassed the entire product market and led to uniform use of Tris, all users of children's sleepwear were exposed to the hazard; that is, government regulation had the unfortunate effect of magnifying and spreading the risk across the population, a point made by key scientists when they first reported that Tris was a carcinogen.[45]

Second, the government-sponsored ban on Tris brings an abrupt end to the magnified demand for Tris-treated products, most likely more abrupt than would be the case from normal market operations. To the extent that there were unestimated financial losses, we believe the losses would be larger in the government regulation case than in the case of unfettered markets, because of the uniformity effects and the abrupt nature of the ban. However, we have not introduced considerations of private suits that might have imposed cost and discipline on free-market firms in our story about those firms.[46]

As a final theoretical consideration, we note that the CPSC had another regulatory alternative available to it that could have generated a totally different outcome. After the demise of Tris, the CPSC withdrew certain features of the flammability standard, which made it possible for new inherently protected yarns to be used in the production of sleepwear and provided an incentive for more firms to experiment with new technologies. But the agency eventually took another important step. The CPSC moved to develop a classification standard that would inform consumers of the weakness in information markets and draws on competition to demonstrate the value of alternative levels of consumer protection.[47] Had the approach been taken earlier, it is doubtful that the Tris episode would have ever transpired. It is also doubtful that rents would have been generated for the participants in the process.

Wealth Effects and Property Rights

If the wealth effects of government actions could be determined perfectly, and if government desired to indemnify damaged firms, part of the congressional debate would be resolved. Evidence of negative abnormal returns in association with a regulation for a particular firm could be interpreted as a taking of property. Positive returns would be interpreted conversely. During an episode like Tris, the net wealth changes induced from a regulation and ban could be viewed as the effect of changes in property arrangements induced by government.

Recalling our first set of empirical findings, we found no abnormal gains or losses for the apparel firms in our portfolio. We also emphasized that the portfolio may not have been representative of the smaller firms most affected by the episode. It is still interesting that apparel firms were the focal point of the congressional debates and that the fabric producers stood to gain if the apparel producers were reimbursed by government instead of by the latter group of firms.

We found no abnormal negative returns for the fiber portfolio in association with the ban and overall negative returns for Tris producers. Reimbursement for fiber firms was included in the congressional action. However, reimbursement for Tris producers was never even debated. While we grant that our estimates offer only tentative evidence of property effects, let alone for making determinations of whether or not adequate due process was provided, we still argue that evidence of net wealth effects is one indication of property effects. The selective indemnification chosen by Congress suggests that reimbursement for property losses had little to do with their legislative effort.

Empirical Tests of Postban Events

Since we found limited evidence of abnormal returns in association with the regulations and ban in our examination of the fiber, fabric, and apparel portfolios, we had little reason to think we would find abnormal returns with the government's move to indemnify affected firms for their alleged ban-related losses. Nonetheless, we tested for abnormal returns and changes in systematic risk for the same three portfolios, recognizing again that the apparel portfolio was hardly representative of the many small firms that operated in the sleepwear apparel industry.

Using daily stock market returns and three-day windows centered on the

Table 9.3
Post-Ban Events

Date	Event	Predicted Effect
May 3, 1977	AAMA obtains expansion CPSC repurchase requirement.	Weak positive for apparel. Weak negative for fiber and fabric.
May 12, 1977	Senator Thurmond introduces first indemnification bill.	Weak positive for all portfolios.
May 24, 1977	Judge Chapman issues temporary order restraining CPSC.	Weak positive for fabric. Negative for apparel.
June 23, 1977	Judge Chapman stays CPSC ban.	No effect.
Aug. 11, 1977	CPSC appeal of stay is unsuccessful.	No effect.
May 5, 1978	CPSC rules against export of banned products.	No effect.
Nov. 8, 1978	Carter veto of indemnification legislation.	Weak negative for all portfolios.
Dec. 30, 1982	President Reagan signs law.	Weak positive for all portfolios.

date of the event, we stabilized the testing period by using 250 days of data prior to the advent of each window. We then tested the three portfolios for each of the eight events listed in Table 9.3. Included in the table are predictions for associated effects. We emphasize that the absence of abnormal returns in association with the regulations and ban caused us to make weak predictions for abnormal returns from the indemnification events.

We generally found weak evidence of abnormal returns across the portfolios in association with the first seven events. Our test of the last event provided suggestive evidence that the apparel portfolio, which included larger firms, may have identified some anticompetitive effects of the Tris episode. There were significant negative returns generated for the apparel portfolio in association with Judge Chapman's ruling. The evidence is consistent with the fact that small apparel firms were to be key recipients of indemnification payments, which were interrupted by the ruling.

V. CONCLUSION

The story of Tris is a story about rules of liability. It describes what can happen when shifting liability rules are accompanied by a technology-forcing regulation. The complex episode offers a rare opportunity to consider the effects transmitted to markets when a regulation that involves a particular chemical treatment is imposed, the treatment is then banned by the regulatory agency, and government assumes liability for damages imposed by the action. Our analysis has emphasized the important role played by the chemical treatment itself, how it formed a screen to be penetrated by imports, and then how the producers of the affected apparel goods and the manufacturers of the chemical treatment and other related producers fared during the episode.

Our findings offer strong support for the case that domestic producers of sleepwear gained market share relative to their foreign counterparts while the regulation was in effect and later when the principal chemical treatment was banned. We also find that the owners of the five chemical companies favored by the regulation first gained and then suffered a net wealth loss during the episode.

When we examined members of a major apparel trade association that formed a committee to monitor the regulation, we found that the producers of synthetic fibers favored by the regulation lost wealth when the chief chemical treatment was banned. We found no evidence of wealth creation or destruction for the fabric and apparel firms that were members of the trade association committee.

Our examination of the postban activity and the question of government liability reveals government accepting private action principles in the debate about loss indemnification. Causality, not negligence, dominates as the standard applied when Congress moved to indemnify losses. In some ways, we find it curious that the chemical producers never entered the debate about indemnification, while our results indicate that they were the losers in the episode. Economic theory suggests that the most inelastically supplied input would gain the most and lose the most from a technology-forcing regulation and lose the most from a ban of that technology. However, the interests of the small apparel producer dominate the congressional debate and the later claims filed for reimbursement.

We conclude from all this that the Tris reimbursement debate stemmed from congressional concerns about adjusting the outcome of the Tris incident through selected redistribution. Apparently, the outcome generated was simply not what Congress intended. While theories of liability were discussed, there was no real effort to come to grips with underlying legal and philosophical issues. We conclude further that specialization in regulation, as elsewhere in the economy, may provide opportunities for highly specialized yet diverse groups to gain from one regulatory episode. We also observe that regulatory gains, like those elsewhere in the economy, are indeed risky.

NOTES

The authors express appreciation to William R. Dougan, Hugh H. Macaulay, Michael T. Maloney, Fred S. McChesney, Robert E. McCormick, Roger E. Meiners, and Robert Staaf.

1. For background on the agency, see W. Kip Viscusi, *Regulating Consumer Product Safety* (Washington, D.C.: American Enterprise Institute, 1984).

2. Stigler's point on this applies to government organizations. (See George J. Stigler, "The Division of Labor Is Limited to the Extent of the Market," *The Organization of Industry* [Chicago: University of Chicago Press, 1968], pp. 129–41.)

3. See Ronald H. Coase, "The Problem of Social Cost," *Journal of Law and Economics* 3 (October 1960): 1–44.

4. Peltzman has argued that gains from regulation will be shared by producers and consumers, thus the joint demand for regulation. However, Tullock has argued that all potential gains from regulation tend to be dissipated in costly efforts to obtain the desired restriction, which may describe the apparel industry outcome. Yandle points out that joint efforts by consumer groups and industry to secure a regulation, such as the one analyzed here, can enhance residual rents for certain participants, which may describe the position of the chemical producers. McChesney has added to the discussion of special interest demand for regulation by noting that firms will engage in costly political struggles to avoid regulations, drawing on quasirents while doing so. (See Sam Peltzman, "Toward a More General Theory of Regulation," *Journal of Law and Economics* 19, 2 [August 1976]: 211–40; Gordon Tullock, "The Welfare Costs of Tariffs, Monopolies, and Theft," *Western Economic Journal* 5 [June 1967]: 224–32; Bruce Yandle, "Rentless Rentseeking and Abnormal Returns," *Public Choice* 48 [1986]: 265–70; and Fred S. McChesney, "Rent Extraction and Rent Creation in the Economic Theory of Regulation," *Journal of Legal Studies* 16 [1987]: 101–17.)

5. While the U.S. and United Kingdom standards were passed in the same year, the testing methods established are not substitutable. For example, a Hong Kong apparel producer must have two test procedures when shipping to the two markets, even though both regulations are designed to achieve similar levels of safety.

6. The second standard was less stringent than the first with regard to the time a molten material can burn after separation from a test specimen. The leniency of the standard was based on the argument that older children were better able to move away from danger than younger ones.

7. Two studies were instituted in 1975. The first, an animal study by the National Cancer Institute, found that Tris was associated with kidney cancer in rats. A second study, sponsored by the Environmental Defense Fund, confirmed the National Can-

cer Institute finding. Tris was banned under the authority of sec. 2(g)(1)(A) of the Federal Hazardous Substances Act. (See *Federal Register*, April 8, 1977, p. 18850.)

8. The five companies were Michigan Chemical Company, Dow Chemical Company, Great Lakes Chemical Company, Stauffer Chemical Company, and Tenneco.

9. The discussion here is drawn from U.S. Congress, House, *Banning Distribution of Tris: Hearing before the Subcommittee on Antitrust, Consumers and Employment of the Committee on Small Business*, 95th Cong., 1st sess., April 28, 1977, and from a review of industry periodicals.

10. The data are based on calculations from "Cotton Counts Its Customers," by the National Cotton Council (Memphis, Tenn.) various years.

11. For background on the cotton dust standards, see Bruce Yandle, "A Social Regulation Controversy: The Cotton Dust Standard," *Social Science Quarterly* 63, 1 (March 1982): 58–69.

12. Data on this are from A. J. Field, *Trade and Textiles: An Analysis of the Changing International Division of Labor in the Textiles and Clothing Sector, 1963–1978* (Queson City, Philippines: New Day Publishers, 1984), p. 147.

13. "Washington Concentrates," *Chemical and Engineering News*, February 2, 1970, p. 23.

14. "Washington Concentrates," *Chemical and Engineering News*, April 20, 1970, p. 27.

15. "Flame Retardants Growth Flares Up," *Chemical and Engineering News*, October 18, 1971, p. 16.

16. U.S. Congress, Senate, Committee on Commerce, *Authorize Appropriations for Flammable Fabrics Act and Fire Research and Safety Act of 1968: Hearings before the Consumer Subcommittee of the Committee on Commerce on S.3765 and S.3766*, 91st Cong., 2d sess., June 2, 1970, p. 44.

17. The effects of such notices on the wealth of stockholders has been estimated by Jarrell and Peltzman and is found to be substantial. Indeed, negative publicity regarding potential violations of regulations is arguably a much larger deterrent than the small civil penalties imposed by agencies. For example, Jarrell and Peltzman find that a major recall of drugs imposes a cost of $12 on that firm's shareholders for each $1 recall cost, and imposes a $25 to $50 cost on the shareholders of related drug companies. The average direct cost of recalls analyzed was $2 million, whereas the wealth effects were estimated to average $100 million. (See Gregg Jarrell and Sam Peltzman, "The Impact of Product Recalls on the Wealth of Sellers," in *Empirical Approaches to Consumer Protection Economics*, ed. Pauline M. Ippolito and David T. Scheffman [Washington, D.C.: Federal Trade Commission, March 1986], pp. 377–409.)

18. The seminal work on regulatory cartels referred to is George J. Stigler, "The Theory of Economic Regulation," *Bell Journal of Economics and Management Science* 3 (September 1971): 3–21, and Sam Peltzman *supra* note 4.

19. See Bruce Yandle, "Bootleggers and Baptists: The Education of a Regulatory Economist," *Regulation*, May/June 1983, pp. 12–14, 18.

20. This feature of the joint effort is discussed in Yandle *supra* note 4.

21. See "Flammability Rule Argued," *Chemical and Engineering News*, April 9, 1971, p. 9.

22. See McChesney *supra* note 4.

23. Data on imported and domestically produced sleepwear cover SIC 2341311–

2341318 and are from U.S. Bureau of the Census, *Current Industrial Reports, Apparel Survey, 1972–1980* and *Current Industrial Reports, Underwear and Nightwear, 1980–1986*, and U.S. Bureau of the Census, *U.S. Imports for Consumption and General Imports, SIC-Based Products by World Areas, 1972–1980*. The SIC designations cover girls', children's, infants', and toddlers' nightwear of all categories. Income and population data are from *The Statistical Abstract of the U.S.*, various issues, and the apparel and all-items CPI are from reports of the Bureau of Labor Statistics.

24. The O.L.S. estimate does not account for the fact that the dependent variable ranges from a minimum of zero to a maximum of 100 percent. We did not transform the model to a logit specification, since we were not seeking to measure the effects of the regulations on penetration, but rather to test the hypothesis that import penetration was affected. We also estimated a model for import shipments, not penetration, using the same independent variables. The coefficients of the variables had the same signs as those reported for penetration, though the coefficient on BAN was not significant. The latter finding suggests that domestic shipments expanded relative to imports during the ban, causing penetration to fall significantly, but that imports did not change significantly.

25. We chose firms whose SIC codes were closely related to the main product categories mentioned in the text. Of the twenty-one NYSE firms included on the committee, we omitted Lehigh Valley Industries, since its SIC code designation was different from the three categories.

26. The financial event analysis we applied is based on the notion of efficient financial markets and has been described in some detail by Schwert. (See G. William Schwert, "Measuring the Effects of Regulation: Evidence from the Capital Markets," *Journal of Law and Economics* 24, 1 [April 1981]: 121–58.) The theory proposes that all currently available information and estimated future cash flows discounted to the present are included in the price of a security at any one time. When new information is available, capital markets adjust instantly. If the information has real effects, a well-specified estimate will show abnormal returns for the test portfolio relative to the market. Regulatory events are notoriously difficult to estimate because of the leaky nature of information flows, since such proceedings are generally long and drawn out, so that few surprises remain when a final rule falls in place. Binder has studied extensively the usefulness of official dates for investigating the financial market effects of regulation and advises researchers to widen the relevant event window when searching for effects. (See J. J. Binder, "Measuring the Effects of Regulation with Stock Price Data," *The Rand Journal of Economics* 16, 2 [Summer 1985]: 167–83.) We examined alternate windows that were expanded beyond the official dates and found somewhat improved results. However, since the official dates provide satisfactory estimates, we report the results for those.

27. The coefficient was significant at the .102 level.

28. We note that Tris was withdrawn from the textile apparel market in May 1977, immediately following the ban. (See Howard J. Sanders, "Flame Retardants," *Chemical and Engineering News*, April 24, 1978, p. 28.)

29. We call attention to the magnitude of these losses, noting that Tris was a relatively small part of the output of the affected chemical companies. Similar large losses have been found by other researchers in their examination of the effects of advertising regulation, a phenomenon somewhat related to the ban of a product.

(See Richard S. Higgins and Fred S. McChesney, "Truth and Consequences: The Federal Trade Commission's Ad Substantiation Program," in *Public Choice and Regulation: A View from Inside the Federal Trade Commission*, ed. Robert J. Mackay, James C. Miller III, and Bruce Yandle [Stanford: Hoover Institution, 1987], pp. 181–204.) We offer three explanations for our results. The first is a brand-name capital argument, which suggests that the credibility of firms that market products found to be hazardous is reduced significantly, so that all future product sales are affected. The second explanation goes to the likelihood of costly product liability suits to be brought by affected firms and consumers. The third relates to the fact that consumers moved away from all chemically treated textile products in reaction to the ban. The value of all ongoing research and development in the flame-retarding and related chemical industry fell to zero following the ban.

30. This discussion draws from United States Congress, Senate, *Claims for Losses Resulting from the Ban on Tris, S.823, Hearings before the Subcommittee on Separation of Powers of the Commitee on the Judiciary*, 97th Cong., 1st sess., May 4–5, 1981.

31. The full text of the ruling is found in U.S. Congress, House, *Reimbursements for Losses Incurred by Government Banning of Tris, S. 823, Hearings before the Subcommittee on Administrative Law and Governmental Relations of the Committee on the Judiciary*, 95th Cong., 2d sess., June 14 and 15, 1978, p. 266.

32. For discussion, see ibid.

33. See *supra* note 30 at 2.

34. See *supra* note 31 at 374–75.

35. The discussion here is taken from *supra* note 31 at 2.

36. Merow's point was well supported in press reports and testimony. According to these, the federal ban on Tris brought an amazing reaction among consumers, who turned away from chemically treated sleepwear and all other chemically treated textile products. The ban was seen as a fundamental setback for all chemical treatment of textiles, especially for flame-retarding chemicals. (See Sanders *supra* note 28 at 22. In addition to the noted setback for the chemical industry, at least one major producer of children's sleeper, The William Carter Company, immediately ceased the production of Tris-treated sleepwear when evidence of its potential hazardous nature was made public. Arguably the Carter firm had the most brand-name capital at stake. (On this see *supra* note 31 at 68–70.)

37. See *supra* note 31 at 322–41, 329.

38. Of course, the debate that took place implicitly deals with government immunity, and an extensive discussion of the deeper philosophical point is not to be expected from Congress. The history of government liability and of the Federal Tort Claims Act itself leaves murky impressions, at best, of the bright lines that distinguish governmentally imposed harm from privately generated harm. (For discussion of this, see Peter H. Schuck, *Suing Government* [New Haven, Conn.: Yale University Press, 1983].)

39. Richard A. Epstein, *A Theory of Strict Liability* (San Francisco: Cato Institute, 1980), pp. 108–11.

40. In this sense, a regulatory taking can be viewed in the same way as government's exercise of eminent domain powers. However, even that blunt instrument has some specified safeguards. (On this, see Richard A. Epstein, *Takings: Private*

Property and the Power of Eminent Domain [Cambridge, Mass.: Harvard University Press, 1985].)

41. Compensation for regulatory effects is discussed in Donald Wittman, "Liability for Harm or Restitution for Benefit," *Journal of Legal Studies* 13, 1 (January 1984): 57–80. Wittman summarizes several key cases and argues that courts provide compensation when government regulation is not efficient. He distinguishes government actions that involve a physical expropriation of property from actions that generate external effects and argues that expropriations are more likely to be anticipated. In the Tris case, we would argue that the ban, which amounts to a physical taking of property, was not anticipated. At the same time, the ban presumably generated positive externalities, or at least extinguished negative ones.

42. Ralph Nader said the signing of the law "stands for the principle that the Government will indemnify companies that use products they know, or should have known, are dangerous to meet federal regulations." (See Ralph Nader and Gene Kimmelman, "A Bad Precedent," *New York Times*, January 1, 1983, p. F2.) He pointed out that asbestos producers were already lining up in Washington for similar treatment.

43. See U.S. Congress, Senate, *Ban on Chemical Tris in Apparel, etc., Calendar No. 564*, 96th Cong., 1st sess., December 18, 1979, p. 3.

44. Calculated by the authors from data obtained from the U.S. Court of Claims.

45. See Arlene Blum and Bruce N. Ames, "Flame-Retardant Additives as Possible Cancer Hazards," *Science*, January 7, 1977, pp. 17–23.

46. We have reason to believe those costs could have been substantial. There had been a flurry of product liability suits involving sleepwear prior to the imposition of the CPSC standard. These suits diminished markedly in the postregulation period. (On this, see Stanley M. Suchecki, "FR: Progress, Problems, . . . and Product Liability," *Textile Industries*, February 1977, pp. 45–47.

47. See "Development of Fabric Classification Standard Appears Feasible, CPSC Staff Says," *Product Safety & Liability Reporter* 16, 38 (September 16, 1988): 905–6.

REFERENCES

Binder, J. J. "Measuring the Effects of Regulation with Stock Price Data." *The Rand Journal of Economics* 16, 2 (Summer 1985): 167–83.

Blum, Arlene, and Bruce N. Ames. "Flame-Retardant Additives as Possible Cancer Hazards." *Science*, January 7, 1977, pp. 17–23.

Coase, R. H. "The Problem of Social Cost." *Journal of Law and Economics* 3 (October 1960): 1–44.

"Development of Fabric Classification Standard Appears Feasible, CPSC Staff Says." *Product Safety & Liability Reporter* 16, 38 (September 16, 1988): 905–6.

Epstein, Richard A. *Takings: Private Property and the Power of Eminent Domain.* Cambridge, Mass.: Harvard University Press, 1985.

———. *A Theory of Strict Liability.* San Francisco: Cato Institute, 1980.

Field, A. J. *Trade and Textiles: An Analysis of the Changing International Division of Labor in the Textiles and Clothing Sector, 1963–1978.* Queson City, Philippines: New Day Publishers, 1984.

"Flame Retardants Growth Flares Up." *Chemical and Engineering News*, October 18, 1971, p. 16.

"Flammability Rule Argued." *Chemical and Engineering News*, April 9, 1971, p. 9.

Higgins, Richard S., and Fred S. McChesney. "Truth and Consequences: The Federal Trade Commission's Ad Substantiation Program." In *Public Choice and Regulation: A View from Inside the Federal Trade Commission*, ed. Robert J. Mackay, James C. Miller III, and Bruce Yandle, 181–204. Stanford: Hoover Institution, 1987.

Jarrell, Gregg, and Sam Peltzman. "The Impact of Product Recalls on the Wealth of Sellers." In *Empirical Approaches to Consumer Protection Economics*, ed. Pauline M. Ippolito and David T. Scheffman, 377–409. Washington, D.C.: Federal Trade Commission, March 1986.

Linneman, Peter. "The Effects of Consumer Safety Standards: The 1973 Mattress Flammability Standard." *Journal of Law & Economics* 23, 2 (October 1980): 461–79.

McChesney, Fred S. "Rent Extraction and Rent Creation in the Economic Theory of Regulation." *Journal of Legal Studies* 16 (1987): 101–17.

Nader, Ralph, and Gene Kimmelman. "A Bad Precedent." *New York Times*, January 1, 1983, p. F2.

Peltzman, Sam. "Toward a More General Theory of Regulation." *Journal of Law and Economics* 19, 2 (August 1976): 211–40.

Sanders, Howard J. "Flame Retardants." *Chemical and Engineering News*, April 24, 1978, pp. 22–36.

Schuck, Peter H. *Suing Government*. New Haven, Conn.: Yale University Press, 1983.

Schwert, G. William. "Measuring the Effects of Regulation: Evidence from the Capital Markets." *Journal of Law and Economics* 24, 1 (April 1981): 121–58.

Stigler, George J. "The Division of Labor Is Limited to the Extent of the Market." *The Organization of Industry*, 129–41. Chicago: University of Chicago Press, 1968.

———. "The Theory of Economic Regulation." *Bell Journal of Economics and Management Science* 3 (September 1971): 3–21.

Suchecki, Stanley M. "FR: Progress, Problems... and Product Liability." *Textile Industries*, February 1977, pp. 45–47.

Tullock, Gordon. "The Welfare Costs of Tariffs, Monopolies, and Theft." *Western Economic Journal* 5 (June 1967): 224–32.

U.S. Congress. House. *Banning Distribution of Tris: Hearings before the Subcommittee on Antitrust, Consumers and Employment of the Committee on Small Business*. 95th Cong., 1st sess., April 28, 1977.

U.S. Congress. House. Committee on the Judiciary. *Reimbursements of Losses Incurred by Government Banning of Tris, S.823, Hearings before the Subcommittee on Administrative Law and Government Relations*. 95th Cong., 2d sess., June 14 and 15, 1978.

U.S. Congress. Senate. *Ban on Chemical Tris in Apparel, etc., Calendar No. 564*. 96th Cong., 1st sess., December 18, 1979.

U.S. Congress. Senate. Committee on Commerce. *Authorize Appropriations for Flammable Fabrics Act and Fire Research and Safety Act of 1968: Hearings before the Consumer Subcommittee of the Committee on Commerce on S.3765 and S.3766.* 91st Cong., 2d sess., June 2, 1970.

U.S. Congress. Senate. Committee on the Judiciary. *Claims for Losses Resulting from the Ban on Tris, S.823, Hearings before the Subcommittee on Separation of Powers of the Committee on the Judiciary.* 97th Cong., 1st sess., May 4 and 5, 1981.

Viscusi, W. Kip. "Consumer Behavior and the Safety Effects of Product Safety." *Journal of Law & Economics* 28, 3 (October 1985): 527–53.

———. *Regulating Consumer Product Safety.* Washington, D.C.: American Enterprise Institute, 1984.

"Washington Concentrates." *Chemical and Engineering News,* February 2, 1970.

"Washington Concentrates." *Chemical and Engineering News,* April 20, 1970.

Wittman, Donald. "Liability for Harm or Restitution for Benefit?" *Journal of Legal Studies* 13, 1 (January 1984): 57–80.

Yandle, Bruce. "Bootleggers and Baptists: The Education of a Regulatory Economist." *Regulation, May/June 1983, pp. 12–18.*

———. *"Rentless Rentseeking and Abnormal Returns." Public Choice* 48 (1986): 265–70.

———. "A Social Regulation Controversy: The Cotton Dust Standard." *Social Science Quarterly* 63, 1 (March 1982): 58–59.

10

Deposit Insurance, Liability, and the S&L Mess

Roger E. Meiners and Bruce Yandle

I. INTRODUCTION

Congress passed the Financial Institutions, Reform, Recovery and Enforcement Act of 1989 (FIRREA) in 1989 to help resolve the insolvency of the Federal Savings and Loan Insurance Corporation (FSLIC) and stabilize the shaky financial structure of the nation's savings and loan associations (S&Ls).[1] The legislation renamed and restructured FSLIC, weakened the independent power of the savings and loan regulators by placing their function within the U.S. Treasury, and formed a new version of the FSLIC, called the Savings Association Insurance Fund (SAIF), which joined its stronger sister institution, the Federal Deposit Insurance Corporation (FDIC), that insures commercial bank deposits.[2] More important from a fiscal standpoint, the legislation appropriated $50 billion in taxpayer dollars to fund the FSLIC restructuring with expectations that several hundred billion more would eventually be needed. Along with a host of new regulatory strictures, the legislation made clear that all deposits in the nation's deposit institutions were backed by the full faith and security of the United States Government.

The signing of the legislation into law by President Bush answered a fundamental question regarding deposit liability. U.S. taxpayers are the insurers of last resort for banking system deposits. The taxpayers are ultimately liable for the solvency of banks, S&Ls, and credit unions.

What led to the demise of the S&L insurance fund? How is it that taxpayers find themselves liable for actions and events that led to the collapse of some 500 S&Ls and their deposit insurer? Does the necessary restructuring of the S&L industry have anything to do with deposit liability and how it was managed? We believe that government (taxpayer) insurance had a great deal to do with the problem Congress sought to solve in 1989. The problem has to do with deposit premiums, how they are set, and the extent to which the premiums charged induce managers of S&Ls and other financial institutions to accept risk. But there is more to the story than just a faulty insurance mechanism.

This chapter tells a story of the demise of FSLIC and some 500 S&Ls that together led to the restructuring of the S&L industry and pushed the industry one step closer to becoming an indistinguishable part of the commercial banking industry. The first part of the chapter traces the development of the FSLIC and the evolution of deposit insurance. The next section identifies the origins of the recent collapse that led to the simultaneous bankruptcy of hundreds of S&Ls and the draining of the insurance fund. That is followed by a discussion of regulatory problems, problems with the insurance mechanism, and the resulting incentives that operated within the S&L industry. It is here that we encounter the heart of the liability problem. The chapter ends with some brief thoughts about future liability problems.

II. SUBSIDIZING RISK IN FINANCIAL MARKETS

The Free Lunch Problem

A primary job of economists is to repeat over and over that there are no free lunches. The origins of the problem in the S&L industry arise from the first cousin of the free lunch—the subsidized lunch. Many lunches not paid for when they were bought are now being paid for by taxpayers who did not enjoy the lunches. In short, there is a massive redistribution of wealth under way.

Despite the high cost of the insurance fund bailout, accompanied by political finger pointing, the popular press pays little attention to the non-mysterious reason why the problem became so large.[3] The free lunch policies of the past have not ended, so that under the right circumstances, the same problem could emerge again.

The story is a common one in government policies. For example, in the 1950s and 1960s federal law kept the prices of domestically produced natural gas and oil well below their market value. The result was more energy consumed than if the price had been higher. Production fell in the United States, as producers cut oil output in response to the low domestic prices or decided to sit on their assets in hopes that prices would rise in the future. This policy might be viewed as a form of deficit spending by the federal government that is not counted at the time the liabilities are incurred. The resulting forces helped OPEC become as powerful as it did, causing the energy crisis of the 1970s—the low-cost lunches of earlier years came back with a big price tag.

Similar stories can be told about financial markets. American banks lend billions of dollars every year to poor foreign nations knowing that there is little likelihood that those nations ever will repay the loans and may not even be able to pay the interest due on the loans. These loans are not as foolish as they first appear because many are underwritten, in one way or another, by the federal government. The loans are really a part of the foreign aid program not carried on the books as a part of the federal budget. As recent policy discussions have indicated, eventually hundreds of billions of dollars in bad loans have to be cleared from the books.

Similarly, the savings and loan fiasco was caused by federal government efforts to have subsidized lunches—deposit insurance that did not place market constraints on the insured. That policy, combined with the financing of some of the federal budget by inflation in the 1970s, triggered the S&L mess. Today, we are paying for the policies adopted (and some continued today) by earlier financial institution policymakers.

Federal Regulation of the S&L Industry

Like most laws governing financial institutions, the statutes that determined the structure and conduct of the S&Ls were set during the 1930s' depression.[4] Federal deposit insurance originated in the backlash that followed the failure of the Federal Reserve to provide liquidity to banks experiencing currency drains in 1929–1933. Arguing that the Fed was not able to perform so as to assure financial stability, in 1934 Congress initiated deposit insurance as a supplement, if not a replacement, for the Fed's insurance function.[5]

The Federal Home Loan Bank Board (FHLBB) was created with its guarantee arm, the FSLIC, to give the public confidence in S&Ls that were members of the FSLIC. The FSLIC and its bank counterpart, the FDIC, provided maximum coverage of $2,500 for each private account. Through the years, the liability coverage has increased fortyfold: to $10,000 in 1950, $15,000 in 1966, $20,000 in 1969, $40,000 in 1975, and $100,000 in 1980.[6] Over those years, inflation rose sevenfold. All along, the insurance carried a fixed premium—a single price—calculated as a percentage of each institution's deposit base. No adjustments were made for the relative riskiness of a financial institution's operations.

An examination of commercial banks reveals that managers reacted predictably in their operations to the full faith and credit of the federal government by changing capital to asset ratios. In 1930 the ratio stood at 15 percent. Depositors also enjoyed the additional protection of double liability borne by bank shareholders. With the introduction of FDIC, shareholder liability was discontinued *and* capital to asset ratios declined. In recent years, the ratio averages 7 percent across all commercial banks; FDIC rules require a 6 percent minimum.[7]

After the creation of the FSLIC, S&Ls were organized primarily as mutual associations, met required dividend payments to depositors (the interest on passbook savings), and had to meet stipulated portfolio investments in fixed-rate mortgages generated within a fifty-mile radius of the principal office. The S&Ls had exclusive access to funds provided by the Federal Home Loan Bank (FHLB), which was organized in 1932 to provide S&L funding, at below market interest rates due to government guarantees of FHLB bonds.

The S&Ls worked within the interest-rate spread that resulted when their regulated cost of funds was subtracted from the average yield on their mortgage portfolios. While the regulated financial structures of S&Ls provided security for depositors, it also set ill-founded bases for action by S&L managers.

Role of the FSLIC

With the exception of some relatively small state-chartered S&Ls that do not belong to the FSLIC, S&Ls chartered either by the federal government or by state governments belong to the insurance fund. Prior to the crisis of 1988, the S&Ls made annual contributions to the FSLIC of one-twelfth of 1 percent of all deposits, or about 8 cents per $100. The proceeds collected were intended to provide a pool of money, the insurance, so that depositors would be paid all of their deposits and interest earned in the event their S&L should become insolvent. But as the S&L failure rate rose, so did the insurance premium—for all S&Ls, again regardless of risk. By the end of 1988, the premium had been raised to 20.8 cents per $100 in deposits.

Every year tens of thousands of businesses fail in the United States for many reasons. Economic misfortune or bad luck, bad management, and large-scale fraud and theft are some of the reasons. Some of the failures happen to be financial institutions. Unlike other businesses, financial institutions seldom go through bankruptcy proceedings. Indeed, the process followed by the deposit insurers and regulators is a substitute for that process. Over the years, the FSLIC has bailed out insolvent S&Ls and has usually arranged for mergers between the failing institution and a stronger one. As in many bankruptcy proceedings, the managers of the failing business are the first to lose their jobs. The regulators supervise operations while the business is being restructured. All along, the depositors are assured their funds are safe; there is no reason to cease doing business with the bankrupt S&L.

In 1980, 11 insured S&Ls were taken over by the FSLIC to rescue depositors. The number rose to 74 in 1982, due to the recession, but fell to 27 by 1984 as the economy moved ahead.[8] In 1988 the depositors of over 200 S&Ls were rescued, and more than 300 additional S&Ls were targeted for restructuring under the 1989 bailout plan. Since the FSLIC insurance pool was insufficient to provide the tens of billions of dollars needed to return hundreds of S&Ls to solvency, intervention by Congress was required to keep the system afloat.

As the demise of FSLIC became certain, some commentators focused on the liability question and claimed the losses should be funded by the S&L industry, not by the federal government (taxpayers). The claim was unrealistic on two counts. First, the solvent S&Ls would have been made insolvent by trying to salvage their insurance agency; the resources simply were not there. In January 1989, some $100 billion of deposit liabilities were at risk in insolvent S&Ls. At the time, the tangible net worth of the entire industry stood at $38.2 billion.[9] Second, and more to the point of liability, there is no logical reason why solvent S&Ls should pay for the mistakes and economic misfortunes of other S&Ls.

S&Ls are independently owned and operated businesses. They are not responsible for each other's actions. Just as no one suggested that Ford and GM should bail out Chrysler several years ago, it makes no sense to say that competent (or lucky) S&Ls should bailout incompetent (or unlucky) S&Ls. The purpose of the bailout is not to save the S&Ls—indeed many are disappearing—the purpose is to insure that the depositors do not lose their money and that the integrity of the financial system is maintained. The fact that Congress had little choice but to do what it did to save the S&Ls does not mean that the policies that helped generate the problem have been abandoned.

There is one last reason for arguing that the insurer, not the insured, should fund the restructuring if the funds can be gathered, even if fraud is the cause of some of the S&L failures. The federal government requires federally chartered S&Ls to buy deposit insurance. Having no choice, they face a monopoly insurance company. The monopoly insurer sets its own price, establishes its own rules, and requires a long list of specific actions to be taken by the insured institutions. While some of those practices contribute to the risk of failure, a point we will discuss later, the liability insurer is free to set the rules of the game. If reserves are too low, the problem is with the insurer, not the insured. Since the federal taxpayer is the insurer of last resort, something akin to the reinsurer in ordinary insurance markets, and is legally put on notice each time FHLB bonds are sold with the full faith and security of the federal government backing them, it is only logical, though sad, that taxpayers and not other S&Ls would provide additional capital when their taxpayer-operated insurance company begins to go under.

The fact that Congress had little choice but to re-fund the monopoly insurer with taxpayer dollars does not mean that the policies of FSLIC that contributed to the demise have been abandoned. We now review the history of the S&L problem and focus on the incentives created for those in the industry.

III. THE ORIGIN OF THE INSURANCE CRISIS

The structure of the S&L industry established in the 1930s worked well for several decades. S&Ls were sound and there were few failures. To a large extent the businesses, which were generally local, small organizations, enjoyed a quiet life. By law, the vast majority of their lending was for homebuilding. And by law, most of their funds came from savings accounts held by millions of individual savers. Later, because of federal regulation of interest rates, S&Ls had an advantage in offering savings accounts. The financial world was a simple place in the 1950s. You saved your money at an S&L; you had a checking account with a bank; and your mortgage (at rates now hard to believe) came from an S&L. In 1965, when inflation was running at 2 percent, the interest rate on savings accounts was about 4 percent, and home mortgage rates averaged about 5.8 percent.

Although the financial system worked quite well, it was highly restrictive and prevented many good investment opportunities from being available to most people. The system also restricted competition in the provision of financial services. While the system was likely to change through time, the inflation of the 1970s broke the system apart.

Impact of Inflation

Today, we celebrate 4 or 5 percent inflation as a reasonable level, not one that causes alarm. Twenty years ago that was such an unacceptably high level that it helped cause President Nixon to impose wage and price controls in a (misguided) effort to control inflation. Since inflation averaged less than 2 percent for many years, 4 or 5 percent in 1970 was considered a crisis.

Had there never been a change in inflation rates, the structural weakness of the financial system might not have become apparent. Since the 1930s the federal government had set, by Regulation Q, the maximum interest rate that federally insured banks and S&Ls could pay to depositors. This system worked reasonably well until, in 1970, the rate of inflation hit 5 percent, about the same as the rate of interest that could legally be paid to people holding savings accounts. This meant that one lost money by saving money; the inflation rate, combined with the taxes paid on interest earned, was higher than the interest earned. The dollar saved last year was worth less than it was the year before.

Unless the interest rate could rise to account for inflation's corrosive effect on the value of the dollar, the incentive to save was diminished. People began to search for new places to save their dollars where the federal restrictions on what they could be paid would not apply. This caused problems in the S&L market, but as inflation subsided in 1971 and 1972 the concern abated.

In 1973 inflation rose and in 1974 it hit double digits (11 percent) for an unheard-of high. Dipping a bit in the mid–1970s, inflation stayed in double digits from 1979 through 1981, after which it dropped to "acceptable" levels. The damage to the old regulatory structure was done. Congress had no choice but to allow the financial system to change.

Citizens could not risk saving money at fixed interest rates when inflation was so unpredictable. In 1974, when the consumer price index rose 11 percent, the legal maximum interest rate on passbook savings accounts was 5.25 percent. Time deposit accounts at S&Ls could pay no more than 7.75 percent interest (which was taxable). Home mortgage rates averaged 9 percent (tax deductible). At these rates, people were being punished for saving and were being paid to borrow money. The S&L system stayed afloat, with difficulty, primarily because there were not many options for most people as to where to save their money. However, in a technical sense the industry was in serious trouble. When the industry's portfolio of mortgages yielding below market rates was priced for the market, the present value was less than that of the industries' liabilities—the funds in savings accounts.

As people sought other places for their money, the pressure grew to relax the restrictions on interest rates that could be paid to depositors. By the time the next round of high inflation rates was finished in 1982, there had been no choice for Congress and the regulatory agencies but to remove most of the restrictions on interest rates and on the types of financial services that could be offered.

The financial world changed quickly. Traditional savings deposits, which in 1970 was where people held 42 percent of the nation's money supply (M2), only held 12 percent of the money supply in 1984. New places to put money in a highly competitive market were now available. Money market deposit accounts, which did not exist in 1981, held more money by 1983 than did savings deposits. Inflation was the primary cause of the pressure to change the structure of the financial system. It also was the primary cause of the insolvency of so many S&Ls.

Inflation and the Solvency of S&Ls

Inflation means a rise in the general price level. If there is 10 percent inflation, some prices may rise 20 percent, while others fall 5 percent; relative prices of various goods change while the general trend is upward. During the inflation of the 1970s, the most notable price change was that of energy products. For the years 1973 and 1974 combined, when the consumer price index rose 17.2 percent, most of the increase was due to the 74 percent increase in fuel oil and coal prices and the 29 percent increase in food (especially grain) prices. In the three years (1979–1981) when the overall consumer price index rose 39.4 percent, the price of fuel oil rose 139 percent and the price of gasoline rose 110 percent. In contrast, the price of home electronic equipment fell slightly.

Despite the high rates of inflation, interest rates remained relatively low until the early 1980s. Savings and loans were issuing fixed-rate mortgages (variable-rate mortgages were prohibited by law until 1981) that were often at or below the current rate of inflation. In 1974, 1979, and 1980 most conventional mortgages issued were at an interest rate below the inflation rate. People were paying a negative rate of interest, especially when considering the tax deductibility of the interest payments; people were being paid to borrow money.

For the eight years between 1974 and 1981, the rate of increase in the consumer price index averaged 10 percent per year. This inflation, combined with the restrictions on interest rates that lending institutions could pay borrowers, kicked up the demand for real estate. The real rate of interest was near zero or negative and, for about a decade, it had been difficult to save money so that it earned more than the rate of inflation. People turned to real assets, such as gold and real estate, to protect their wealth.

Expectations of continued or even higher rates of inflation (remember talk of 20 percent inflation or of inflation "out of control"?) increased the demand for real property. The price of real estate—farmland, existing and new homes, and vacant land held for speculation—was bid up rapidly. Prices rose most quickly in the high growth areas, especially in California and Florida, and in the energy and mineral boom areas, such as Texas, Oklahoma, and Louisiana. In farm states such as Iowa, Nebraska, and South Dakota, the price of farmland often doubled in a few years. Farmers were optimistic about grain prices, and investors looked to hold real estate in the form of farm property.

The story at the other end, as inflation was rapidly brought under control—3.2 percent in 1983 and 1.9 percent in 1986—accompanied by a recession in the early 1980s, is recent history. As inflationary expectations were dampened and many people came to believe that 10 percent inflation would not be common, and as energy and farm product prices fell, the real estate market took a dive.

Especially in Texas, where real estate prices fell as much as 50 percent in the mid- and late 1980s, those who gave mortgage money to buyers when prices were high were left holding the title to property worth less than the mortgage as the property owners simply walked away, cleaned out by the crash. Similar stories, on a less grand scale, are told in the farm states where farm land prices have fallen (as have grain prices) and farmers had property worth less than the money they borrowed to buy it.

While the fall in inflation rates from the 10 percent plus rates of the 1970s and early 1980s is a generally positive economic event, it meant that there were bills to pay for the economic follies imposed by inflation. The reduction in inflation and in inflationary expectations caused a disaster for many S&Ls (and many property owners).

The other side of the inflation disaster came earlier. As inflation and interest rates rose through the 1970s and into the 1980s, S&Ls were stuck with portfolios dominated by mortgages made in the days of 6 percent mortgage money. In short, back in the 1960s the S&Ls paid depositors 4 percent and made fixed-rate mortgages at 6 percent. When inflation jumped to 10 percent the old mortgages rose in value to the homeowner but were losing assets for the S&Ls. As indicated earlier, many S&Ls were technically bankrupt through the 1970s. Their assets were mortgages carried at book value, which was fine when they were issued, but not at market value, which had fallen due to the rise in interest rates. Most S&Ls weathered that financial problem only because their deposits were quite stable and they did not have to sell their assets at discount prices.

The Rising Insolvency Problem

The mid-1980s collapse of oil and grain prices that followed on the heels of the 1982 recession, deflation, and the accompanying forces associated with the restructuring of America's industrial sector left an indelible imprint on the nation's regional economies. The states that were more specialized in grain, energy, and heavy machinery suffered worse than other regions. Within the affected sectors of the economy, activities tied to land and real estate became major recipients of the adjustment burden.

As the number of bad loans increased, along with more defaults on mortgages, the buck stopped with the lending institutions, hitting hardest in the energy and farm belts. A record number of commercial banks failed; the federal farm credit system trembled and called for an infusion of tax money;[10] and S&L associations in the troubled regions simply could not recover from insolvency.

The cumulative financial effects of nonperforming loans and defaults on mortgages held by S&Ls pushed the earlier insolvent S&Ls deeper in the red after the sharp oil price decline that began in 1985. At the same time, some of the weaker but still solvent S&Ls in the older industrialized states were gaining ground. The insolvency problem is seen vividly in Figure 10.1, which graphs the total number of FSLIC-insured S&Ls that became insolvent in the period 1976 through 1988.[11] In 1975 there were 17 institutions with zero or negative net worth (insolvent). The number rose sharply in 1982, in association with the severe recession and commodity deflation, and jumped sharply after that. By 1988, there were 364 insolvent S&Ls and during the period 1,092 insolvencies had been resolved by the FSLIC. Simply put, the industry was shrinking rapidly through FSLIC-led consolidations and mergers.

Figure 10.2 uses June 1988 data to identify the share of each state's S&Ls that are insolvent. The states are then arrayed in six groupings, starting from the most to the least insolvencies by state. States in the worst tier contain more than one-fourth of the insolvent institutions nationwide. As can be seen, most of the states in the tier specialize in energy and grain production. That characteristic follows the states in the second tier. The

Figure 10.1
Insolvent S&Ls: 1976–1988

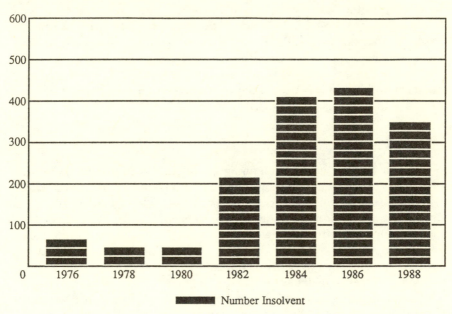

Number Insolvent

third tier represents a kind of transition group of states, where insolvencies have less to do with highly specialized economies and more to do with a combination of industry adjustments related to the new competitive environment created by deregulation, the economic tremors that came from the 1982 recession, and the energy shocks. Some of the states in the third tier, like Alabama, had fairly significant energy sectors, which included coal and oil production. Others, like California and Florida, have lenders that were deeply committed to land and real estate development. The tier also includes a few heavy-industry states, like Indiana and Michigan. Finally, the last tier contains nine states that have no insolvent S&Ls and Kentucky, where just 1.6 percent of the S&Ls were insolvent.

IV. THE REGULATORY CHALLENGES

Unusual economic forces such as high inflation and energy shocks took their toll on the nation's S&Ls. Beyond the control of any financial institution, the problems generated were compounded by weaknesses in the regulatory system, which became all the more apparent in the 1980s. Some regulatory strictures prevented S&Ls from making logical changes that would have cushioned the negative economic effects and strengthened their financial soundness. As noted earlier, only since 1981 have S&Ls been

Figure 10.2
Percent of S&Ls Insolvent, by State, June 1988

TIER ONE (11) Over 25%		TIER TWO (7) 15 to 24.9%		TIER THREE(10) 10 to 14.9%	
Alaska	66.7%	Colo.	24.3	Idaho	14.3
Texas	49.1	N. Mex.	24.0	Calif.	14.0
Neb.	41.7	Minn.	22.2	Fla.	13.7
Ark.	37.8	Miss.	21.4	Mo.	13.6
Okl.	36.7	Ill.	20.8	Ala	13.5
Ore.	33.3	S. Dak.	16.7	Wash.	11.4
N. Dak.	33.3			Ga.	11.3
Utah	30.8			Va.	11.1
La.	29.8			Ind.	10.1
Kans.	27.3			Mich.	10.1
Wyo.	27.3				

TIER FOUR (7) 5 to 9.9%		TIER FIVE (6) 0.1 to 4.9%		TIER SIX (9) 0%	
Tenn.	9.8%	N.C.	4.4%	Del.	0.0
Ariz.	9.1	S.C.	4.1	Haw.	0.0
Mont.	9.1	Conn.	3.8	Mass.	0.0
N.J.	8.1	Pa.	3.0	Me.	0.0
Ohio	8.0	Wisc.	2.7	Nev.	0.0
Md.	6.1	Ky.	1.6	N.H.	0.0
N.Y.	5.9			R.I.	0.0
				Ver.	0.0
				W.V.	0.0

allowed to offer variable-rate mortgages, which move with changes in interest rates so that the borrower is protected when rates decline and the lender is protected when rates rise. The spread between fixed- and variable-rate mortgages indicates that lenders adjust for the riskiness of the fixed-rate instrument. When rates fall, borrowers can obtain a new, lower-interest-rate mortgage and pay off the old higher-rate loans. When interest rates rise, the lender cannot force borrowers to pay off the old mortgages in favor of new higher-rate loans.

The necessary deregulation of S&Ls that introduced adjustable-rate mortgages and allowed S&Ls to offer checkable deposits and a richer array of savings instruments was not easily digested by the industry because of the timing of the changes. Deregulation first allowed S&Ls to compete aggressively for savings dollars, but did not allow them to offer adjustable-rate mortgages. The old fixed-rate mortgages were still producing low revenues, and the new higher-yielding savings instruments systematically increased S&L payouts and eliminated profitability.

The old regulations restricted opportunities for investors, forcing them to put money in time deposits that often paid far less than they might have earned in the absence of the government restrictions. On the other side of the ledger, S&Ls were the mechanism that supported homebuilding markets at lower rates of interest. The S&Ls did not reap high profits from the cheap money provided by savers because competition in the mortgage market forced them to pass the savings to the borrowers. Housing was supported at the expense of other more profitable investments. Income was transferred from numerous unknown investors and the savers who earned low rates of interest to homebuilders and buyers.

The ending of the federal controls terminated the cheap lunches that came with them. But the move to a more rational financial system means that we have to pay the costs imposed by the old regulations and the costs that came with restructuring the system. The 1989 act that restructured S&Ls is a mixed bag. Some things are ended, but oddly enough, in an effort to force prudent behavior by the S&Ls that remain in operation, a greater percent of their portfolio must be in mortgage assets than was required for years, which in a sense is a return to one feature of the old artificial division between banks and S&Ls.

Problems with FSLIC Insurance

Federal insurance for S&Ls, FSLIC, and for banks, FDIC, was established in the 1930s. The system worked well as long as inflation was stable and there was no change in the basic structure of the operations of financial institutions. The economic swings of the 1970s and 1980s and the deregulation of many aspects of the financial markets made clear—to the tune of over 100 billion dollars—weaknesses in the FSLIC system that were always present.

FSLIC insurance has been required of all federally chartered S&Ls (over 1,000 nationwide) and available to state-chartered S&Ls that wanted to join the system (over 1,000 nationwide). Unlike most federal regulatory schemes, which require state regulations to be subservient to federal standards, state-chartered S&Ls were allowed to follow state regulations of their activities—which may not be as strict as federal regulations—and yet belong to FSLIC.

In the early 1980s, several states liberalized the investment powers of their state-chartered S&Ls. An element of moral hazard entered the already crude insurance scheme. S&Ls in those states could take on risks not allowed for S&Ls in other states. Prominent among the states with expanded powers were California, Florida, and Texas. Given the high-flying nature of their economies at the time, especially in real estate, some S&Ls ventured further than would ordinarily be prudent. As the data presented earlier show, S&Ls in those states dominate the pack of those in serious trouble.

A major reason these S&Ls and others, state or federally chartered, could venture into risky areas, while most S&Ls maintained their conservative investment and expansion programs, is because of the existence of fixed-rate federal insurance. For years, every FSLIC-insured S&L paid one-twelfth of 1 percent of its deposits to the FSLIC as their "insurance premium." The premium continued until 1988 when an emergency surcharge was added, making the new fee 20.8 cents per $100 of deposits and still yielding a flat premium.

In a real insurance program, the insurer adjusts the premium to account for the riskiness of the insured and will cancel or not write insurance for highly risky exposure units; that is, prudent S&Ls with solid capital structures would pay lower insurance rates than high-risk S&Ls. An S&L approaching insolvency would have difficulty renewing its insurance contract, which would obviously warn investors about the prudence of doing business with that company. Similarly, S&Ls in areas of stable economic activity would pay lower rates than S&Ls in volatile economic regions. Under the FSLIC, by law, everyone buys insurance and everyone pays the same premium. Prudently operated S&Ls in Texas that avoided the lure of gaudy rates of return in risky ventures paid (and still pay) the same premium to the FSLIC as their high-flying competitors who went billions into the red. There was no market discipline.

Private insurers would be unlikely to allow such behavior to continue without taking action to force high-risk S&Ls to limit such investment activities to reduce the damage done to the insurance pool. Instead, to clean up the S&L mess, not only are the taxpayers going to pay the bill, but also all other S&Ls are required to pay special assessments to the Savings Association Insurance Fund (SAIF), the replacement for the FSLIC, to put more cash in the till for the insolvents. Under FIRREA, all S&Ls continued to pay 20.8 cents per $100 of deposits to the new insurance fund, SAIF, through December 31, 1990. After that, the premium rose to 23.8 cents until December 31, 1993, when it is supposed to fall to 18 cents and continue at that level until the end of 1997, when the rate will fall to a flat 15 cents.[12] Again, the special assessments are a flat fee—no adjustment is made for the current behavior or riskiness of the individually owned and operated S&Ls.

The comparison of S&L insurance fees with those of commercial banks is interesting. They too are required to pay higher premiums to a new deposit insurance fund, the Bank Insurance Fund (BIF), which like SAIF is part of FDIC. Banks paid 8.3 cents per $100 through December 1989, and will pay 12 cents until December 31, 1997. A fee of 15 cents is required after that. Obviously, commercial banks are given a seven-year competitive advantage. They also pay a flat fee that ignores risk.

Private Insurance and Liability

Companies that provide insurance that places them at substantial risk closely monitor the insured and often insist on certain changes in the methods of doing business to keep the insurance in force—at least at the rates offered. In part, insurance companies set rates for businesses based on their estimates of the relative riskiness of the operation. Mistakes are made, of course, but far fewer than when all members of an industry are given the same insurance at the same rate, regardless of how safe the insured appears to be. This major defect in the structure of the FSLIC and all other federal insurance for financial institutions has not been revised. Instead the problem is supposed to be reduced by dramatically increased vigilance on the part of federal bank examiners and a host of financial regulations that severely limit the investment options available to members of the industry.

The behavior of the federal monopoly insurer is partly explained by the fact that it is a monopolist that can draw on taxpayer money for bailouts. Competitive insurance companies, which must purchase reinsurance in the market rather than depend on taxpayer bailouts, cannot behave like federal monopolists. Private insurance companies are liable for the losses up to the point of their own bankruptcy, which causes them to monitor insured who pose major risks.

Having uniform premiums leads to more uniform rules, which is to say the implied goal of deposit insurers is homogeneity across financial institutions, loans, and customers. The highly structured regulations that accompanied the 1989 legislation will lead to the production of a more homogeneous stock of houses that are covered by mortgages, the elimination of more borrowers who fail to meet the uniform lending rules spawned by the rules, and more uniform lenders, who are now limited in inventing new lending and saving programs.

Incentives of S&L Participants under FSLIC

The bankruptcy of hundreds of S&Ls produced numerous stories about fraud on a massive scale (and some convictions) and even more stories about poor judgment on the part of S&L executives.[13] U.S. attorneys have brought hundreds of actions and convicted 140 individuals in the last few years.[14] In addition, congressional committees have held many hearings about these "shocking" revelations only to find that prominent members of Congress appear to be involved in the S&L mess.[15] The failure to do much to change the incentives of those in the industry, except to claim that there will be more vigilance in the future by federal watchdogs, means that the same problems can be expected to occur in the future. As Soviet rulers from Stalin to Gorbachev have discovered, shooting a few bad managers and exhorting the rest to do better has little impact on the productivity of an industry.

Insulating depositors from liability and helping insulate the owners of S&Ls from liability, by the existence of flat-rate public insurance to cover losses incurred for any reason, eliminates many of the market discipline devices that help constrain the behavior of managers of private firms. The fact that more S&Ls did not go under is, if anything, a tribute to the high degree of integrity that exists despite governmental programs designed to reward foolish or careless managers, and even some who intended to commit fraud.

So long as depositors are sure that their deposits are guaranteed by the federal government, there is a clear incentive to seek the S&L that offers the highest interest rate. When inflation and interest rates were high and changing rapidly in the 1970s and early 1980s, savers were enticed to send their money to institutions that they did not know by reputation and might deal with only by mail. If High Flyer S&L in Dallas, in its first year of operation, advertised nationwide that it paid higher interest than anyone else, given the FSLIC guarantee, savers had no reason not to send money to High Flyer.

So long as accounts are insured by the FSLIC or the new SAIF, it is of little concern to depositors that an institution may have poor lending habits or limited capital that increase the likelihood of failure. Capital structure matters little when there is a federal guarantee behind those who accept savings deposits. The system still fails to impose the market discipline of liability on the major participants, replacing such contractual liability with a mandated standard that leaves the taxpayers again liable.

During the years of high inflation, the price explosion in real estate, and the oil boom, most S&L managers continued to use prudent investment rules when setting interest rates for savers and borrowers. Their reputations were at stake. At the time, they were punished for their prudence by institutions that took advantage of the FSLIC guarantee to offer higher rates of interest to savers and lent a greater portion of their assets to more risky borrowers than business judgment would normally allow. That many of the S&Ls with riskier portfolios went bankrupt was to be expected whatever happened to the economy. When inflation rates and petroleum and real estate prices unexpectedly fell rapidly, the number of bankruptcies jumped to monumental levels.

The effect of government regulation of the S&L industry has been to reduce market incentives to adjust for risk, to reduce concern that there are dishonest people who want to steal depositors' money, and to eliminate much of the premium for reputation. With flat-rate insurance, lenders have incentives to have riskier portfolios and savers have no reason to be concerned about that. These effects are understood; what has been discussed less are the consequences that arise from the lack of importance of reputation or goodwill.

Reputation as Guarantee of Quality

Reputation or goodwill is a valuable asset. The *name* Coca-Cola is probably worth billions of dollars. Companies work hard to build and maintain reputation as a key asset. Unlike physical assets such as buildings and trucks that have alternative uses as a company goes under, reputation or goodwill is an intangible that is of value only as it exists. If a company ruins its reputation through mismanagement and bankruptcy, there is no salvage value.

Similarly, the reputation of individuals is important. Arnold Palmer has earned far more by endorsing products than he ever did by winning golf tournaments, because many people trust him. He puts his reputation on the line when he endorses a product. Suppose he endorsed a new product that turned out to be worthless or dangerous. His reputation and market value as an endorser would diminish. Hence, he has an incentive to think about product quality, as does the producer of the product. Producers of quality products hire expensive endorsers, like Arnold Palmer, because it signals to buyers that the producers are willing to risk substantial capital on expensive promotion campaigns that are utterly worthless if the product turns out to be deceptive in quality and consumers reject the product.

People who have a lot at stake beyond a single business deal can act as quality assurance to others. If the chairman of General Motors or IBM accepts a seat on a board of directors of a company, he places much of his career at stake. What would the likelihood be that persons of such quality reputation would sit on the boards of S&Ls with dubious lending practices that could end in a fiasco? In general, people with high-quality reputations end up on boards of directors of high-quality companies. It is a signal to investors and buyers that many people with a lot at stake are putting their reputations on the line to keep quality high.

Obviously, if enough is offered in compensation to some people of valuable reputations, they will risk that reputation for the big score. Some of the S&L collapses in Texas have seen people of presumed stature throw away their reputations—for chances at high gains that were made available because of the regulatory structure of the industry that caused many depositors to have no concern about where their money went.

Market Review of Investment Opportunities

Compare the situation in the S&L industry to that of investments via the stock market. Investors have heard of blue chip companies like IBM and, for good reason, presume their money will not be subject to gross mismanagement if they buy IBM stock. Suppose investors are offered stock in Meiners-Yandle Corporation. As promoters of this fine company, we advertise that we expect to earn above market rates of return. Obviously, you should invest with us, not with IBM. Some investors may believe this line, but most investors will either try to evaluate carefully what is going on at Meiners-Yandle Corporation or they will rely on a brokerage firm, such as

Merrill Lynch, that has a reputation to maintain by providing investors information about stocks that have no reputation value.

Investors have incentives to protect their funds that would largely be eliminated if the government promised that no one would lose money by investing in any stock. More investors would pick Meiners-Yandle Corporation over IBM if we claimed the return on investment would beat IBM—and had a government agency there to guarantee that no stock purchasers could lose money. Investors would have little incentive to inquire what was going on at Meiners-Yandle, since their investment would be guaranteed.

As managers, we would not be subject to normal market evaluations about our prospects. Meiners-Yandle could go forward with whatever scheme we had in mind. If we were lucky we would succeed and everyone would be paid. If we were wrong, we could end up out of business, but would be likely to have risked less of our capital than would be the case without the government insurance.

In the case of federally insured financial institutions, we would have strong incentives to make risky investments in hopes of large gains. The principals in the operation need have little at stake. If we ran losses on investments, we could continue to pull in more investors by paying interest out of deposits. Eventually, the financial house of cards could collapse if our schemes did not pay off, but given the difficulty that even diligent federal investigators have evaluating the true market value of what is carried on the books, huge losses could be incurred for a long time before a halt would be called. Then the government would pay off the depositors. Obviously, if we were so inclined, fraud could be involved too, but that is not necessary for above-normal rates of losses to be incurred.

Because investors have less reason to try to evaluate the quality of operation of firms that are guaranteed by the federal government, it is to be expected that, especially among the high-risk operations, their boards of directors would be composed of individuals less well known (of lower reputation value) than would be the board members of firms of similar size that intended to maximize the long-run value of the firm—and protect the reputation of the board members and top managers—by engaging in investment strategies of ordinary prudence. Not only are higher risk investment strategies encouraged by flat-rate government insurance for depositors, but more fraud can be expected to occur. While fraud is always a danger because getting rich at others' expense is a fine temptation, there will be fewer monitors watching for fraud when the government is not saying, "Don't worry, we will cover any losses." Investors will not scrutinize firm operations, nor will there be a private insurance firm with its own capital at stake to watch for evidence of fraud, and, since there is less concern about who constitutes the board of directors, firms will be able to attract large quantities of dollars without offering a high-quality board as another assurance to investors. It is no accident that despite the size of the S&L

industry, there never was a major S&L with a national brand name. There was no incentive to invest in reputation since the government accepted responsibility for all competitors in that market regardless of quality.

Government Review of Investment Opportunities

Much has been made of the role of government examiners who check the books of guaranteed financial institutions, such as S&Ls. Any hope that a large, well-intended, well-trained staff of examiners will prevent more fraud or, more commonly, imprudent decisions than will private evaluators, is misplaced. Government examiners are supposed to play a role that is to replace such things as insurance company evaluations and numerous private investor (depositors and stockholders) examinations of various aspects of the operation. These multiple investigators in the private market, who often have different incentives, make mistakes. But, given the benefits of multiple independent evaluations by individuals and firms with profit motives, the number of mistakes made must be smaller than the number of mistakes made by government examiners who are given one set of objectives and personally have little at stake from mistakes made about the institutions they examine.

There has also been discussion about improving the quality of government examination of lending institutions to reduce the number of mistakes made by examiners. Increasing the number of government examiners raises the costs of all S&Ls as they provide staff and material to deal with the examiners. Perfectly well-managed S&Ls will have to bear the same review costs as will the poorly managed S&Ls that regulators are to help prevent. Increased examinations are also likely to result in more regulatory constraints on managerial decision making across the industry that may or may not make sense.

The policy imposed by the 1989 legislation, which is so complicated that few regulators much less industry executives fully understand it, sets detailed requirements for balance-sheet management and lending authority. As the rules now stand, the S&Ls will be among the most tightly regulated institutions in our economy, perhaps in the history of federal regulation. Just to mention one example, investment officers with S&Ls will likely be required to state their intentions as to whether or not they intend to sell or hold when purchasing portfolio securities.

If interest rates rise or fall—offering opportunities to secure capital gains or deflect loss—those investments purchased as permanent assets must be held. Only those securities that were marked initially as tradable can be sold when market opportunities arise. To be successful, the investment officer must either have perfect foresight or be unusually lucky. The new regulations set restrictions on lending that focus S&Ls on traditional homebuilding markets and lower-income housing within those markets. But that is just the beginning. S&Ls may not invest in unrated bonds, other than those of quasi-government agencies. In addition, minimum capital requirements have been tightened to the point that 600 additional S&Ls are expected to fail to meet the new standards, while other strong S&Ls will operate in an ironclad jacket for years to come.

All the rules simplify the examination process, but also limit the ability of S&Ls to compete with other financial intermediaries. For the S&Ls to exist, let alone flourish, in the new regulatory environment, they will need interest rate protections similar to those they previously had under Regulation Q. Alternatively, the S&Ls will have to enjoy interest rate subsidies when borrowing funds from the Federal Home Loan Bank, which will not likely happen.

V. CONCLUSIONS

Failure by government to allow for risk-determined deposit premiums, which allows private insurers to be liable for losses, is the fundamental cause for the recent S&L crisis. While the failure is understandable given the political incentives that motivate elected officials, the resulting uniform insurance fees led managers and owners of S&Ls to accept riskier loans and to engage in other opportunistic behavior. The question of liability—who should bear the losses that ultimately arose—is itself fundamental to the socialized deposit insurance system. As it now stands, the U.S. taxpayer has learned where the buck stops. The liability, and therefore the risk, is spread across the backs of the burdened taxpayer.

While that is clearly the case, it is not the end of the story. FIRREA, the massive legislative package intended to salvage the S&L insurance fund and put the industry on a sound footing, again contains the seeds of a future collapse. Just as in the past, deposit insurance has a flat fee. But unlike the past, the fee is significantly higher for S&Ls relative to their bank competitors. On top of that disadvantage and mainly because of the fixed-rate insurance, the S&Ls will work under a heavy blanket of regulation, perhaps the heaviest of any industry in the United States.

How long will the current fix last? To answer that question, we must recall the conditions that triggered the 1980s' collapse. The four-part problem of inflation, then falling commodity prices, then deregulation, and then a recession destroyed the old structure of the industry. Inflation is always a possibility, given the record of the monetary authorities. Recessions come and go periodically. And commodity price changes are always a potential fact of life. When the nation is hit again by economic turmoil, we can watch for another chapter in the story of deposit liability and the S&L mess.

NOTES

1. See *Washington Notes* (August 11, 1989), p. 32.

2. "FIRREA: A Closer Look Reveals New Realities," *Savings Institutions*, October 1989, pp. 28–35.

3. The source of the problem we discuss has been recognized by others. For example, see *Economic Report of the President* (Washington, D.C.: Government Printing Office, 1989), pp. 200–204.

4. For an excellent history that covers this discussion and more, see John C. Weicher, "The Future Structure of the Housing Finance System," in *Restructuring Banking and Financial Services in America*, ed. William S. Haraf and Rose Marie Kushmeider (Washington, D.C.: American Enterprise Institute, 1988), pp. 296–336. Also in the same volume, see George J. Benston and George G. Kaufman, "Regulating Bank Safety and Performance," pp. 63–97.

5. Benston and Kaufman argue that had the Federal Reserve Bank performed, government-provided insurance would not have been needed then and now. See *supra* note 4 at 65.

6. Ibid., p. 67.

7. Ibid., p. 71.

8. This discussion is based on "Thrift Industry Trends and Industry Performance: December 1977 through June 1987" (Washington, D.C.: U.S. General Accounting Office, GAO/GGD 88–87-BR, May 1988).

9. See Christopher Ellis, "Thrifts Face Uncertain Future as Buoy-Up Costs Keep Rising," *Insight*, December 21–January 2, 1989, pp. 31–38.

10. There are rough estimates that the Federal Farm Credit Banks may require about a $10 billion annual subsidy through the 1990s to stay solvent.

11. The figure is based on data taken from Edward J. Kane, "The High Cost of Incompletely Funding the FSLIC Shortage of Explicit Capital," *Journal of Economic Perspectives* 3, 4 (Fall 1989): 31–47, at 35. Note that meaningful comparisons of insolvencies cannot be made after 1988 due to the federal government's restructuring activities that began in 1989.

12. See "FIRREA: A Closer Look Reveals New Realities," p. 32.

13. For example, see "The Verdict's In: Crooks Are Out," *Savings Institutions*, March 1989, pp. 36–42.

14. Ibid., p. 37.

15. Lincoln Savings and Loan of California, managed by Charles Keating, was the nation's worst S&L failure, requiring some $2.1 billion of taxpayer funds to handle it. Mr. Keating and five U.S. Senators were investigated on charges that the senators intervened when the regulators attempted to rein in Mr. Keating's operations. The five senators had received $1.46 million in campaign contributions. (See Brooks Jackson, "How Regulatory Err Led to the Disaster at Lincoln Savings," *Wall Street Journal*, November 20, 1989, pp. A1, A8.

11

Insurers, Automakers, and the Political Debate over Air Bags

Robert Kneuper

I. INTRODUCTION

The federal government has been involved in automobile safety regulation since the 1966 passage of the National Highway Traffic and Motor Vehicle Safety Act, and over the decades that have followed, government officials have put forth regulations involving everything from seat belts to bumpers to child seating systems. While legislators and regulatory agencies have been successful in mandating these changes, many were met with resistance by both industry and consumers. Perhaps the most controversial of these regulations involved the National Highway Safety Board's attempt to require air bags on all newly produced automobiles.[1] Confident of the substantial safety benefits from air bags, government regulators, supported by a wide variety of special interest groups, began pushing for an air-bag mandate in the late 1960s. But, as it would turn out, the air bag was not your ordinary safety device; it was costly, controversial, and unlike its predecessor (the seat belt), involuntary. The attempt to mandate this unique safety device set off one of the longest and most intense political battles of our time—a battle that still remains unresolved over twenty years after it began.

This chapter will examine the debate over air bags—a debate normally characterized as a conflict between civil liberties groups, who value freedom of choice with respect to automobile safety, and automobile safety groups, who value reduction of automobile-related fatalities and injuries. Behind the scenes, the air-bag debate pitted two financially powerful and politically influential groups against one another: auto producers and insurers. This chapter will discuss the economic motivations that drove these two groups toward opposite ends of the debate.

The chapter is organized as follows: The next section looks at automobile safety regulation and its effect on consumers and industry. This is followed by a chronological discussion of the air-bag saga starting with the original introduction of an air-bag rule in 1969 and ending with a controversial decision made by then Transportation Secretary Elizabeth Dole in 1984.

The next major section examines the special interest groups involved in the struggle: the insurance industry, automakers, air-bag manufacturers, and other smaller, but important interest groups. In addition to providing details on the relative merits of air bags and their predicted financial impact on the various interest groups, the section puts forward some theoretical notions to explain why the various groups were either for or against the mandate. The chapter ends with some final thoughts on the passive restraint struggle.

II. THE EFFECTS OF AUTOMOBILE SAFETY
REGULATIONS ON CONSUMERS AND INDUSTRY

In 1898, traffic safety was hardly a public concern; barely one hundred cars were on the road at that time in the United States. When Dr. Truman J. Martin of Buffalo, New York, took out the first automobile insurance policy that year, his main concern was the damage caused by horses scared by the noisy machines.[2] Then, as mass markets grew, the price of the automobile plummeted, and by 1921 cars were being driven over 55 billion miles a year.[3] The joys of driving were not free; there were 13,900 traffic fatalities in 1921 and 40,000 in 1941.[4] But over that same period, the fatality rate fell from 25.3 to 12 deaths per 100 million miles driven. Safer driving, cars, and highways had combined to provide safer automobile transportation.

Beginning in the early 1960s, the traffic fatality rate began to rise, opening the door for a debate over the "highway safety problem."[5] Fueled by professed concerns over unsafe automobiles and consumers' failure to wear seat belts, automobile safety advocates began pushing regulations that would not only change the construction and cost of automobiles, but that would also change the nature of the automobile business.

For consumers, ensuing regulations would imply a reduction in utility, since a government-mandated safety choice would replace the voluntary choices of automobile drivers and passengers. For example, requirements for shatterproof glass reduce a real hazard to passengers in a collision. Such requirements also eliminate a lower-cost choice for consumers willing to produce their own safety by driving more carefully or by demanding other safety features, paid for by the income saved by purchasing the less expensive, but riskier, autos without safety glass. Denial of such choices means the loss of benefits to those who valued something else more than safer windshields.

An elimination of consumer choices is often justified on the grounds that government regulations improve automobile safety. Reductions in automobile deaths and injuries supposedly offset losses in individual liberties. But, ironically, mandated safety protection can lead to more, rather than less, automobile-related deaths and injuries. Sam Peltzman argues that when drivers believe an automobile to be safer, they will tend to drive faster and exercise less care.[6] The results of this "lulling effect" can more than offset the benefits from a safer automobile, resulting in a net increase in automobile-related fatalities and injuries.

For auto producers, mandated safety equipment implies the provision of a specific bundle of product attributes that were formerly unbundled and sold separately to consumers. Without regulation, some producers might provide superior brakes and less safe interiors. Others may offer faster acceleration and quicker steering to assist in avoiding accidents. Each producer can provide similar safety outcomes with different portfolios of safety-producing attributes. Uniform regulations eliminate these options and often require safety protection that would otherwise be unmarketable. And even when a form of mandated protection is desired by consumers, automobile safety regulations impose costs in the form of uncertainties introduced into the automobile business. This is because government intervention forces automobile producers to anticipate the decisions of government regulators in addition to other market-related outcomes.

Automobile safety regulations can, of course, benefit auto producers in their quest for profits and predictability. Uniform rules simplify producer decision making, eliminate the necessity of meeting diverse state standards, and allow producers to focus their political influence on the single regulator, the monopoly producer of rules. The adept industry lobbyist can use regulation to raise the costs of international and some domestic competitors. The possibility of enhanced profits from the anticompetitive effects of regulation can more than offset the costly, mandated technological changes.

Other interest groups play a subtle but important role in driving automobile safety regulations. For auto insurers, a coordinated reduction in deaths and injuries means a reduction in underwriting claims. Additionally, uniform regulations create a more homogeneous driving force, which can simplify actuarial estimation.

The producers of safety equipment have an obvious interest in rules that mandate devices, particularly ones covered by patents or that are produced with highly specialized inputs. Doctors and other health professionals have also played an important role in automobile safety regulation. Changes in the nature and number of deaths and injuries not only affect the medical profession as a whole, but also redistribute wealth within the profession.

Overall, automobile safety regulations can affect a variety of groups in many ways. By changing the rules of the game, these regulations create new winners and losers and change the final outcome, resulting in an automobile product that is drastically different than that which would have been produced under an unhampered market system.

III. THE PASSIVE RESTRAINT SAGA

Background

On January 31, 1967, soon after the passage of the National Highway Traffic and Motor Vehicle Safety Act, the National Highway Safety Board (NHSB) issued the first federal motor vehicle safety standards, which included requirements for lap-shoulder belts in both front-seat positions and lap belts for rear-seat passengers.[7] Long recognized as being highly effective in reducing fatalities and severe injuries in a technical sense, seat belts have one problem: Their effectiveness depends on voluntary use by drivers and passengers.

Passive devices, on the other hand, provide protection automatically to automobile occupants.[8] On May 7, 1970, the NHSB (which later became the National Highway Traffic Safety Administration [NHTSA]), dissatisfied with consumers' disregard for seat belts, began moving toward passive safety protection by requiring that cars manufactured on or after January 1, 1973, must have restraints requiring "no action by vehicle occupants such as fastening belts."[9] By attempting to mandate passive restraints, NHSB had opened the door for one of the longest and most intense regulatory debates of our time.

Passive Restraint Regulation: Round One

The passive restraint story actually began in 1952. That was when J. W. Hetrick patented an air cushion that inflated automatically when a vehicle suddenly decelerated.[10] Twelve years later, Eaton Yale and Towne, Inc., began developing air bags, and in 1968 the company began selling the idea to NHSB director William Haddon, Jr. With the industry announcement that a passive system would be ready in three to four years, the NHSB was prepared to mandate its use.[11] As one NHSB official put it, "There's no longer any question but that we can build cars that are both beautiful, and in which it will be all but impossible to kill yourself. We're heading in that direction now. Auto safety is becoming a very sexy field."[12]

In June 1969, NHSB issued an advance notice of proposed rule making for "inflatable occupant restraint systems" with an anticipated effective date of January 1, 1972.[13] (A chronology of further passive restraint events is contained in Table 11.1.) The mandate became official in May 1970, but with two major changes. First, the effective date of compliance was delayed until January 1, 1973. Second, NHSB did not specify the use of air bags, but allowed for any passive form of protection that could be shown effective in a thirty-mile-per-hour barrier crash.[14] Many air-bag suppliers did not anticipate a performance standard as proposed by NHSB, but were "dreaming of a $1 billion to $2 billion a year market starting in 1975."[15] Their

Table 11.1
Selected Events Involving Passive Restraint Legislation

Date	Event
1966 Sept. 9	National Traffic and Motor Vehicle Safety Act Signed by the President
1967 Feb. 3	National Highway Safety Bureau (NHSB) requires manual belts on all newly produced cars
1970 May 7	National Highway Traffic Safety Administration (NHTSA) requires passive restraints by Jan. 1, 1973
Sept. 25	NHTSA changes compliance date to July 1, 1973 for front seats and until July 1, 1974 for all seating positions
1972 Feb. 24	NHTSA permits compliance with interlock system
Dec. 5	U.S. Court of Appeals forces NHTSA to review its testing standards and to give automakers reasonable time in complying with the passive restraint law
1974 Oct. 29	Congress outlaws interlock standard
1977 June 30	NHTSA proposes new passive restraint standard to be phased in starting on Sept. 1, 1982
1981 April 6	NHTSA delays compliance of large cars by one year
Oct. 23	NHTSA rescinds passive restraint standard
1982 June 1	U.S. Appeals Court rules that NHTSA's rescission was "arbitrary and capricious"
1983 June 24	Supreme Court upholds earlier decision
Sept. 1	NHTSA delays compliance by one year
1984 July 11	DOT Secretary Dole announces new passive restraint phase-in program beginning in September 1986, unless two-thirds of the country's population is covered by state seat belt laws

Source: Supra n. 5 at 1-5.

disappointment was shared by General Motors (GM), which had made a major commitment to an air-bag program and had hoped to sell the system to other car makers.[16]

While air-bag suppliers were understandably shaken by a turn away from a technology-based standard, the uncertainty generated for GM and other auto companies was more complex. Firms that share a market are caught in an intense competitive battle for market share that depends on prices and product features, among other things. For car makers, the lead time between the design and actual production of automobiles can be as long as five years. Given a distribution of anticipated features and prices demanded by consumers, the major producers tend to go for the heart of the distribution, since large-volume production is necessary for lower costs and prices. This implies a substantial commitment of capital in anticipation of what the future automobile market will look like.

The air-bag technology was not cheap. Estimates of the cost of air bags ranged as high as $1,000, and if one producer chose to use air bags and purchased the expensive tooling for doing so, it might later learn that a competitor had found another lower-cost way to find a regulatory solution. Capital losses would be sustained by the first producer in the adjustment process. If all producers were required to follow a similar mandate, the problem would be simpler. In effect, price increases for safety would be coordinated by the federal government, and that seemed to be the preferred route. As one auto executive put it, "If the government doesn't require air bags, you won't get them. Nobody's going to be the only virgin in the sorority house. No one can afford to be."[17]

But what seemed like a simple regulatory solution to the air-bag problem became complicated by the realities of marketing the device. For one thing, questions began to arise concerning the reliability and feasibility of air bags. Consequently, auto producers requested additional time for testing and developing the necessary tooling.[18] Automakers were also pursuing other alternatives for complying with the performance standard. Ford Motor Company began considering an interlock system, which required the front seat belts to be fastened in order to start a car. Supporting that alternative, Irvin Industries, a safety belt producer, stated that "the government can achieve the quantum jump in safety belt usage and death and injury reduction it is seeking by mandating the adopting of ignition interlock systems in all cars until air bags are fully developed and proven."[19] After a reported meeting between President Nixon, Henry Ford II, and Chrysler Corporation's Lynn Townsend, the NHTSA decided to allow interlock systems as an alternative to passive restraints.[20]

Despite regulatory delays and the introduction of the interlock, GM still supported the air-bag alternative. The company had promised to produce 100,000 bag-equipped cars in 1974 and 1 million by 1975, but eventually failed to meet these goals.[21] Frustrated in the technical development of air bags, GM blamed part of their difficulties on the uncertain regulatory environment. GM President Edward N. Cole pointed toward NHTSA for the failure, claiming, "We cannot justify the expenditure in the area of $200 million for fully-automated tools and facilities"—until GM knew whether a passive restraint system would be mandatory or optional in 1976 or beyond.[22]

Following court actions by Ford, Chrysler, and American Motors Corporation (AMC) to delay the passive restraint ruling, it became increasingly clear that NHTSA's ruling and air bags in particular were losing the day. The technology being forced was highly complex and expensive. Even a lower bound cost estimate for air bags of $300 was close to 5 percent of the price of the average automobile at the time. There were also questions regarding product liability. Neither air-bag producers nor auto companies knew exactly how much liability insurance on air bags would cost. The insurance carriers for one air-bag manufacturer originally estimated the cost to be $10 per unit, later raised the figure to $50, and then declined to give any quotation.[23] Expectations were further upset in April 1972 when an experimental vehicle failed a 50 mile per hour barrier crash as the car's air bag failed to inflate, allowing the two passenger dummies to be "killed."[24] One month later, a demonstration sponsored by the National Motor Vehicle Safety Council also failed.[25]

Despite these setbacks, air-bag proponents, led by the insurance industry, held their ground. Allstate Insurance Company Vice President Donald L. Schaffer wrote to the NHTSA Administrator urging that "Front Seat Air Bags should be required on all automobiles sold in this country."[26] Allstate had a strong vested interest in the cause. Back in 1968, the company had joined forces with Ford and the Eaton Corporation by "helping with the testing of a pro-bag campaign."[27] According to Carleton H. Swanson, president of Eaton's automotive components group, "Allstate saw a benefit in air bags that nobody else had noticed. Bags do save lives. But in the total insurance payoff for auto accidents, the greatest dollar cost is not the death benefit—it's plastic surgery for the girl who hits the windshield."[28]

To the insurers' disdain, this first episode of the air-bag debate ended on October 29, 1974, when Congress outlawed the ignition interlock standard and sent the passive restraint regulation back to NHTSA. After this and the OPEC embargo, passive restraints became a dormant issue. Regulating automobiles took a back seat to forming policies that might salvage the beleaguered auto industry. If automobiles were to be regulated, particularly under a Republican administration, it was necessary first to have a viable industry.

Round Two

While the battle had ended, the passive restraint war was not over. In June 1977, President Carter's Transportation Secretary Brock Adams proposed a new standard to take effect in 1982. This new passive restraint mandate went far beyond the previous administration's agreement with GM

Table 11.2
Members of the National Committee for Automobile Crash Protection

```
Aetna Life and Casualty Insurance Company
Alliance of American Insurers
Allstate Insurance Companies
American Academy of Pediatrics
American Congress of Rehabilitation Medicine
American Insurance Association
American Nurses Association
Automobile Club of Missouri
Susan P. Baker, Associate Professor, Johns Hopkins School
    of Hygiene and Public Health
Center for Auto Safety
Center for Concerned Engineering
Consumer Action Now
Epilepsy Foundation of America
Ralph Nader, Attorney
National Association of Independent Insurers
National Association of Mutual Insurance Companies
National Representatives Conference of Governors' Highway Safety
Nationwide Insurance Companies
Physicians National Housestaff Association
Prudential Property and Casualty Insurance Company
Safeco Insurance Company of America
State Farm Insurance Companies
Travelers Insurance Companies
United Automobile, Aerospace, and Agricultural
    Implement Workers of America (UAW)
```

```
Source:  Status Report.  Insurance Institute for Highway Safety,
         July 26, 1977, p. 4.
```

and Ford calling for the voluntary production of 440,000 air-bag-equipped cars to be produced in fall 1979.[29]

This time, a passive restraint coalition was formed with strong supporters that included consumer interest groups, doctors, nurses, and even the United Auto Workers (see Table 11.2). The insurance industry was also able to gather substantial support for the proposal. A spokesman for the American Mutual Insurance Alliance stated that the providers of "more than 95 percent of all auto insurance written in the country...join together for the third consecutive year to offer...unequivocal support for the mandatory passive restraint standard."[30] Also supporting Adams' decision were a number of air-bag manufacturers including the Eaton Corporation, Thiokol Chemical Company, Allied Chemical Company, Rocket Research Corporation, and Talley Industries.

The passive restraint coalition was armed with substantial evidence supporting both the need for and benefits from mandated air bags. NHTSA had found that only 11 percent of the driving public fastened their seat belts.[31] There was also some evidence that supported the reliability of air bags. By 1980, NHTSA could report that air-bag-equipped cars had traveled

some 800 million miles while maintaining exceptional performance records.[32] Of the 10,281 GM-produced cars sold with air bags between 1974
and 1976, 378 had successfully deployed with no inflator malfunctions and
no failures to deploy, a record that caused NHTSA to rate that system as
99.995 percent reliable.[33]

On the anti–air-bag side, the strongest evidence came from the GM effort
to sell air-bag-equipped cars. The firm had committed substantial funds to
the design, development, and marketing of its 1974 Oldsmobile, Buick, and
Cadillac cars with driver-side air bags. GM had planned to produce 300,000
cars with bags and had absorbed $250 to $300 per car to offset the cost
of the option. In spite of the plans and marketing efforts, only 10,000 bag-
equipped cars were sold. In 1980, GM equipped 415,000 Chevettes with
automatic belts, selling only 13,000 of them (about 3 percent).[34] Other
manufacturers including Ford, AMC, Volkswagen, and BMW expressed
similar concerns, though Volkswagen had successfully sold its Rabbit model
with passive belts.

In congressional hearings on the Adams' proposal, Chrysler Corporation
stated its opposition to a passive restraint mandate:

Secretary Adams' decision will force the American public to pay triple the cost for
a second best safety system. Mr. Adams' ruling ignores his own agency's data which
show that present belt systems will save 50% more lives than air bags. These lives
could be saved right now with today's belts rather than waiting several years for
air bags.[35]

Chrysler even went so far as to distribute an ad of a huge exploded air bag
and a surprised gas station attendant, the caption reading, "Honest, all I
did was slam the hood."[36]

Representatives of AMC found Adams' ruling equally distasteful, claiming
that it had been made "without clear evidence of [the bags'] lifesaving
effectiveness over present belt systems [and] is a multi-billion-dollar gamble
with consumers' money."[37]

Beginning in 1978, the hopes of passive restraint proponents again began
to fade. It was becoming clear that most automakers intended to comply
with the rule by way of passive belts rather than air bags. Anticipating the
diminishing market for bags, air-bag manufacturers such as Eaton Corporation and Allied Chemical Corporation stopped production in 1978. Eaton
had been a pioneer in air-bag development, "spending thirteen years and
more than $20 million on research."[38] Ironically, Eaton blamed NHTSA
for the failure by pushing air bags too fast and too hard. A spokesman for
the firm stated: "Every technical development in the auto industry, from
automatic transmission to cruise control, has had a long lead time. The
industry gets a chance to work out the problems and the people can learn
to appreciate the new product."[39] By mandating passive restraints, NHTSA
had overridden this "natural law of product development."

In early 1981, President Reagan came into office having promised the ailing auto industry regulatory relief. Later that year, NHTSA rescinded the air-bag requirements.[40]

Round Three

The Reagan administration's decision to end the passive restraint requirement did not go unchallenged. Petitions for judicial review were filed by members of the auto insurance industry. On June 1, 1982, an Appeals Court ruled that NHTSA had acted arbitrarily in rescinding the regulation. On June 24, 1983, the Supreme Court upheld that decision.[41] NHTSA was required to review its decision and to offer evidence of a full review in its next action. After the remand, NHTSA again delayed compliance with the former regulation for another year while it reviewed the record in light of the Court's ruling.[42]

A final twist in the debate came in July 1984 when Department of Transportation Secretary Elizabeth Dole announced that all cars sold in the United States would be equipped with passive restraints by September 1989 unless two-thirds of the country's population was covered by state-ordered mandatory seat belts.[43] Dole's proposal required compliance by 10 percent of the 1987 models, 15 percent of the 1988 models, and 40 percent of the 1989 models, while progressing toward the mandatory 100 percent for the 1990 models. Once again, the insurance industry mounted a court battle attacking the Dole decision as just another effort to delay the adoption of the technically superior air bag. Meanwhile, state legislatures began to wrestle with mandatory seat belt laws, and the political struggle over air bags moved from Washington to the fifty states.

IV. WHAT EXPLAINS THE POSITIONS OF THE SPECIAL INTERESTS?

The opposition of mandatory passive restraints shown by the auto industry is reasonably straightforward, especially in light of the failed experience by GM. Passive restraints were costly and not valued sufficiently by consumers of highly popular, mass-produced autos. Unilateral action to market the device as standard equipment, or as an option, by one major producer was a highly risky venture. If the industry was to move in that direction, a uniform standard would be required. The industry needed certainty, especially for a product that consumers might not buy.

Even if passive restraints were mandated, the auto industry still had a problem, and that was price elasticity of demand for automobiles. Higher prices inevitably lead to lower sales, and the domestic industry was already in a tough struggle with foreign producers who enjoyed a cost advantage. To the extent that air bags were not valued by consumers, the air-bag mandate was nothing less than an industry-wide tax. Lower-cost safety alternatives were preferred such as an interlock standard or mandatory use of seat belts. Given widespread consumer discontent with the former device, automakers turned toward a seat belt mandate. The seat belts were already standard equipment; enforcement cost would fall on the states, not on the auto manufacturers. In addition, seat belts did not raise new questions about potential product liability issues as did air bags and other passive restraints.

Perhaps these problems would not have been so pressing had the auto industry been experiencing good times, but that was far from the case. The oil embargo had permanently changed the way automobiles would be built. The industry was putting forth a massive effort to redesign engines, frames, and bodies to meet the demands of higher energy prices and ward off Japanese penetration into the domestic market. It was a time for realignment, not for gambling on safety regulations when a substitute was readily available.

Given their apparent opposition to air bags, how is it that automakers failed to overturn the passive restraint mandate? At the forefront, the opposition came in the form of various public interest groups such as Ralph Nader's Center for Auto Safety. Behind the scenes, however, were automobile insurers that provided substantial funding for these groups.[44] Perhaps the most interesting question in the air-bag saga is why auto insurers were such staunch supporters of the device.

In answering this question it is important to understand the economic environment faced by auto insurers over the period of the debate. As with auto producers, the economic events of the 1970s and 1980s dramatically changed the nature of the insurance business. Hit by a combination of high inflation, higher real interest rates, the transition to smaller and less safe cars, a rise in court-awarded liability claims, and changes in state insurance laws, the industry suffered heavy underwriting losses in the late 1970s and early to mid-1980s.

Losses in the area of automobile liability were particularly dramatic. As indicated in Table 11.3, underwriting losses increased annually between 1981 and 1985 in this area, accounting for roughly $24 billion in losses over the entire period. In contrast, losses from automobile physical damage, which accounts for slightly less than half of automobile premiums written, amounted to $1.5 billion over the same period.

But how could an air-bag rule help to solve auto insurers' underwriting problem? One hypothesis maintains that auto insurers were attempting to reduce costs. Air bags, like other mandated safety devices, would lower automobile-related deaths and injuries and associated insurance claims (assuming that the Peltzman effect does not result in a net increase in fatalities and injuries). This could offset rising claims resulting from inflation, large court awards, and the shift toward smaller cars. From this perspective, an air-bag rule would be particularly attractive in states where premium in-

Table 11.3
Underwriting Experience of Automobile Insurers

Year	Liability Net Premiums Written $000	Liability Statutory Und. Gain After Divs. $000	Physical Damage Net Premiums Written $000	Physical Damage Statutory Und. Gain After Divs. $000
Stock Companies				
1981	14,183,345	-1,885,977	9,414,148	-181,161
1982	15,122,394	-2,532,478	10,126,718	-492,567
1983	15,937,704	-2,984,519	10,999,447	-135,701
1984	17,090,600	-3,994,923	12,162,533	-577,829
1985	20,380,000	-4,685,540	13,885,000	-248,480
5 Yrs	82,714,043	-16,083,437	56,587,846	-1,635,738
Mutual Companies				
1981	7,819,467	-727,528	5,469,781	135,168
1982	8,444,892	-806,372	5,876,640	-64,337
1983	9,256,149	-950,819	6,595,202	244,844
1984	9,910,697	-1,454,139	7,324,532	-38,135
1985	11,565,000	-2,090,540	8,440,000	-5,160
5 Yrs	49,996,205	-6,029,398	33,706,155	273,380
Reciprocals				
1981	2,388,027	-198,673	1,856,302	62,171
1982	2,656,383	-332,994	1,994,426	-59,446
1983	2,882,376	-507,939	2,144,891	7,518
1984	3,244,184	-276,657	2,292,441	-148,611
1985	3,735,000	-545,850	2,605,000	-14,290
5 Yrs	14,905,970	-1,862,113	10,893,060	-152,658
Total Industry				
1981	24,390,839	-2,812,178	16,740,231	16,178
1982	26,223,669	-3,671,844	17,997,784	-615,350
1983	28,076,229	-4,443,277	19,739,540	116,661
1984	30,245,481	-5,725,719	21,779,506	-764,575
1985	35,680,000	-7,321,930	24,930,000	-267,930
Tot	144,616,218	-23,974,948	101,187,061	-1,515,016

Source: "The Liability Insurance Crisis," Hearings Before the Subcommittee on Investigations and Oversight, Ninety-Ninth Congress, January 21 and 22, 1986, p. 111. Figures are in nominal dollars.

creases were difficult to get approved. In other cases, cost reduction could result in short-term profits for auto insurers.

While reducing expected claims may have been part of the reason for insurers' support of air bags, the cost reduction hypothesis is only logical up to some limit. In the long run, less automobile-related injuries and fatalities imply a fall in the demand for automobile insurance. Where expected losses are low, individuals may choose not to buy automobile insurance or, in states where coverage is mandatory, may opt for minimum coverage. At the extreme—if traffic fatalities and injuries became nonexistent—a market for automobile liability insurance would not exist.

An alternative hypothesis is that auto insurers were out to reduce uncertainty in the prediction of future automobile claims. From this perspective, the poor underwriting experience that auto insurers suffered was an indication that actuaries could not accurately forecast insurance claims, prompting insurers to turn toward government to enhance predictability.

Two features of the air bag point toward this increase in predictability. First, the air bag has a distinct advantage in protecting the upper chest and head of front seat passengers in a head-on collision. As pointed out in a statement made by Brian O'Neill, President of the Insurance Institute for Highway Safety:

The various laboratory tests indicate that lap/shoulder belts and air bags can provide significant protection in frontal crashes but that air bags can offer superior protection as crash severity increases. There are a number of possible reasons for this: air bags distribute the impact forces over a wider area of the torso than is possible with any belt system; unlike belts, air bags restrain the head; and the distance over which the energy of the torso is absorbed is greater with bags than with belts.[45]

In this sense, the air bag is a unique type of safety device that could markedly reduce serious auto-related injuries such as paraplegia, epilepsy, and brain damage. It could also guard against facial injuries that result in disfigurement and plastic surgery. At the same time, air bags are less effective in side and angular collisions. Indeed, it is possible for bags not to inflate when collisions come at 90 degrees to a vehicle's path. Thus, while total deaths and injuries from air bags are comparable to belts (when used), the nature of the injuries is quite different between the two devices.

Research reported by the Rand Corporation on jury awards in liability cases ties the technical safety advantage to a courtroom advantage, where most costly insurance claims are generated.[46] This research examined data for Cook County, Illinois, for the 1960s and 1970s. It found that the median value of automobile injury awards remained constant in real terms across the two decades. Jurors had an uncanny ability to reckon damages in constant dollars. However, the awards for serious injuries, such as those associated with paraplegia, rose markedly across the decades, with the highest awards going to those who suffered nerve damage and paralysis. The second highest category of awards was related to eye and ear injury. These awards were also the most difficult to predict. The ratio of the mean to the median was the highest for paralysis and nerve damage (4.3), with serious eye and ear injury (3.5) and permanent facial injury (3.0) close behind.

A second feature that attracted insurance companies to air bags was the fact that they are passive: that is, the automobile occupant has no choice in the matter of safety protection. This means that the expected injuries and fatalities resulting from accidents involving air-bag-equipped cars can be estimated largely by looking at the engineering performance of the bags. In this sense, by removing the safety choice decision from the spontaneous whims of consumers, auto insurers can better predict the expected loss distribution for each insured individual. Moreover, if this change can be mandated across all automobiles, the driving force would become more homogeneous with respect to safety, further reducing uncertainty in predicting automobile claims.

Overall, the uncertainty hypothesis appears consistent with other political positions taken by insurers such as their support of other passive safety devices (i.e., reinforced bumpers, automatic braking systems, etc.) and their push for various types of tort reform including no-fault insurance.[47] In this sense, insurers are attempting to change the nature of the automobile safety hazard by pushing for passive homogeneity (nonvoluntary safety protection that is uniform across the driving population) and by moving insurance claims out of the difficult-to-predict court system.

Other interest groups also played a role in the passive restraint debate. Air-bag suppliers generally favored passive restraint legislation, although there were a few exceptions. While a passive restraint mandate would increase the market for bags, it would also introduce uncertainty into the air-bag supply business, just as it would for auto producers and insurers. Disappointments such as the original shift from a technology-based to a performance standard certainly did not help. If the government was to get involved, air-bag producers desired predictability.

Doctors were also heavily involved in the battle for bags. A special interest motivation on their part is not clear since the systematic reduction of head, back, and neck injuries would reduce the demand for medical services. Uncertainty reduction may have again been the motive, since these injuries are most often associated with difficult-to-predict malpractice suits. Difficulty in prediction implies high malpractice premiums. Considering this and the substantial nonpecuniary costs associated with the provision of health-care services for severe automobile injuries, the support for air bags is a logical one.

Uncertainty Reduction and the Bag/Belt Trade-Off

The insights discussed in the previous section are even more interesting when one considers the trade-offs created by the 1984 Dole decision. This

Table 11.4
Annual Incremental Reduction in Fatalities and Injuries

	Fatalities			Moderate-Critical Injuries		
	Low	Mid-point	High	Low	Mid-point	High
Airbags only	3,780	6,190	8,830	73,880	110,380	147,580
Airbags with lap belts	4,410	6,670	8,980	83,480	117,780	152,580
Airbags with lap-shoulder belts	4,570	6,830	9,110	85,930	120,250	155,030
Automatic Belts Usage:						
20%	520	750	980	8,740	12,180	15,650
70%	5,080	6,270	7,510	86,860	105,590	124,570
Mandatory Belt Use Laws Usage:						
40%	2,830	3,220	3,590	47,740	53,440	59,220
70%	5,920	6,720	7,510	100,430	112,410	124,570

Source: _Federal Register_, July 17, 1984, p. 29886.

is because a vote for (against) mandatory seat belt laws was indirectly a vote against (for) passive restraints, forcing interest groups to choose between the two regulatory alternatives.

An idea of the relative effectiveness of the two alternatives is shown in Table 11.4. As indicated in the table, which shows a range of estimates within confidence limits, air bags without belts would avoid some 17 percent more fatalities annually at the high range of the estimate than seat belts used 70 percent of the time. Air bags are also superior to belts at the high range of the estimate for the reduction of moderate to critical injuries. The midpoint estimate, which is normally used in statistical studies, tells a slightly different story. Mandatory belts (used 70 percent of the time) are superior to bags in reducing fatalities and moderate to critical injuries.

Since air bags could not be delivered to the entire auto population for at least ten years, the promised benefits would be long in arriving. Not so for mandatory belts. Effective state laws could bring immediate benefits. If the bag benefits are discounted to account for the present value of human life, which is assumed to be greater than a future fatality avoided, the mandatory belt option becomes all the more attractive. From a present value perspective, mandatory seat belt laws generate a greater reduction in automobile-related deaths and injuries than does a national air-bag rule.[48] This means that interest groups hoping to increase automobile safety should have preferred the mandatory seat belt alternative, while those groups against mandatory seat belt laws must have preferred something else to increased safety.

For the auto industry, the choice was clear. Automobile producers could not predict political outcomes, nor could they accurately predict the response of consumers to passive restraint options. On the other hand, seat belts were a known technology that was already included in the price of automobiles, and enforcement of use would fall on the police, not on the auto producers. A lower-cost and effective technology, from the standpoint of the auto industry, was preferred to a higher-cost, uncertain, new technology. Like the insurance industry, which hoped to shift the cost of injury reduction to purchasers of automobiles, the auto industry sought to shift the cost to taxpayers who fund police and highway safety programs. Enforcement of mandatory seat belt laws would not come cheap, but the cost would not show up on auto price stickers.

For the insurance industry, the trade-off was more complex. Air bags were a way to guarantee that any driver would be effectively "buckled up." Further, air bags could selectively reduce injuries associated with the most difficult-to-predict insurance claims. The mandatory seat belt alternative would, on the other hand, result in a greater reduction in the expected value of insurance claims.

As it turns out, statistical evidence indicates that insurers favored a national air-bag rule over the state mandatory seat belt alternative, refuting hypotheses that they were out to save lives or reduce underwriting claims.[49] Safety and cost reduction may have been important concerns, but reduction of uncertainty was crucial.

V. CONCLUSIONS

This chapter has examined the twenty-year political struggle over passive restraints. The struggle officially involved the potential reduction of automobile-related injuries and fatalities. Unofficially, the debate was an intense political struggle between automakers, insurers, and others.

The reduction of uncertainty was a major motivation for all of the groups, particularly insurers. Air bags would mean a more homogeneous and predictable driving force. Seat belts, on the other hand, would leave the safety decision in the hands of millions of heterogeneous consumers. The problem was that bags appeared unmarketable and automakers were not in a position to accommodate insurers in their attempt to mandate passive homogeneity.

A political compromise was needed but none was found. Instead, the battle was shifted from federal regulators to state legislatures.

Caught in the middle was the consumer, whose preferences for safety or danger took a back seat to the lobbying resources generated by well-organized interest groups. All the while, the "safety problem" remains, despite legislators' professed desires to eliminate it.

NOTES

1. The government's mandate actually involved passive restraints, which include both automatically fastening seat belts and air bags. In many cases, however, the terms air bags and passive restraints are used interchangeably, since air bags were the focus of much of the debate.

2. *Insurance Handbook for Reporters*, 2d ed. (Northbrook, Ill.: Allstate Insurance Group, June 1985).

3. Stanley Lebergott, *The Americans: An Economic Record* (New York: W. W. Norton & Company, 1984), p. 435.

4. Robert Crandall et al., *Automobile Safety Regulation* (Washington, D.C.: The Brookings Institution, 1986), p. 48.

5. Rising fatality rates are not necessarily a reflection of increased negligence on the part of drivers (i.e., failure to wear seat belts) or reduced quality of automobile safety protection. In many cases, changing fatality rates are simply the result of shifting demographics.

6. See Sam Peltzman, "The Effects of Automobile Safety Regulation," *Journal of Political Economy* 83, 4 (1975): 677–725. For discussion of subsequent literature that questions and supports the Peltzman findings, see *supra* n. 4.

7. *Supra* n. 4 at 48.

8. Originally a term used in medical journals, the word *passive* is used to describe preventive measures that do not require any action on the part of the patient. Examples include "pasteurizing milk . . . flouridation and chlorination of water and iodination of salt; enriching foods; providing electrical systems with fuses and insulation." In contrast, "active" approaches require participation by the patient and include "fastening seat belts; taking 'the pill'; and wearing helmets." Dr. William Haddon, Jr., claims to have coined the term *passive* in an early 1961 medical journal article. Coincidentally, this same doctor later became administrator of NHSB and later President of the Insurance Institute for Highway Safety, a public interest group supported by insurance companies that avidly supports passive restraints, particularly air bags. Haddon's remarks on this subject are contained in the Institute's February 21, 1974 *Status Report* 9, 4:7.

9. *Federal Register*, November 3, 1970, p. 16927.

10. *Background Manual on the Passive Restraint Issue*, Insurance Institute for Highway Safety, August 1977, p. 6–4.

11. Ibid.

12. "Safe at Any Speed?" *Newsweek*, September 7, 1970, p. 54.

13. *Supra* n. 10 at 6-5.

14. *Supra* n. 9 at 16927.

15. "A Hard Letdown for Air Bag Backers," *Business Week*, December 9, 1972, p. 29.

16. Ibid.

17. "The Deflated Airbag," *Newsweek*, December 18, 1972, p. 90.

18. NHSB granted the request as the compliance date was pushed back one year. See *supra* n. 9 at 16928.

19. *Supra* n. 10 at 2-16.

20. Ibid. at 2-17.

21. *Status Report*, Insurance Institute for Highway Safety, February 21, 1974, p. 2. Eventually, GM committed to production levels of 100,000 units annually for 1974, 1975, and 1976.

22. Ibid.

23. Donald D. Holt, "Why Eaton Got Out of the Air Bag Business," *Fortune*, March 12, 1979, p. 148.

24. "A Jarring Letdown for the Airbag," *Business Week*, April 29, 1972, p. 19.

25. Statement of William Haddon, Jr., M.D., President, Insurance Institute for Highway Safety, before the Senate Committee on Commerce, Science and Transportation Subcommittee, September 8, 1977, Attachment 4, p. 3.

26. *Supra* n. 21 at 3.

27. *Supra* n. 23 at 147.

28. Ibid. In October 1973, Allstate announced a 30 percent discount on medical and no-fault personal injuries for air-bag-equipped cars. Other insurance companies soon followed suit.

29. "Green Light for Air Bags," *Time*, July 11, 1977, p. 51.

30. *Supra* n. 10 at 1-8.

31. *Automobile Occupant Crash Protection*, Progress Report No. 3, National Highway Traffic Safety Administration, July 1980, p. 4.

32. Ibid. at 82. One report that looked at the performance record of air-bag-equipped cars noted that: "If these vehicles had not been equipped with air bags, approximately 11 fatalities and 131 injuries from all types of crashes would have been expected during this amount of travel. The accident performance of this fleet, however, resulted in only 6 fatalities and only 67 injuries ranging from moderate to critical."

33. Ibid at 86.

34. Hearings before the Subcommittee on Telecommunications, Consumer Protection and Finance, April 27–28, 1981.

35. *Status Report*, Insurance Institute for Highway Safety, July 26, 1977, p. 10.

36. *Supra* n. 10 at 6-27.

37. *Supra* n. 29 at 51.

38. *Supra* n. 23 at 146.

39. Ibid.

40. *Federal Register*, July 17, 1984, p. 29863.

41. Ibid.

42. *Supra* n. 40 at 29863.

43. Ibid. at 29862.

44. For example, the State Farm Companies Foundation has supported the Center since 1975. In 1986, this single foundation provided 22 percent of the Center's

budget. See *Organization Trends* (Washington, D.C.: Capital Research Center, April 1987).

45. Brian O'Neill, "A Note on Air Bag Effectiveness," Insurance Institute for Highway Safety Submission Docket 74–14, No. 32, Occupant Protection, December 19, 1983, p. 8.

46. See Mark A. Peterson, *Compensation for Injuries*, Santa Monica, Calif.: Rand Corporation, 1984.

47. Researchers have found that payments per insured motorist are actually higher in no-fault states, while the number of court cases is higher in traditional states. Hence, evidence that property/casualty insurers support no-fault insurance supports the uncertainty hypothesis but goes against the cost-reduction hypothesis. See "Compensating Auto Accident Victims: A Follow-up Report on No-Fault Insurance Experiences" (Washington, D.C.: U.S. Department of Transportation, May 1985).

48. This assumes that safety belt usage under mandatory seat belt laws will be greater than 50 percent. Most studies have found this to be true. See Adrian K. Lund, et al., "Motor Vehicle Occupant Fatalities in Four States with Seat Belt Use Laws," *SAE Technical Paper Series* (Washington, D.C.: Insurance Institute for Highway Safety, 1987); Allan F. Williams and Adrian K. Lund, "Seat Belt Use Laws and Occupant Crash Protection in the United States," *American Journal of Public Health* 76 (1986); and William B. Wilson, "Seatbelt Usage Attitudinal Study, A Report for the National Highway Traffic Administration"(McLean, Va.: Teknokron, Inc., Feb. 1979).

49. A statistical analysis of state mandatory seat belt votes shows that states with a relatively large number of insurance personnel per capita tend to, *ceteris paribus*, be against state mandatory seat belt laws. This result is consistent with the claim that auto insurers are out to reduce uncertainty with regard to actuarial estimation. For more information on this analysis see Robert Kneuper and Bruce Yandle, "Insurers, Auto Producers, and the Air Bag/Seat Belt Vote," unpublished manuscript, Department of Economics, Clemson University, 1989.

Selected Bibliography

Brennan, Geoffrey, and James M. Buchanan. *The Reason for Rules*. Cambridge: Cambridge University Press, 1985.

Buchanan, James M. *Cost and Choice*. Chicago: Markham, 1969.

Buchanan, James M., and Gordon Tullock. *The Calculus of Consent*. Ann Arbor: University of Michigan Press, 1962.

Calabresi, Guido. *The Cost of Accidents: A Legal and Economic Approach*. New Haven, Conn.: Yale University Press, 1970.

Commons, John R. *Legal Foundations of Capitalism*. Madison: University of Wisconsin Press, 1968.

Epstein, Richard. *Takings: Private Property and the Power of Eminent Domain*. Cambridge, Mass.: Harvard University Press, 1985.

Hayek, F. A. *Law, Legislation and Liberty*. Chicago: University of Chicago Press, 1977.

Holmes, Oliver W. *The Common Law*. 1811. Reprint. Boston: Little, Brown & Co., 1963.

Huber, Peter M. *Liability: The Legal Revolution and Its Consequences*. New York: Basic Books, 1988.

Hurst, James Willard. *Law and Markets in United States History*. Madison: University of Wisconsin Press, 1982.

Landes, William, and Richard A. Posner. *The Economic Structure of Tort Law*. Chicago: University of Chicago Press, 1987.

Leoni, Bruno. *Freedom and the Law*. Los Angeles: Nash Publishing Co., 1972.

Litan, Robert E., and Clifford Winston, eds. *Liability Perspective and Policy*. Washington, D.C.: The Brookings Institution, 1988.

Polinsky, A. Mitchell. *An Introduction to Law and Economics*, 2d ed. Boston: Little, Brown & Co., 1989.

Pollock, Frederick. *The Genius of the Common Law*. New York: Columbia University Press, 1912.

Posner, Richard A. *Economic Analysis of Law*. Boston: Little, Brown & Co., 1986.

Pound, Roscoe. *The Spirit of the Law*. 1921. Reprint. Boston: Beacon Press, 1963.

Viscusi, W. Kip. *Regulating Consumer Product Safety*. Washington, D.C.: American Enterprise Institute, 1984.

Yandle, Bruce. *The Political Limits of Environmental Regulation*. Westport, Conn.: Quorum Books, 1989.

Index

About the Contributors

David D. Haddock is Associate Professor at the School of Law, Northwestern University, specializing in law and economics. He has been a faculty member at UCLA and Emory University and was chief antitrust economist at Ford Motor Company.

James L. Huffman is Professor of Law at the Natural Resources Law Institute, Northwestern School of Law, Lewis and Clark College. Huffman's current research focuses on government insurance programs and liability as they relate to natural disasters. He has been a visiting professor of law in Greece and Guatemala.

Robert Kneuper is an economist at the Bureau of Economics, Federal Trade Commission. His views do not necessarily reflect those of the FTC. Kneuper holds a doctorate in economics from Clemson University.

Hugh H. Macaulay, Clemson University Alumni Professor of Economics Emeritus, researches market solutions to environmental problems. He has been a faculty member at Texas Tech University, Texas A&M University, Holy Cross College, and Taiwan National University. His most recent teaching assignment was at Dumphries University, Australia.

Fred S. McChesney, Professor of Economics and Robert T. Thompson Professor of Law and Business at Emory University, is recognized for his contributions to the theory of government regulation and consumer protection. A former visiting scholar at the University of Chicago's School of Law, McChesney served for two years on the senior staff of the Federal Trade Commission.

Roger E. Meiners is Director of Clemson University's Center for Policy Studies and is a Professor of Law and Economics at Clemson. He has been a faculty member at Texas A&M University, Emory University, the University of Miami, and a visiting professor at Guatemala's Universidad Francisco Marroquin.

Gordon Shuford did his graduate work in economics at Clemson University, where his research focused on the political economy of regulation. He is presently on the staff of the South Carolina Tax Commission; previously he worked as a research economist at the Federal Trade Commission.

Robert J. Staaf is Professor of Law and Economics at Clemson University. Staaf's research focuses on the evolution of common law rules and intellectual property rights. Staaf was formerly a faculty member at Virginia Tech and the University of Miami, and he was a senior economist with the Federal Trade Commission.

Bruce Yandle is Alumni Professor of Economics at Clemson University and is Director of the Strom Thurmond Institute. Author of books and numerous articles on environmental economics and regulation, Yandle's research focuses on political economy and legal institutions. He has served as Executive Director of the Federal Trade Commission.